THE SAFFRON ROAD

A JOURNEY WITH BUDDHA'S DAUGHTERS

Christine Toomey

Portobello

First published by Portobello Books 2015
This paperback edition published by Portobello Books 2016

Portobello Books
12 Addison Avenue
London
W11 4QR

A CIP catalogue record is available
from the British Library

9 8 7 6 5 4 3 2 1

ISBN 978 1 84627 493 0
eISBN 978 1 84627 497 8

www.portobellobooks.com

Typeset in Arno by M Rules
Printed and bound by CPI Group (UK) Ltd, Croydon, CR0 4YY

To my mother Diane Inglis,
my beautiful daughter Ines
and all Buddha's Daughters

CONTENTS

PART IV Japan

WEST

PART V North America

PART VI British Isles

PART VII France

PART VIII Beyond Bounds

ILLUSTRATIONS

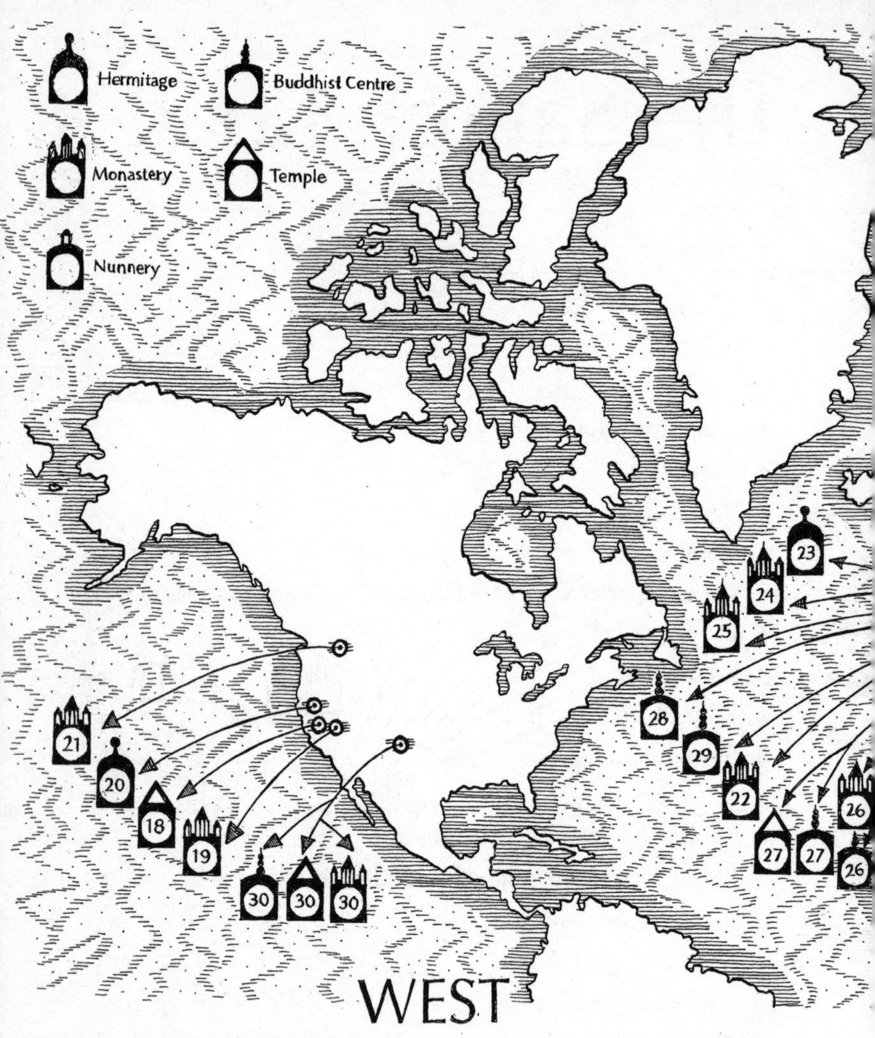

18. Tien Hau Temple, San Francisco
19. Gold Mountain Sagely Monastery, San Francisco
20. Aranya Bodhi, Awakening Forest Hermitage, California
21. Sravasti Abbey, Washington State
22. Cittaviveka, Chithurst Monastery, West Sussex
23. Milntuim Hermitage, Perthshire
24. Samye Ling Monastery, Southern Uplands
25. Throssel Hole Abbey, Northumberland
26. Plum Village, Monastery and Buddhist Centre, Dordogne
27. La Gendronnière Temple, Blois
28. Jamyang Buddhist Centre London
29. Drukpa Buddhist Centre, London
30. Upaya Institute and Zen Center, New Mexico

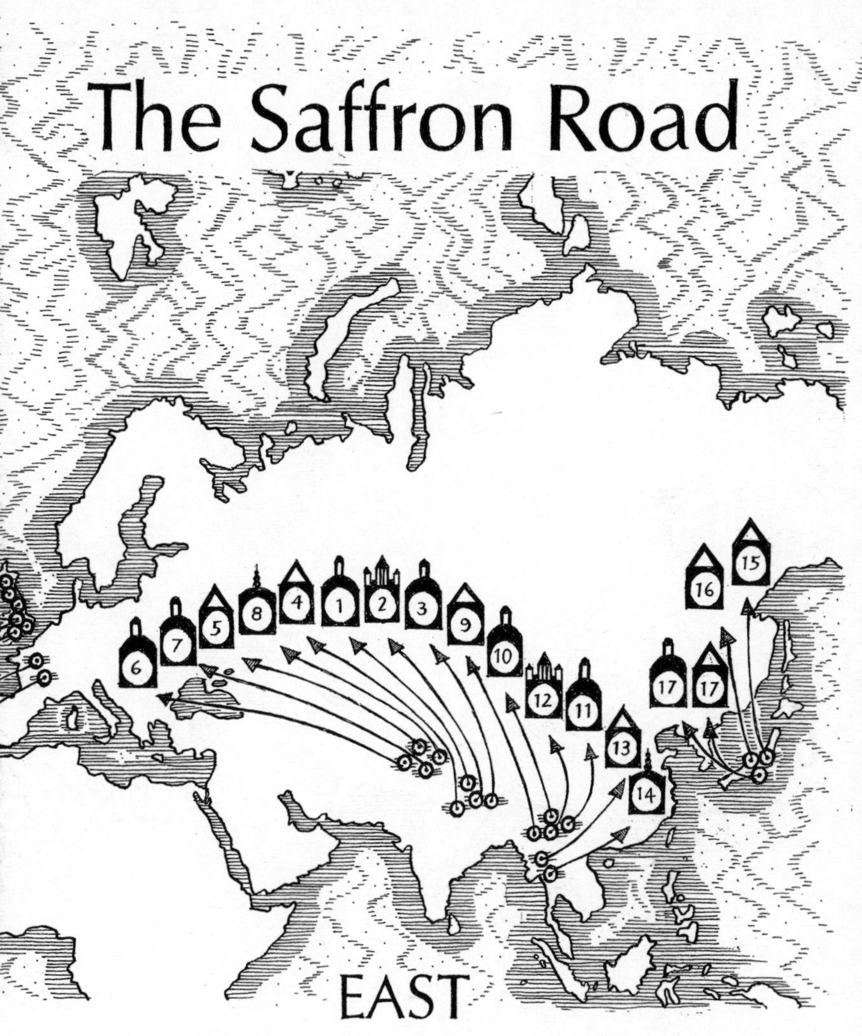

1. Druk Gawa Khilwa Nunnery, Kathmandu
2. Kopan Monastery, Kathmandu
3. Khachoe Chakyil Ling Nunnery, Kathmandu
4. Mayadevi Temple, Lumbini
5. Tsuglagkhang Temple, Complex, Dharamshala
6. Dolma Ling Nunnery, Sidhpur
7. Dongyu Gatsal Ling Nunnery, Kangra Valley
8. Tushita Meditation Centre, Dharamshala
9. Bagan Ancient Temple Complex, Bagan
10. Sakyadhita Thilashin Nunnery School, Sagaing
11. Mauka Thiwon Chaung Nunnery, Sagaing
12. Masoeyein Monastery, Mandalay
13. Shwedagon Pagoda Temple Complex, Yangon
14. Dhamma Joti Vipassana Centre, Yangon
15. Tokeiji Temple Kitakamakura
16. Jakuan Temple, Kyoto
17. Aichi Senmon Nunnery & Training Temple, Nagoya

Preface

CROSSROADS

My interpreter Tsering strides ahead, sure-footed and mindful that, if we are late, the woman we are to meet might take fright and flee. As we hurry along this rocky path behind the Dalai Lama's private compound, edging past mothers holding the hands of small children, maroon-robed monks and elderly devotees, some smile and wave, looking puzzled at our haste. This narrow path that circles the Tsuglagkhang Temple in the Himalayan foothills of Dharamshala, northern India, is meant to be trodden slowly, as a form of Buddhist meditative practice. To walk its length clockwise is to perform a *kora*, a pilgrimage intended to calm the mind.

While pilgrims tread the path, many slip strings of mala beads between their fingers, lips fluttering with the silent chant of chosen mantras. At one point, where the path widens, a row of giant brass prayer wheels gently rolls to the touch of those who pass. Inside the drums are sheaves of prayers, said to gain force from movement. Dotted amongst the pine trees flanking the hill ahead are brightly painted *mani* stones, some carved with prayers that Tenzin Gyatso, the Fourteenth Dalai Lama, will one day return to Tibet, where he once ruled supreme before Chinese troops invaded his strategically critical homeland, forcing him into exile more than fifty years ago.

As we reach our meeting place, there is no sign of Nyima and I fear that we have missed our chance. But then we glimpse her, head bowed, half hidden from view by a white stupa reliquary. She doesn't have long to talk. That night she must work in the kitchen of a small restaurant in the valley below. A cool wind blows up as Nyima starts to speak, carrying her words away and forcing us to lean close. Now and then, she turns to look over her shoulder, as if to make sure no one else is listening, though the place is all but deserted.

Even as a young girl Nyima had felt a calling to become a nun, she tells us. She was barely fourteen when, with the support of her family, she presented herself at the doors of a local nunnery close to the ancient Tibetan capital of Lhasa to be accepted as a novice. In years gone by, most Tibetan families would send their youngest son to become a monk, sometimes at the age of just three or four, to bring the family honour and often because they could not afford to feed large numbers of children. But with girls, it has traditionally been more a matter of the girl's own choice. When a girl expressed a wish to join a nunnery, most families would look on it as the child's karma, even if it meant they would see little of their daughter from then on.

For two years, Nyima immersed herself in monastic life with deep contentment. But then her young world collapsed. When she was just sixteen, she and a small group of fellow novices dared to make a stand on a street corner in Lhasa to protest against the Chinese authorities' recent decision to deny future generations of girls the right to enter Buddhist monastic orders under the age of eighteen. The protest lasted only a few minutes before the group was arrested and imprisoned in Lhasa's notorious Drapchi jail.

Nyima spent the next five years in prison. She tells us how, in summer, she was forced to stand all day outside on a box with sheets of newspaper stuck under her armpits and between her legs. If the newspapers slipped, she was savagely beaten. In winter, she was made to stand barefoot on blocks of ice until the skin of her soles peeled away. Once, when she replaced the words of a song inmates were instructed to sing in praise of Chairman Mao with her own version paying tribute to the Dalai Lama, she was locked for two years in solitary confinement and tortured with electric cattle prods.

Broken physically and mentally by her ordeal, by the time she was released Nyima had abandoned her dream of living as a nun. Her only goal was to escape what the Chinese euphemistically call the Tibet Autonomous Region, which covers only half of the land that Tibetans claim as their ancient territory. After fleeing across the Himalayas to Nepal, she made her way into exile in India. Regret for her lost vocation is written in Nyima's soft features as she speaks.

This brief meeting is my first encounter with a Buddhist nun, albeit one forcibly disrobed, and it haunts me long after we have parted.

A few days after speaking with Nyima, I visit a nunnery near Dharamshala where I encounter hundreds more young nuns, some barely into their teens, some having also escaped Tibet. One pretty young nun with a shaven head named Dawa Dolma trekked across the Himalayas for two months without her family when she was just eleven years old. Inspired by the deep Buddhist faith of her grandmother, she too had decided at a very young age she wanted to become a nun and sought novice ordination as soon as she reached India. When I ask her how she feels now about her chosen path, her features light up. 'It makes me feel as if I'm standing on a tall mountain,' she says. 'It makes me feel as if I can see a long way.'

There is something that impels me to want to understand more about what led women such as Nyima and Dawa Dolma to enter holy orders in the first place, especially at such a young age. But on this, my first visit to Dharamshala, there is little time. It is early May 2011, and I am here to record a seismic shift in the lives of exiled Tibetans. For more than three centuries, successive Dalai Lamas have fulfilled the dual role of supreme spiritual guide and political figurehead for their people, but two months earlier, Tenzin Gyatso, the Fourteenth Dalai Lama, announced his intention to retire from such temporal duties. That summer an energetic Harvard-educated lawyer, Lobsang Sangay, would be stepping into the Dalai Lama's earthly shoes as elected prime minister of the Tibetan government-in-exile. As I sat beside Dr Sangay in a small plane hugging the snow-capped peaks of the Himalayas as we fly north, we talk about this historic transfer of power and how, despite being the child of Tibetan refugees who had witnessed atrocities in their homeland, he was determined to stick to pacifist principles in tackling the leadership challenge he was about to face.

Later, in the sunlit antechamber of the Dalai Lama's private residence, I talk to his nephew about the sensitive issue of the spiritual succession. In the past, Tenzin Gyatso has spoken of the role dying with him if his people feel they no longer need such a spiritual leader. If they do want a successor, and he dies in exile, Tenzin Gyatso has made it clear that the one who takes his place will also come from outside Tibet. On more than one occasion, he has also raised the possibility that his successor could be a woman, noting his belief that women have a greater capacity for compassion.

'If a female Dalai Lama comes, then that female must be very beautiful,' he has told devotees, before adding, with the mischievous chuckle that sometimes belies his gravitas as recipient of the Nobel Prize for Peace, 'If the female Dalai Lama is very ugly, then fewer people will show interest.'

This comment about prerequisite beauty has caused offence to some feminists, but the moment of what the Dalai Lama says has not been lost. Imagine if the Pope were to announce he expected a woman to rule the Holy See one day, or if the Grand Ayatollahs of Iran decreed their successors could soon be wearing chadors – there would be gasps worldwide. Yet, amongst the world's community of more than half a billion Buddhists, the possibility that one of their most revered spiritual leaders could one day be female appears to be acknowledged with little dissent.

Such an enlightened stance also has me intrigued. And so I vow one day to return to this Himalayan hill station to explore the lives of Tibetan Buddhist nuns and the strides they are making towards equality with their monastic brethren. But no sooner has this seed of an idea taken root than it starts to grow into something far bigger. The more I explore the unfamiliar world of Buddhist nuns, the more extraordinary it becomes. First, I hear of nuns in Nepal practising kung fu in search of physical and spiritual empowerment. Then I learn of one British woman who, finding herself the only nun in a monastery of 100 monks, took herself to a remote cave in the Himalayas for twelve years, surviving avalanches, wolves and temperatures of –35°C, in search of silence, solitude and enlightenment. I unearth news of a nun in Burma being imprisoned for 'impersonating a monk' because she dared challenge the country's authoritarian regime. Further afield, I discover a Zen Buddhist nun in Japan, regarded by many as a national treasure, who has won many of country's most prestigious literary prizes, several of them for erotic fiction.

Delving deeper, I locate women who have come from widely diverging backgrounds, not only in the East but also in the West, to follow the path to becoming a Buddhist nun. One in Nepal is a princess, another a former anti-terrorist policewoman, another a former Bollywood star and Miss India finalist. Others from the West include a former presenter of the television show *Top Gear*; an acclaimed composer; a concert violist of international standing; a former BBC news journalist; Switzerland's first female commercial airline pilot; a former political aide to the mayor of Washington, DC; a former Paris catwalk model; a one-time advertising executive in New York; and a former banker in the City of London. Most of these women I only encounter after embarking on the journey of this book. But as I set out, I feel certain I will come across some of the most extraordinary women I am ever likely to meet.

For more than two decades, as a foreign correspondent and feature writer for the *Sunday Times*, I have travelled to parts of the world riven by conflict and war. Much of my time has been spent writing about men and women, particularly women, whose lives have been marked by suffering and tragedy. Some of these stories have had a deep and lasting impact on me. They include a series of reports on the mass rape of women and girls in Bosnia and Kosovo. One of the women I spent hours interviewing talked of the fierce love she felt for the daughter born as a result of rape and how this love had saved her from despair. Another spoke of witnessing her son being beheaded in front of her and how she had been forced to bury his body before being deported to a rape camp. She had been determined to speak to me so the truth would be known, but after we finished talking, I stood by helpless as an ambulance drove her back to hospital to treat her for renewed trauma.

At a border crossing in the West Bank, I have stood berating Israeli soldiers refusing safe passage to a Palestinian mother whose young son was shot dead by the Israeli military and who then donated his heart and other organs to save the lives of Israeli children. In Iran, I have sat, barely able to breathe, as women told me about the suffocating restrictions placed on them. One woman, during nine years of marriage, was not once allowed by her husband to draw back four layers of curtains in their apartment in an affluent neighbourhood of Tehran; she repeatedly attempted suicide. In Russia's Arctic north, defying a ban on foreign press in the area, I have reported on the way the state gagged women widowed by the sinking of the Kursk nuclear submarine. In India, I have stood in the oppressive heat of an abortion clinic and listened to the sickening justification of doctors participating in the abortion of female foetuses on an unimaginable scale. And in Guatemala, I have ventured into some of the poorest drug-and-gang-infested barrios to write about the torture and mass murder of women and girls, in a country where those who kill women enjoy legal impunity. All of these women were ignored, devalued and degraded simply because of their gender.

After so much time spent shedding light on some of the darkest corners of humanity, the consequences of such tragedies have become frighteningly familiar. Yet over the years I have been deeply moved by the courage many of the women I interviewed had discovered in themselves, my belief being that, ultimately, it could inspire us all. So when, in the course of writing about the Dalai Lama's political successor, I begin to encounter the stories of Buddhist nuns, I am touched by their strength and conviction, and heartened too. Because the courage these women show is born not only of tragedy or brutality, but also of something more uplifting: a longing to achieve their own enlightenment, and a compassion and determination to help others achieve it too. In a world numbed by the amount of attention paid to violence, terrorism, and political and religious power struggles, I find it profoundly refreshing to come across women whose lives are dedicated to nurturing the opposite.

Although Buddhist monks tend to have a much higher profile in the West than Buddhist nuns, the internet readily yields videos of many nuns who have stepped into the public arena to deliver wise talks on every aspect of Buddhism. They are often able to present profound eastern philosophy in an accessible and sometimes humorous way, typical of a down-to-earth, female approach to life's problems. While the greatest numbers of Buddhist nuns still reside in the East, women are now being ordained into Buddhist monastic orders in countries around the world, many of them pushing the frontiers of what it means to be a nun in today's materialistic world. As Buddhism has spread from one society to another the experience of women who have chosen this life has changed significantly.

To explore these changes, I resolve to follow some of the paths Buddhism has travelled through the East and from East to West. I have little understanding in advance of the scale of this journey, which will eventually lead me to travel a distance equivalent to circling the globe twice. Nor do I appreciate the logistical difficulties involved. Nuns' lives, I soon discover, flow to a very different rhythm; in this age of instant electronic communication, I must sometimes revert to writing letters to those in distant lands or wait months before hearing back from women emerging from silent retreat.

But what began as an essentially journalistic endeavour soon took on a more personal sense of urgency. In the months before I embarked on this journey both of my parents died. First, my father became ill, passing away soon afterwards. Then my mother, who had not lived with my father for more than thirty years, suddenly collapsed. As my sister and I sat at her bedside every day my heart broke as I saw life slip from our mother, who just weeks before had been so full of energy and love for her family. I grew up listening to my mother tapping away on a typewriter next to my bedroom; a self-taught journalist, it was her love of writing that first inspired me to follow the same path. When my mother died, I sank into a deeper sorrow than I have ever known.

There had been painful losses and estrangements before this, but the shock of losing both my parents so suddenly and within just a few months of each other brought my life to a standstill. I felt at a crossroads. After so much time spent bearing witness to the suffering of others, I realized I barely knew how to handle my own. It was then that I came to see the writing of this book as a gift. At the heart of Buddhism lies an acknowledgement that suffering is an inevitable part of human existence and it is how we face this that defines us. A true understanding of this fact is the basis of the wisdom Buddhist nuns dedicate their lives to awakening, not only for their own sake but also for the benefit of others whose lives they touch.

With this realization came an awareness that the journey I was about to undertake would comprise three interwoven journeys: one following the paths that Buddhism has travelled from East to West, the second tracing the extraordinary individual paths taken by women to becoming Buddhist nuns, and the third pursuing my own search for deeper understanding and a wisdom that would heal.

For far from running away from life, those who choose to become Buddhist nuns make it their business to deal on a daily basis with some of the most profound and intractable problems of human existence. While many in the male hierarchies of most of the world's major religions argue over, or simply ignore, the contributions of women to their faith, Buddhism has from the beginning recognized and embraced the value of the feminine, even if centuries of ritual have obscured this in some traditions. But then Buddhism is not a proselytizing religion. Many would argue it is not a religion at all, more a philosophy and way of looking at life. It is certainly not a religion that encourages anything to be taken on blind faith; its rigorous discipline demands that no teachings be accepted until proven true through personal enquiry. In an age when scepticism of all kinds is fashionable, this is one reason for Buddhism's growing appeal amongst those with some sense of life being bigger than the confines of scientific certainty.

Throughout my travels, most of those I meet became nuns as young women, even girls. But some have come to this spiritual life later, after marrying, in some cases more than once, and having had children. One nun I meet in Japan is still married. Despite my initial expectation that Buddhist nuns would observe vows of poverty and chastity like their Christian sisters, in Japan, through a historical quirk, neither monks nor nuns within the Zen tradition are required to be celibate.

Some of the nuns I meet are schooled in seminaries or live in nunneries, temples or abbeys, only travelling beyond these cloistered walls when invited to give Buddhist teachings or to carry out specific duties. Others live and work in the wider world, fully integrated with their communities. All are engaged, in one way or another, in furthering understanding of the now-fashionable concept of 'mindfulness', which lies at the very heart of all Buddhist practice dating back 2,500 years. By following the nuns' journey I begin to appreciate the ways in which this most ancient of philosophies has subtly infused many aspects of modern life. It underpins some of the most revered teachings on meditation, which is practised regularly, according to one report, by more than ten million people in the United States alone.

In some ways, I come to see the Buddhist nuns' journey as a metaphor for the struggles and triumphs of women the world over and through time, the alternative way of life they have chosen a testimony to the way women survive and adapt. What all the women I encounter have in common is that they feel a calling to a larger purpose in life. In this rapidly changing age, which is forcing many of us to question what is meaningful, the path these women have chosen is not just different but somehow defiant. Our modern world has grown to disdain the inner life, often disparaging it as 'navel gazing'. Yet theirs is a journey inwards, rather than outwards in search of material success, security or personal triumph. It is a passage through a spiritual landscape fraught with hardship but offering great reward. When I witness the uncertainties of my daughter's generation, and remember those of my own, about role models, career building and what being a successful and happy woman means in a society obsessed with body image and material possessions, exploring the lives of those drawn to asking different questions about life, and finding different answers, offers a refreshing alternative perspective.

Few women ever feel a calling to become a Buddhist nun. And few of us would have the strength, courage and stamina that the rigours of their vocation demand. But all of us can sit quietly for some minutes each day and begin to touch what these women devote their lives to nurturing: the essence of what is in our hearts, our intuition, our true self.

To step inside the world of Buddhist nuns, East and West, is to journey to a very different place, one with something to say to us all. This, then, is the story of the road walked by Buddha's Daughters. It begins long before dawn, in the Himalayas of Nepal, the land where the Buddha was born.

EAST

PART I

NEPAL

1

KUNG FU NUNS

At the Druk Gawa Khilwa nunnery, nestled in mountains an hour's drive from Kathmandu, each day begins at 3 a.m. with the sound of a bell. Dawn will not seep across the highest Himalayan peaks for several more hours. As the young nuns stir from sleep, only a dim light filters through the dormitory windows from lit pathways beyond.

No words are spoken and no glances exchanged as the young women slip from their beds and wrap their slender frames in burgundy and saffron robes. First, an underskirt and shirt without sleeves, worn even on the coldest of days. Over this, a wide lower robe is folded and tucked at the waist. Finally, a long shawl, a *zen*, is tossed around the shoulders to keep out the chill. After smoothing out sheets and blankets, each woman steps up onto the firm mattress of her bed and sits cross-legged facing the wall against which her pillow rests. Each then turns within, entering the realm of meditation.

While most of the sisters spend the next two hours treading their own inner path, repeating secret mantras and recitations given to them individually by the head of the Buddhist order to which they belong, alternate groups of nuns take it in turns to follow a very different form of practice. Instead of monastic robes, they lift a different set of clothes from the storage boxes under their beds: loose brown trousers and long-sleeved martial-arts jackets cinched at the waist with a cloth sash. Tying the laces of white canvas shoes, they pass quietly from their dormitories into the night air.

It is mid-October when I join them and together we snake up a stairway that leads from their residential complex, along a steep incline bordered on either side by scented flowers and shrubs. The stairs lead to a large hall in front of which stands a giant gilded statue of the Buddha. If the weather is too cold, the nuns take up formation inside the hall. But today, as it is warm enough to practise outside, I follow the women as they climb three further flights of stairs onto the roof and space themselves out with a few low whispers. As their instructor brings the group to order they draw their feet together, pull two clenched fists back towards their waists and stand waiting.

At the opening command they raise their arms to shoulder height, thrust their right fist into their left palm and spring into such sharp action that it seems a temporary affront to the calm devotions of those meditating below. In the background, the only sound is a gentle symphony of cicadas, but high on the nunnery roof the peace is now pierced by the shouted instructions in the practice of kung fu. With each position counted out, the nuns move through a series of steps that flow from graceful hand gestures through fierce air punches and swinging chops to soaring kicks and acts of fighting.

Most of the exercises are carried out with each nun going through the motions individually, either with bare hands or with the long fighting sticks known as *bo* staffs. The most startlingly beautiful are performed with blood-red fans swirled above the head and around the nuns' waists. At times the fans are spun open, at others flipped closed, the effect more dance than martial art. Other exercises involve two nuns sparring, circling each other with clenched fists, thrusting, shoving, grabbing the other's neck in the crook of their arms and pushing their opponent to the ground. Some of the moves are conducted with the fighting sticks held in both hands and used as both shield and weapon. As each series of manoeuvres comes to an end, the nuns again draw their fist into their palm then push their open hands slowly down by their sides. It is only this subtle closing movement that returns to the women the gentle demeanour of their monastic calling.

What I am witnessing in this striking pre-dawn display is more than 1,000 years of tradition being turned on its head.

For more than a millennium this practice of kung fu was reserved only for monks, its roots lying far to the north in the legendary Chinese monastery of Shaolin. It was here in the fifth century that kung fu was said to have originated, after Bodhidarma, an Indian prince turned Buddhist monk, set out to take the teachings of the Buddha to China. On finding temples there vulnerable to attack by thieves, and many of the monks struggling with the rigours of monastic life, the monk devised a system of fitness and defence that drew heavily on the ancient traditions of Indian yoga. Like yoga, Shaolin kung fu developed from an observation of the way animals move. Over the centuries the Shaolin monks incorporated many different animal postures into their practice until eventually the mastery of many of these styles developed into a form represented by a dragon. Unlike the fire-breathing dragon of western mythology, the Chinese dragon is a powerful spiritual creature.

It is telling, then, that the nuns of Gawa Khilwa belong to the Drukpa order of Himalayan Buddhism, *druk* being the Tibetan word for both 'dragon' and 'thunder'.

As the first blush of sunlight bleeds over the horizon, the nuns draw their morning kung-fu practice to a close. A deep rumble of drums can be heard in the distance and high on the roof of the nunnery's main temple I see the silhouettes of two figures blowing hard into gold-and-jewel-encrusted conch shells. This piercing bugle call is the Buddhist call to prayer. It is barely 5 a.m. and two hours of elaborate ritual and worship in the temple will follow before the nuns and I sit down to breakfast.

The ferocity of these morning exercises at Gawa Khilwa seems the antithesis of spiritual endeavour. But this practice I am privileged to have observed not only builds the women's physical and mental strength, it also instils in them a growing sense of confidence. This is an entirely new experience for Buddhist nuns, who, through the centuries, have often been neglected and overlooked.

From the moment I began planning this journey, I wanted to start here, on this rooftop in Nepal. Seeing young nuns engaging in kung fu seemed to offer the perfect introduction to a story of spiritual empowerment. That it was happening so close to the place where the Buddha was born more than 2,000 years ago added to its symbolism. But this is not a straightforward tale, nor was it to be an easy one to follow, as I began to realize on the tortuous route to Gawa Khilwa.

When I descended through the smog to Kathmandu airport in the autumn of 2012, I knew little about Nepal. I knew that today it is one of the poorest countries in the world, beset by the aftermath of ten years of Maoist insurrection. This conflict only petered out in 2006, when the King of Nepal agreed to restore parliamentary democracy. Two years later, a Maoist-led parliament reduced the king's status to that of a figurehead and declared the country a republic. But it was not the self-declared Maoists who dealt the Nepali royal family its harshest blow: rather, the bloody vengeance of a lovelorn prince. In 2001, fuelled, many believe, by rage at his parents' disapproval of the woman he wanted to marry, Crown Prince Dipendra had gone on a bloody rampage in Kathmandu's Narayanhity Palace, gunning down almost every member of the royal family before committing suicide. To rid Nepal of the murdered royals' ghosts, a high-caste priest volunteered to take on the negative karma of the tragedy by donning the king's golden suit, shoes and sunglasses and riding an elephant out of the Kathmandu Valley into symbolic exile.

But as I arrive in Kathmandu it feels as if the departed spirits of these murdered royals still breathe misfortune on those who remain in their former kingdom. When I leave the airport, I discover a place sunk in chaos. The city's roads are dug up, its buildings are crumbling, the streets are full of hawkers and beggars, and it has the unenviable reputation of being one of the most polluted cities in Asia.

For centuries the country's strategic position, caught in a pincer between China and India, meant that trading caravans laden with silk, wool and salt traversed high mountain passes here, bestowing great wealth on Nepal. As Kathmandu grew rich, many gilded pagodas and ornate temples, both Buddhist and Hindu, were built in the city. But those who pass through Kathmandu today leave a slurry of waste. Rubbish is piled high along the city's roads and throughout the countryside beyond. Nepal's greatest good fortune now is that its mountainous north contains ten of the world's fourteen tallest mountains, including the highest point on earth, Mount Everest. With an appetite for adventure, hordes of foreign trekkers and mountaineers descend on Nepal each year in ever-growing numbers. Yet even the base camps around these high peaks are now strewn with the detritus of a throwaway modern society.

This seems an incongruous location to seek the origins of Buddhism. But it was here, in the far south of modern Nepal, in a ramshackle town called Lumbini, that the man who came to be known as the Buddha, or 'Awakened One', was born. At the time of the Buddha's birth, around 480 BCE, Lumbini lay in a small north Indian kingdom ruled from Kapilavastu, the capital, by a tribe of kinsmen known as the Sakya. For this reason the Buddha is sometimes referred to as Buddha Sakyamuni, or 'Sage of the Sakyas'.

There are many versions told of the Buddha's life, though few details exist of the time before he became a wandering monk. Certainly his youth must have been more complex than the later poetic tales suggest, but for the purposes of this book their version of events will suffice. According to legend, the Buddha was born into great privilege, as a prince named Siddhartha Gautama, whom sages immediately predicted would one day become either a great ruler or a revered holy man. To ensure that his son succeeded him on the throne, King Suddhodana virtually imprisoned him within the walls of a royal compound and, in order that he should never want to leave, made his life one of luxury and ease. As a young prince, Siddhartha was provided with three palaces for the three seasons of the year and was surrounded by beautiful courtesans. His marriage to a cousin, Yasodhara, resulted in the birth of a son, Rahula. But by the time his son was born, Siddhartha was twenty-nine and overcome by curiosity about the world.

During secret night-time journeys beyond the palace walls, he is said to have come across four sights – of a sick man, an old man, a decaying corpse and an ascetic – none of which he had ever been allowed to see in his life of indulgence. When he turned to his charioteer to ask if sickness and death would eventually be part of his life too, the answer, that they would, is thought to mark Siddhartha's awakening from innocence and prompted him to seek an alternative existence. After gazing tenderly at his wife and child as they slept, he set out secretly one night from the palace and for the rest of his life lived as a simple monk, wandering widely through the Ganges plains of northern India.

Following years of extreme asceticism, he is said to have sat down one day beneath a bodhi tree where, after weeks of intense meditation, he came to a series of realizations. His enlightenment embraced a deep understanding of the true nature of human suffering and a way of being released from it, into a state sometimes referred to simply as nirvana, principally by banishing ignorance and craving. These realizations formed the basis for teachings that spread so widely across the globe that today more than half of the current global population is said to reside in parts of the world where Buddhism was once a dominant force.

At the start of my journey, I understand little of the rich and complex world of Buddhist teachings. I know that 2,500 years ago the Buddha summed up the reality of human existence in what came to be known as the Four Noble Truths. The first truth is a clear recognition that in life there is suffering, and the second that we suffer because everything is impermanent, but because we don't want to accept that fact, we cling to what we think will make us happy and our attachment only makes us suffer more. The third and fourth truths recognize that there is an end to suffering and this can be achieved through a way of life summed up as the Noble Eightfold Path, namely: right understanding, right thought, right speech, right action, right livelihood, right effort, right mindfulness and right concentration. The endless cycle of clinging and suffering, referred to in Buddhist teachings as *samsara,* is the condition in which humans everywhere are said to find themselves. Acknowledging this is as relevant today as it was in antiquity.

For the jetlagged traveller, the journey from Kathmandu to Gawa Khilwa nunnery is itself an initiation into the sorrows of mankind. After leaving the polluted city's choked thoroughfares behind, the steep, deeply pitted road leading into the mountains is precarious and prone to frequent landslides. More than once I clamber out of the taxi to lighten its load as its wheels spin, trying to gain purchase on loose gravel, unnervingly close to the edge of a precipice.

From some distance away, as the taxi twists and turns, I begin to glimpse a striking white edifice that towers above the valley. As we draw closer I get a sense of the size of the nunnery: not just one building but a complex of many, adorned with traditional designs of brightly coloured tiles around the eaves. The tall steel gates of the nunnery remain firmly shut as we draw up to the main entrance. One of the persistent power cuts that besiege Nepal has disabled the electric lock. Beyond the metal grille, I watch a portly nun disappear into the bowels of a gatehouse with a wrench in her hand. Minutes later she emerges, rearranging her robes and smiling broadly. A generator growls to life, the gates swing open and I enter a different world.

By now it is already early evening and after being shown to my room in the nunnery's guest quarters, I am left to my own devices. Most of the nuns are busy with their duties, so I take a stroll alone through the grounds towards a large hall.

In front of the hall, close to the towering gilded Buddha, are a number of smaller dragon statues. This is one external sign that Gawa Khilwa is a seat of the Drukpa, or Dragon order of Himalayan Buddhism. The Drukpa order was founded a millennium ago and over the course of hundreds of years, many of its followers became adepts at a powerful form of spiritual practice believed to lead to enlightenment within a single lifetime.

I have only just begun to unravel the complex threads of different Buddhist lineages, but I am struck that the head of the Drukpa order, known as the Twelfth Gyalwang Drukpa, chooses to live for most of the year here at Gawa Khilwa nunnery rather than in a monastery like most other senior male lamas. His encouragement of the nuns in practising kung fu is only one aspect of a highly unusual degree of support he shows the women in his care. Most significant of all is his direct teaching of the nuns. This breaks with Buddhist tradition, which, throughout much of history, has held nuns to be inferior to monks. So much so that in the past many were treated as little more than domestic servants in monastic settings.

There is nothing subservient about the demeanour of the nuns I watch striking fighting poses against the dawn sky the following morning. When their practice is over and they return to their dormitories to change into their monastic robes, I make my way to the nunnery's main temple for the start of the first period of daily worship. The temple itself is a feast of rich colours and imagery, its tall ceiling supported by a succession of pillars around which the golden tails of dragons are entwined. The walls are lined with nearly 2,000 glass-paned alcoves containing delicate golden statues of male and female deities and seated Buddhas.

But it is the throng of women already gathered inside that astounds. Enveloped within this soaring space, surrounded by walls glistening with reflected light, are more than 200 nuns sitting cross-legged on row after row of long low mattresses covered with rugs fringed in red and gold. In front of them brightly painted tables hold ancient scriptures, from which they recite, their chanting accompanied by ringing bells and the constant throb of ceremonial drums beaten with long curved sticks.

Raised above the main floor where the nuns are seated is a dais on which the Gyalwang Drukpa sits when in attendance. To one side, hung in a wooden mount, is the temple's biggest drum, whose deep sound echoes far beyond the nunnery and into the valley below. Beside the nun whose task it is to beat the drum sits the mistress of chants. Her sonorous voice leads the gathering of nuns through at least four hours of devotions each day: two in the morning and another two or more in the early evening. Spread before the dais, at a lower level, the nuns sit in rows facing each other on either side of the main entrance. At the end of each row, left and right, are Gawa Khilwa's most recent arrivals: more than a dozen novices below the age of fourteen. One, I later learn, is just ten years old.

As I join the morning gathering, I am motioned to sit on a cushion on the floor just inside the entrance, to one side of the temple's heavy wooden doors, right next to the nunnery's discipline mistress, Wangmo. Her watchful gaze surveys the nuns in her charge, taking note of those falling short in their endeavours. When Wangmo catches a distracted eye, her stern frown ensures a quick return to concentration. But on me, the visitor, Wangmo bestows only smiles.

Much of the focus of the rituals and chanting the nuns engage in is centred on 'cutting through the ego', curbing craving and desire and seeking enlightenment for the benefit of all. Yet watching the nuns seated before me go through their devotions, weaving their hands in sequences of graceful movement known as mudras and singing sutras from stiff sheaves of ancient scriptures, I can't help but wonder. What experience of suffering have these women and young girls had that they would choose to devote their lives to extinguishing it both within themselves and others? For most, I imagine, can have known little life beyond the nunnery.

In the days that follow, their stories unfold, haltingly, cautiously.

These women are not used to talking about themselves. There are also linguistic differences to be overcome. At the beginning, it is made clear to me by one of the sterner nuns working in Gawa Khilwa's administration office that many here would feel uncomfortable with me bringing in an outsider to act as translator and interlocutor. Given the rare access I have been offered into some of the nuns' most private practices, I both understand and respect this, and accept the help of two Gawa Khilwa nuns who offer to work with me as my interpreter. Occasionally they struggle to understand the question I am asking, but there is another problem that I did not foresee. From a Buddhist perspective, the constant self-dramas in which most people wrap their lives are considered so ephemeral they have little inherent meaning, and I sometimes have the impression that they struggle to understand the point of my questions. For everything I ask is inevitably informed by a western perspective on life, one that is imbued with certain cultural assumptions about individuality and society, one that relies heavily on logic and critical analysis.

And yet, here I am, surrounded by women who have taken their destiny into their own hands, whose lives are highly disciplined but unfurl according to deeper ley lines in the human spirit. As I sit for many hours observing the elaborate rituals of the nuns at Gawa Khilwa, I realize quite clearly this is why I am here. So many years spent writing about the sorrows of others has left me drained. The loss of both my parents has rendered me temporarily incapable of taking in more sadness in forsaken corners of the world. I know I need to take stock.

Looking back at some of what I have witnessed as a journalist, there are times I have struggled to understand the madness of the world. How can you truly explain why one human being has taken another, taped her hair to a post in a remote Bosnian hunting lodge and raped her repeatedly in the name of that chilling euphemism 'ethnic cleansing'? No matter what political framework or theatre of war you place such inhumanity within, at its root lie the poisons of hatred and ignorance.

As the Dutch theologian Henri Nouwen observed, the cruel reality of the world is the cruel reality of the human heart, our own included. We all have these impulses within us. Nuns too feel anger, desire, jealousy and resentment. It is how they transform such feelings within the microcosm of monastic settings and in the world beyond that interests me. And I must begin by challenging my own preconceptions.

One of the assumptions I held is that the monastic existence must be one of quiet contemplation, untroubled by everyday concerns. But from the moment I step within the walls of Gawa Khilwa, I see that the reality is very different.

With a neck pass granting me 'Nuns Compound Special Access' I am left free to wander through their quarters, and everywhere I go I see nuns engaged in hard physical work. The nuns are responsible for the smooth running of every aspect of daily life at Gawa Khilwa, from chopping wood for the kitchen stoves to shovelling sand and cement for further construction work and shouldering much of the maintenance of the nunnery's buildings and gardens, along with running an administration office, a small coffee shop, guest quarters and a library. The only day they have to rest is Sunday, when they wash their clothes and living quarters. But even then, they still get up at 3 a.m. to begin their devotions and spend four to five hours praying and chanting in the temple.

It is this almost total lack of free time that prevents tensions and quarrels erupting, according to Rigzin, the nun who acts as my interpreter throughout most of my stay. Rigzin is one of the older nuns at Gawa Khilwa and has a broad smile that lights up otherwise serious features. Though warm and generous with her time, she retains a slightly formal air, as she rarely takes off the distinctive hat that marks the Drukpa nuns out from those in other Tibetan Buddhist traditions. This maroon cloth hat, known as a *thandal*, gathered at the top and held in place by a blue brim at the nape of the neck, is worn tilted forward and bulges strangely over the nuns' foreheads. Most of the nuns I observe only don the *thandal* when leaving the nunnery, preferring otherwise to remain bareheaded, their shaven heads a sign that they have shed worldly concerns along with their hair and are intent on cultivating only inner beauty.

With so many women living in such close quarters, I expected there to be occasional moments of tension. But in the time I spend at Gawa Khilwa I observe little disharmony or disagreement. Whatever free moments the nuns find in their busy schedule are given over to devotional practices that channel their energy into a world beyond constant self-grasping. Looking in through the window of a dormitory one morning, I watch as a young nun sits cross-legged on her bed tossing handfuls of vibrantly coloured gemstones onto a tower of copper dishes as she repeatedly chants a chosen mantra. This ritual offering of precious stones signifies a symbolic offering up of the riches of the universe. On the bed next to her, another nun is committing sutras from ancient Buddhist texts to memory. Copies of these sacred sutra sheets are kept wrapped in fine silk brocades and stacked in simple bookcases that separate the nuns' beds. Each bookcase contains the few personal items the nuns possess: a toothbrush, soap, pairs of glasses, a mug for tea, on some a few family snapshots.

In many quiet corners of the nunnery I find nuns performing

traditional Buddhist prostrations, a gesture symbolic both of laying down the individual ego and of offering up the body, speech and mind for a higher spiritual purpose. With hands clasped in a prayer position the nuns touch their fingers first to their forehead, then their lips and then their heart, before falling to their knees, and sliding their open palms out in front of them while bringing their foreheads to the ground. It is a movement requiring both agility and stamina. Each novice is required to perform 100,000 prostrations before being able to progress from taking the five most basic root vows of the novice – not to steal, kill, lie, become intoxicated or engage in sexual activity – to a more elaborate series of thirty-six vows known as *gitsul*, which qualify her as an advanced novice or *getsulma*. These additional vows include promises not to wear perfume or any ornamentation, not to sing, dance or play musical instruments, not to accept or keep money and not to take more food than is needed. One vow even stipulates the maximum height from the ground of the bed a nun should sleep on: no more than the distance from the elbow to the fingertips.

Despite such exhortations against singing, the nunnery seems full of lilting, evocative sound, from the early-morning chorus of chanting in the temple to the whispered mantras the nuns recite by themselves. In hidden corners of the gardens I watch small groups of nuns gather to practise playing what appear to me to be musical instruments: pipes, long horns, drums and bells. From this I deduce religious chanting and instruments are excluded from the vows. It seems the spirit of the vows, rather than their literal acceptance, is what matters. One afternoon, in the large hall where the nuns sometimes practise kung fu, I stand captivated by the sight of a group of nuns performing what has all the appearance of a graceful dance. Treading softly in a large circle, they twist their hands close to their faces and then push their palms down towards the floor in a series of intricate moves executed to the chanting of nuns in the centre of the circle. These movements form part of a special ritual, known as *chöd*. Performed every month in evening ceremonies at the temple, *chöd* sometimes involves practitioners imagining their own flesh being pared from their bones as a way of cutting through the ego and overcoming mental demons such as ignorance, anger and fear of adversity. Such intricate and complex mental work seems far removed from the western concept of learning, the goal being not to accumulate knowledge in a sterile academic way, but rather to train the mind to understand the way the mind itself works.

One evening, as I sit watching the sun dipping below the horizon, Gawa Khilwa's chanting mistress, Zangmola, comes to show me the meaning of the expressive hand movements the nuns use when chanting in the temple. Zangmola is a twenty-six-year-old nun from Ladakh, with striking features, high cheekbones, a finely chiselled nose and large brown eyes that flicker earnestly between mine to check if I understand her explanations. Patiently, Zangmola goes through a sequence of eight gestures where fingertips are touched together in different ways to form mudras, and palms are woven in intricate patterns to signify various symbolic offerings of water, flowers, incense, light, perfume, delicious food and harmonious sound. As Zangmola passes from one sequence to another, she clicks her fingers in a gesture signifying a request that these offerings be accepted. An hour spent observing these manual dances instils in me a longed-for sense of peace.

After observing the nuns' busy routine, I am keen to discover some of their personal backgrounds. On my first morning in the main temple at Gawa Khilwa, I had noticed a slender figure seated behind Zangmola. I am intrigued by the way she sits apart on the raised dais, so I seek her out early on in my stay. Her name is Choying Khandro, but the other nuns refer to her simply as 'Cemola'. *Cemola,* I discover, is the Tibetan word for 'princess'.

Amongst the nuns of Gawa Khilwa, 'Cemola' is spoken of with an air of reverence. This is not only because of her noble heritage, but because the region from which she comes in eastern Tibet, Nangchen, is regarded by her countrymen as a deeply spiritual, almost mythical kingdom. More than 800 years ago Nangchen was one of five independent kingdoms in the area of Tibet called Kham, now known by its Chinese name, Qinghai. Once home to many hundreds of monasteries, nunneries and hermitages, and with more nuns and monks per head of population than any other area of Tibet, this sparsely populated mountain kingdom gradually became known as 'The Land of Meditators'.

The most renowned of Nangchen's nunneries were founded in the nineteenth century by the revered Buddhist master Tsoknyi Rinpoche. His unique vision, at a time when nuns were virtually ignored by both the religious establishment and the communities in which they lived, was that the women in his charge should become some of the most accomplished spiritual practitioners in the world. It was in the remote and mystical terrain of Nangchen that the largest nunnery in Tibet, Gebchak Gonpa, was built. Over time, Gebchak became home to a spiritual lineage of more than 300 nuns famed for their achievements in some of the most profound forms of Buddhist teachings. When Chinese troops invaded Tibet in the early 1950s, eventually destroying most of the region's 6,000 monasteries and nunneries, many of Nangchen's nuns, including those at Gebchak, were sent to work camps and perished. Others returned to their nomadic lives. But some retreated to caves in the mountains to continue their meditation practice and wait. Two decades later, they emerged and began to rebuild their demolished nunneries brick by brick.

In the days before I arrive at Gawa Khilwa, Choying Khandro has emerged from seven months of secluded retreat here. During this time her days have been spent almost entirely in meditation, her only contact being with an attendant nun preparing her meals and with the Gyalwang Drukpa himself, from whom she receives private teaching. After I pass a message via her attendant that I would like to speak to her, Choying Khandro takes some time before making up her mind. When she finally agrees, I am asked to wait in a quiet upstairs seating area in the guest quarters. Before she arrives, a rather nervous nun specially designated as my interpreter for the occasion quizzes me on what sort of questions I will ask. Before I have time to answer, Choying Khandro steps lightly up the stairs and takes a seat by my side. She has a regal bearing and holds herself perfectly erect, hands neatly folded in her lap. There is an unconventional beauty and innocence about her. She has an open face, high forehead, full lips and almond-shaped eyes framed by rimless glasses. She is still only twenty-three years old and her direct, clear gaze and constant smile as we speak lends her an otherworldly air.

It is hard to unravel precise details of Choying Khandro's family and, despite repeated gentle prompting, she appears to want to reveal little about her childhood, as if it is somehow now irrelevant. Though Tibetans still recognize and honour royal heritage, all concept of such a tradition was abolished under China's communist government. But gradually I learn that her grandfather was the last king of Nangchen formally to sit on the throne. He died during the Cultural Revolution of the 1960s and 1970s after attempting to defend his kingdom against China's Red Army troops. Two of his three sons have also since died, including Choying Khandro's father, who passed away shortly after she was born, leaving two young daughters.

One of the palaces where the family lived, near the Nangchen capital of Sharnda, is attached to a monastery called Tsechu. This is the palace Choying Khandro refers to as home. As children, she and her sister were sometimes dressed in fine gold brocades and Tibetan ornamental headdresses made of turquoise and coral. A picture of her from this time, which she later brings for me to see, shows her sitting in a meadow as a smiling baby, propped up in a pink and white woollen jumper beside her elder sister. Her sister can't be more than four or five but appears to be wearing silk brocade and a fine shawl.

'When we were young my sister and I used to travel around the countryside on holiday,' Choying Khandro recalls. 'One day, when I was eleven years old, I was taken to visit a nunnery.' The nunnery she visited was Gebchak. Some of Gebchak's older practitioners, who survived the ravages of the Chinese invasion, are now toothless and live out their days in isolated hermitages close by that are little more than mountain caves, where their shaven heads gradually become a tangle of matted locks. Encountering such a harsh and extreme environment might have been alarming, if not frightening, for a young girl of such privilege. But Choying Khandro says that what struck her most was the supreme sense of peace the nuns at Gebchak exuded.

'As soon as I entered that place I knew I wanted to stay there and become a nun,' she says. 'I felt completely at home. Even at that young age I knew that more than anything else I wanted to experience the contentment and happiness you could feel and see in the nuns there.' When news of Choying Khandro's wish to stay at the nunnery reached Tsechu monastery, her mother travelled to Gebchak to fetch her youngest daughter home. But Choying Khandro refused to leave and, as an indulgence, her mother agreed that she could stay for a short while. 'After my mother left me there in that remote place, she used to write me letters pleading with me to come home. She would send my favourite lollipops. But I knew I wanted to stay.'

It was only when one of Gebchak's high lamas eventually convinced her mother of her sincere vocation that Choying Khandro's training as a novice began. She was just eleven years old, but initiation at such a tender age is not uncommon. For many of the young nuns here, however, the lives they leave behind are considerably less luxurious than Choying Khandro's childhood was. Several of the novices I meet have escaped poverty and, sometimes, domestic violence, becoming nuns in search of peace and an education. When asked what brings these young women to the nunnery, most will simply answer that it is their karma, reluctant to talk of any difficulties because it transgresses the central Buddhist edict of 'right speech' – speaking about others without harshness. Karma, at its most fundamental, holds to the scientific principle that for every action there is a reaction, and it is a central tenet of Buddhist philosophy. It is only when karma is linked with the consequences of action from previous lives and a belief in reincarnation that I, personally, struggle. But, unsure that a belief in reincarnation is necessary for sympathy with Buddhist wisdom, this is an inner debate I choose to delay.

Choying Khandro too refers to her karma. 'It was because of my good karma that I was able to become a nun,' she says with a tranquil smile. 'So many people ask, "You are a princess, why did you become a nun?" But from my point of view, I feel more proud of being a nun than being a princess,' she continues. 'Many people could say that the life of a princess is easy. But I don't feel that. Maybe if I wasn't a nun, I could be happy. But my happiness is much deeper now.'

During the time she was expected to carry out solitary meditation retreats at Gebchak, one of which lasted a year in an isolated mountain hut, she concedes she did receive a little preferential treatment due to her royal status. While the staple diet of most nuns in Tibet consists of *tsampa,* rolled balls of dried roasted barley mixed with salty Tibetan tea made with yak butter, she tells me that 'When village people nearby heard there was a princess meditating in the mountains, they brought fresh vegetables for my personal assistant to prepare.' But Choying Khandro's standing as a princess did not spare her from other hardships. While her teachers would prostrate themselves in front of her as a mark of respect, one would beat her when she didn't apply herself sufficiently. 'I still tremble when I remember the sound of his voice,' she says. 'But by his grace I learnt a great deal.'

Choying Khandro was eighteen when she first met the Gyalwang Drukpa on one of his rare visits to Tibet in 2007. 'His Holiness is regarded in Nangchen as an important master and my teachers at Gebchak saw it as a great honour when he asked if I would like to return with him to Gawa Khilwa,' she says. When she left Gebchak for the long drive to Lhasa before flying on to Kathmandu, the people of Nangchen turned out to line the streets and wish her well. Days of celebration were held.

While the majority of the several hundred nuns at Gawa Khilwa are from Nepal or Ladakh, within the Indian border state of Jammu and Kashmir, a number have escaped from Tibet under difficult circumstances, often trekking across the Himalayas for weeks. These Tibetan exiles stand little chance of ever seeing their families again.

By contrast, Choying Khandro's privileged position means her mother and sister have been able to visit her in Nepal.

Her sister, recently married, is a doctor. From an outside perspective, it might appear to many that her work is of more direct benefit to others than the vocation of a nun. But the conviction that the monastic calling creates a vital positive energy for wider society is deeply ingrained in all the nuns I meet. Certainly this is the intention of the nuns' teacher and protector, the Gyalwang Drukpa. He keenly promotes the nuns in his care becoming involved in a variety of social programmes to help the impoverished local communities. In recent years, a small but well-equipped clinic and dental surgery, staffed by volunteer doctors and dentists but largely run by medically trained nuns, has been built at the rear of the nunnery to serve local villagers.

During my time at Gawa Khilwa, however, the clinic's beds slowly fill with ailing nuns. Nepal is in the grip of a flu epidemic and illness steadily sweeps through the nunnery. Many of the nuns take to wearing masks. Kung fu practice is temporarily suspended so the women can conserve their energy. Eventually my patient interpreter, Rigzin, succumbs and is admitted for a night. But, despite my protestations that she should rest, the following morning she is back by my side.

Rigzin's own path to the nunnery is more typical than Choying Khandro's, for her story reflects the hardship faced by many in these parts. Born in the Nubra Valley of Ladakh, she ran away from home to become a nun when she was twenty-two, she explains, because she dreaded the prospect of domestic drudgery and remorseless toil that is the fate of most women in these Himalayan communities. 'I would have been married young, had two or three children and spent the rest of my life working the fields. But I wanted to dedicate my life to other people and not just myself and my immediate family,' says Rigzin, now in her mid-thirties, citing Mother Teresa as her inspiration. She offers to help me converse with some of the other novices, the youngest of whom is a girl called Lanzom.

During morning and evening ceremonies in the temple I have watched as Lanzom, sitting on the end of a row, constantly observes those around her to see what she should be doing. Each time she catches me looking in her direction, she starts furiously leafing through a large book she keeps tucked under the table in front of her and begins to chant, a little theatrically, in a loud, high-pitched voice.

Lanzom, I am told by one of the older nuns, was born in a village close to Nepal's border with Tibet and was sent to work in the fields when she was eight years old. Her brothers became shepherds. But there were too many mouths to feed. When she was nine, her father walked with her for seven days to reach Gawa Khilwa, where the nuns took her under their wing. One afternoon I find Lanzom playing a skipping game outside the nunnery's guest quarters. For a short while I join in her game, but she is shy and unsure of herself. I have been told that she is now ten years old, but in truth this child, who has had no childhood, seems much younger than that. Lanzom is one of more than a dozen novices under the age of fourteen at Gawa Khilwa. All will be given the choice to leave the nunnery if they wish when they reach eighteen. Few ever do.

While the majority of the nuns I meet at Gawa Khilwa have come to the nunnery with little adult experience of lay life, this is not so for Thubten Palmo. Sitting cross-legged on the floor of one of the nunnery's classrooms late one afternoon, she spreads out a handful of photographs to show me something of the time before she became a nun. The picture that catches my eye is of a young woman in a plumed beret and khaki jumper with military epaulettes bearing the letters JKP, a white leather pistol holster slung at her hip; she appears to be receiving a gift while a crowd looks on. 'This is when I was made a police captain,' Thubten says, handing me the photograph for a closer look.

It is almost impossible to equate the uniformed officer in the photograph with the shaven-headed figure seated before me. Even more difficult to fathom is the metamorphosis she has undergone; Thubten was once an anti-terrorist officer in the Jammu-Kashmir police force. 'I felt I wanted to become a nun when I was very young because I loved to read dharma [Buddhist] teachings,' she says. Thubten's father had been an army officer but died when she was eight years old. 'My mother wanted me to join the police and so I did,' explains Thubten. 'As a police officer, I was taught to always be suspicious of people, to think of them as the enemy, a possible terrorist carrying a gun or a knife. I went through all the firearms training, but I knew I could never shoot anyone. The dharma teaches us to treat our enemies as friends. It teaches peace. That was where my heart lay.'

Beside the photograph of Thubten in uniform is another of a small boy in a striped woollen jumper and hat. His hands are clenched and he looks startled and sad. This is Thubten's son. When she was twenty-five, Thubten says she asked her mother for permission to become a nun, but her mother refused. The following year Thubten was married. It was a love-match rather than the customary arranged marriage and the couple were happy. 'But in my heart I knew my feelings hadn't changed,' she says. 'I decided to run away.' Though it is hard to imagine, Thubten tells me her husband bore her no ill will and he is now remarried. When I speak to her about how she was able to leave her child, she clutches the photograph of her son to her heart. 'I loved my son and I miss him very much. But I knew he would be well looked after by my mother.' Her son is only twelve years old but is already considering becoming a monk, she tells me. 'I believe he should be older before he makes such a decision. But I would not stop him.'

It is time for her to return to her daily practice, but as she gathers up her photographs and prepares to leave she turns to me with a wistful smile. 'My life was happy. I used to make my colleagues laugh,' she says. 'But a nun's life is happier. There is no tension and all we have to concentrate on is the dharma. I think I made a good choice.'

Each day that passes, I renew my request to meet the head of the Drukpa order, the Gyalwang Drukpa, keen to learn more about the man who has made such life transformations possible and to understand the origins of his unusual commitment to the nuns in his care. On the morning of my sixth day at Gawa Khilwa, I am granted an audience and shown along a path that skirts the rim of the nunnery, leading to his private quarters. These are set slightly apart, partially shielded from view by tall fencing, and I am struck by their more modern design. While the nuns' quarters have a closed-in feel that seems to fit with the inner journey they are taking, here the entire front wall is comprised of floor-to-ceiling glass windows looking out across the valley leading to Kathmandu. It is as if the Gyalwang Drukpa must live more open to the world; for much of the year, he travels to give teachings to Drukpa monks, nuns and lay followers in Nepal and beyond.

The décor inside the room in which he receives me is full of established Buddhist imagery. But as we begin to speak I quickly gain an impression of the Gyalwang Drukpa as a man whose monastic robes mask a forward thinker impatient with some of the constraints of tradition. Early on in our discussion, he shows me a picture of his mother and I come to understand that her absence when he was boy perhaps provides some key to his unorthodox views. The Gyalwang Drukpa had a harsh childhood. After being recognized as a reincarnation of a previous holder of the title, at the age of four he was taken from the care of his Tibetan parents to a monastery near Darjeeling, in India, to begin training to become a monk. He admits openly to the hardship involved. From the age of five, he was expected to memorize vast volumes of Buddhist teachings and when he failed, or reverted to his natural tendency to write with his left hand, he would sometimes be beaten. This reminds me of Choying Khandro's experience of being beaten by her tutors and seems at odds with the Buddhist ethic of non-violence. But the Gyalwang Drukpa dismisses the contradiction by saying such an education engendered in him tremendous confidence and knowledge of his own strength.

During the course of his monastic training, the Gyalwang Drukpa rarely saw his parents and enjoyed little female influence. The few nuns he encountered were regarded as inferior to monks and invariably treated badly. 'By nature women embody the wisdom of the Buddhist teachings. They are more loving and compassionate than men because of their mothering instinct,' he says. It seems quite a leap from this nurturing vision of womanhood to introducing his nuns to kung fu – a move that has been criticized in more conservative Buddhist circles.

The idea came to him, he explains, after seeing nuns in Vietnam being taught the martial art by police officers taught combat skills to fight the Vietcong. 'Some people say kung fu, knocking somebody down, is the opposite of love. And I too wondered if I was doing the right thing, introducing my nuns to the practice,' he says. 'But love comes in many forms. Love is not accepting failure and it is not failing to defend against attack. I want the nuns that I teach to be strong and confident. Becoming a monk or a nun is not a comfortable experience, but it is good training for the skills they will need in life.'

The essence of Buddhism, he continues, is a process for improving the quality of one's own life and that of others. 'Buddhism is not a religion. It is not an "ism" at all. I prefer to talk about Buddhist teachings,' he says, leaning forward on the elegant sofa, lending his words a sense of urgency. 'You can call it a philosophy of life. But there are many people who misunderstand this term too, thinking of it as something academic. I'm talking about a philosophy of how you stand, sit, drink tea and do everything in life with awareness. This is the essence of meditation.'

Returning to the changing status of women within Buddhism, he reminds me that Buddhist teachings encourage a questioning nature. 'From the religious point of view, this could be quite troublesome,' he says, with a throaty laugh. 'But from a Buddhist point of view, it is very welcome.' The impact of such questioning on improving the position of women within many Buddhist monastic communities is profound. 'The answer to many questions being asked in modern society is that more empowerment of women is needed, because it is quite clear that in nature the feminine principle is of equal importance,' says the Gyalwang Drukpa.

Far from envisioning his nunneries as sanctuaries from everyday reality, his intention is that they should act as training grounds for spiritual warriors. And there are now more women queuing up for the privilege of this training than any of his nunneries are able to accommodate. Gawa Khilwa, for instance, at the time of my visit, has a waiting list of between fifty and sixty women. 'We need women now more than ever,' says the Gyalwang Drukpa, as our meeting concludes. 'In this dark age more female energy is certainly needed.' His intention is that the nuns at Gawa Khilwa, and other nunneries over which he presides in Ladakh and India, will eventually emerge into society to carry out practical work. 'The nuns must see these nunneries as schools from which they will one day emerge, putting their strong female energy to good use,' he concludes.

From the mild, even timid, attitude typical of the nuns I have encountered so far at Gawa Khilwa, I am not convinced this radical vision has yet dawned on many. But as my time there draws to a close, I take a walk with one young novice who seems to encapsulate the spirit the Gyalwang Drukpa is nurturing. Migyur is one of the few nuns I meet who appears curious about life in the West, and one evening she suggests we take a walk beyond the walls of the nunnery to enjoy the cool air. The mountain path that leads away from Gawa Khilwa to a nearby village snakes through rough pasture and fields of crops. We pass mothers and daughters bent double, working, dressed in saris of turquoise, scarlet and emerald green. Some raise their heads and wave.

Migyur is a striking twenty-one-year-old, with bow-shaped lips, a freckled face, smiling eyes and a composed manner. As we walk she asks me a little about myself, then talks of how she became a novice at the age of fourteen, at her father's urging. 'My father told me the life of a nun is both honourable and hard. But as a nun I knew you didn't need to ask anyone's permission to help others,' she says. 'I was very young, but I knew I wanted to be a great woman, a great person.' The clarity with which she speaks suggests that, one day, she will be just that.

As the weekend approaches Gawa Khilwa prepares to open its doors. Every Saturday certain parts of this monastic complex are open to the public. The heavy main gates swing back and a large open space near the entrance slowly fills with motorbikes carrying mostly young couples. While the men, dressed in jeans and T-shirts, dismount from their bikes with a swagger, their wives or girlfriends riding pillion step down from behind them more demurely. Adjusting their colourful saris, some pull shawls up to their faces, leaving only their eyes uncovered to take in the women who have chosen a path different from their own.

Slowly, Gawa Khilwa starts to hum with the chatter of those who have come to make offerings at the temple or are simply curious about the nuns' lives; the atmosphere changes as the bustle and confusion of the world outside intrudes on this oasis of calm. It is a meeting of two worlds, but one the Gyalwang Drukpa encourages. He does not want the nuns in his charge to remain cosseted within the confines of a nunnery. His intention is to prepare them for a wider mission beyond.

After spending a week with the nuns of Gawa Khilwa, I head back down the treacherous road to Kathmandu and meet with nuns who have embarked on such a mission.

2

TO KATHMANDU

From the moment I set eyes on Ani Choying Drolma, it is clear she is a woman in a hurry. We have arranged to meet by the entrance to one of Kathmandu's greatest temples, or stupas, in the neighbourhood of Boudhanath, the hub of Tibetan exile life in Nepal. Boudhanath's central stupa is a thing of beauty, its vast whitewashed central dome gleaming in the morning heat. Rising from the dome, a square tower is painted with four sets of eyes of the Buddha gazing out in all directions and, above this, myriad lines of brightly coloured prayer flags fan out, snapping and fluttering in the wind, each breeze carrying messages of peace to all corners of the world. As I stand watching Tibetans, young and old, walking clockwise around the stupa, murmuring incantations for good fortune, out of the corner of my eye I catch sight of a small, determined-looking figure approaching at speed.

The woman bearing down on me does not look like a nun. Instead of traditional robes and simple sandals, she wears a mustard-yellow polo shirt, white sports shoes suited for fast movement, a wide-brimmed sun visor and an oversize pair of sunglasses. She could pass for an amateur golfer. The visor and sunglasses, she explains as she bustles me through the narrow lanes of Boudhanath, help make her less recognizable. But even so, every few minutes, someone spots her and waves. For Choying Drolma is something of a celebrity in Nepal. Her honeyed voice won her the country's top music award for best female singer and best album of the year in 2004. Far beyond Nepal, her singing has attracted accolades and famous fans, including Celine Dion and Tracy Chapman. She has performed at the Barbican Theatre in London and goes on regular concert tours around the world. But Choying Drolma's performances owe little to the pop style of the West's best-known contemporary singing nun, Suor Cristina, the Ursuline Catholic bombarded with record deals after winning *The Voice of Italy*, or the more staid renditions of the fictional postulant Maria in *The Sound of Music*. Choying Drolma's performances do not transgress the monastic rule against singing, since each song is inspired by traditional Buddhist mantras dating back more than 2,000 years, though some have been adapted and arranged in musical compilations with western artists.

The beauty of her music belies the brutality of her early years, when she grew up in such poverty that her entire family slept in one room and she and her mother were regularly subjected to violent abuse at the hands of her father. As we take our seats in an airy conservatory on the upper floor of her home in a backstreet of Boudhanath, her voice changes tone when she begins to speak of her childhood. At the age of thirteen, after another of her father's drunken attacks, Choying Drolma finally took refuge in a nunnery called Nagi Gompa, in the mountains north of Kathmandu. 'I was so full of anger, I was like a wild thing when I arrived there. I was always getting into trouble,' she says. But under the patient guidance of her teacher, a great meditation master, she gradually learnt to tame her own rage.

'My teacher would say, "Instead of cursing the darkness, why don't you try to light a candle?" He helped me to see everything in a different way. I learnt to perceive the best out of every situation in life,' she says. 'I came to see that my father suffered from a kind of sickness. I began to feel pity and compassion for him. I wouldn't wish anyone to go through what I went through. But also, I have to accept that all the qualities I learnt to develop in myself were as a result of my experience. It drove me to the dharma. I had to develop a strong will to survive and that gave me the strength to succeed. I have come to see situations as my friend not my enemy, learning from them whatever I can, and that has helped me to have a lighter life.'

As she talks, I once again feel ashamed at my initial questioning of how much young nuns can know of suffering. While most may not have experienced the violence Choying Drolma did, the climate of low expectation, subservience and often brutish treatment in which many girls in the region are raised is hardship enough. In order to help others, Choying Drolma set up an organization called The Nuns' Welfare Foundation in 1998 to collect funds for a school for young nuns she has built on the outskirts of Kathmandu. The Arya Tara School now caters for more than seventy girls from the age of five to twenty-two from remote areas of Tibet, India and Nepal. Some former pupils have already gone on to university in India. Once their education is finished, they can choose to return to lay life. 'During the time they are at the school, they have the feeling that they are someone special,' she says.

Her next project, in memory of her mother, who died of kidney disease, is to found a specialist hospital in Kathmandu for treating kidney disorders. It seems an ambitious goal, but one of her friends in Germany has nicknamed her 'Ani Bond' – Ani being a Tibetan honorific for 'nun' – because, like James Bond, she takes on seemingly impossible missions.

Before we part, Choying Drolma closes her eyes, folds her hands in her lap, and sings for me. 'When I sing I remember my teacher, Tulku Urgyen Rinpoche. He taught me how to sing with joy,' she says, her joy clear in the smile that plays on her lips as the sound of her singing fades.

*

In all my meetings with nuns at Gawa Khilwa, and with Choying Drolma, I have been hesitant about enquiring into more intimate aspects of their lives, both out of respect for their natural cultural reserve and because I fear the sensitivity of such questions might be lost in translation. But in my last days in Kathmandu, through a friend of a journalist colleague, I hear of two western women living there who have become nuns in the Tibetan Buddhist tradition. Both agree to a visit. Several years ago, one of the women, Ani Dominique, helped found a clinic and hospice close to Boudhanath's Shechen monastery, which offers rare free treatment to those unable to pay. My brief meetings with both women give me an initial glimpse into the challenges faced by westerners becoming Buddhist nuns and into the attraction that such a different way of life holds.

It has been raining heavily the night before I meet Ani Dominique and the road leading to the apartment where she lives in Boudhanath is a sea of mud. With buses and cars at a standstill, there is no alternative but to take off my sandals and squelch through the quagmire barefoot. When I arrive, covered in muck, Ani Dominique laughs and shows me where to wash my feet before inviting me to join her for lunch. From the outset, she exudes warmth and her conversation is punctuated by infectious laughter.

Born Dominique Marchal to a Catholic family in Brussels, she moved to the Swiss Alps in her early twenties and, with the help of a family inheritance, started taking flying lessons. By the age of twenty-three, she was Switzerland's first female commercial pilot and in the years that followed became a private pilot to wealthy businessmen in different parts of the world. One photograph from her youth shows her perched on the wing of a small aircraft, wearing large dark glasses and a billowing headscarf, a look reminiscent of a young Jackie Kennedy. Another shows her posing in front of a

Learjet, arms crossed, wearing a braided uniform. 'It was all extremely glamorous,' she says with the intonation of a native French-speaker. 'But at the same time I was never free. I was always on standby in case I was needed.'

At twenty-six, Dominique married the first of her three husbands and gave birth to her first son. When the couple divorced, she lost custody of her child and was left heartbroken. Her second marriage also ended in a divorce, after the birth of a second son, as did her third. 'All three men fell in love with me because of my adventurous nature. But then they wanted me to be a conventional wife. I made three abominable choices and I take full responsibility for that,' she says, her bright eyes creasing with amusement. 'The whole thing about love is this endless wish to appropriate another person. The point about the dharma teachings on detachment is not that you cease to care but that you enjoy everything without grasping.'

When I ask her to explain more, Dominique carries on with candour. 'I had a very passionate nature. You could even say I was addicted to passion,' she admits with a deep laugh. 'But once I started understanding something of the Buddhist teachings, I came to realize it really was an addiction. Of course, having orgasms is a wonderful thing. But I think it is extremely important to realize that sexuality is something that can be transcended rather than repressed. If you become a monastic and repress your sexuality, you are bound to have problems. But people who understand that sexuality is a fantastic energy and that this energy can be used in a different way are on the right path.'

Dominique started reading books on Buddhism and in her early forties visited Tibet and Kathmandu. In 1995 she returned and helped set up the Shechen clinic while continuing to deepen her

Buddhist studies. A little over a decade later, when she was sixty-three, she attended a course near Dharamshala in India for women interested in becoming nuns. 'After that, it felt very logical to become a nun,' she says. 'In Buddhism the more you see how it works, the more you want to go deeper,' she explains. 'You become absorbed.'

Returning to the subject of celibacy, she says, 'When you accept that part of your life is over, it creates a lot of mental space. As a woman, you can sometimes think that you will go somewhere and the right guy will be there and you will be able to seduce him, and this occupies a lot of your mind. When you move beyond that, you become a lot freer.'

Did this mean that Dominique was content with the life of a nun because she had led such a full life previously, I wonder? She says not. 'I have never been happier in my life than I am now. I had to go through all the hurt and emotions centred on my own needs, which I prefer to call learning rather than suffering, but in another life I hope I will become a monastic at a much younger age.' Dominique concludes our discussion with apologies – she has a meeting at the clinic she must attend – and embraces me warmly as we part.

The following morning, I take a road leading north from Boudhanath to Khachoe Ghakyil Ling, the largest Tibetan nunnery in Nepal, on the outskirts of Kathmandu. The nunnery is affiliated to Kopan monastery, which has a reputation for welcoming foreigners. Ani Fran, the nun I have come to see, helps organize year-round meditation courses there. She looks tired when I arrive and asks that we rest in the shade of a tree outside during her brief break. Ani Fran was raised by a conservative Catholic family in Bavaria, Germany, before emigrating to Australia, and offers an interesting perspective on the difficulties faced by western women who become Buddhist nuns.

'For westerners, monastic life can be harder in some ways,' she says. When I ask her what she means, she explains that, for some, this is because of mistaken motivation. 'It is important to understand that you become a nun principally for your own good. Because obviously you can help others without being a nun.'

Like Ani Dominique, Ani Fran was once married, for sixteen years, to a man she describes as 'a golden beach boy'. 'It was just a normal marriage – a disaster,' she says with a weary smile. Her own path to monasticism began when she was introduced to Buddhism by an Australian friend who had become a Tibetan Buddhist nun. But it was not until she attended a talk by one of the founders of Kopan, Lama Thubten Zopa Rinpoche, that her interest deepened and she decided to travel to Nepal to visit his monastery. At the time, she thought she would return to Australia within a few months. Instead, she stayed, and when she was in her early forties took the vows of a novice.

Ani Fran is also now in her sixties and it seems clear as she speaks that her chosen path has brought her the peace she was seeking. This is not always the case, she tells me. 'A lot of western women become nuns because they have some sort of messianic feelings that they want to save the world.' This false sense of 'self-sacrifice' leads them to believe the monastic order they join has an obligation to look after them materially for the rest of their lives. 'When this doesn't happen, they become bitter and frustrated and disrobe,' she says. In reality, unless a nun lives within a monastic setting which is able to raise funds from donors to survive financially, she has to find her own way of meeting her living costs. While many eastern families traditionally give some financial backing to those who become nuns, western women often need to find some form of work to support their spiritual practice. For some this can be an impossible challenge.

In addition to financial difficulties, Ani Fran says westerners sometimes feel lonelier than their eastern sisters, who often derive more comfort from the sense of belonging to a community. 'Some disrobe and get a relationship,' she tells me, adding that this very often ends in disappointment. 'When someone has been a monastic – a monk or a nun – it is very hard to be part of a couple,' she explains. 'You become very self-contained. This is very difficult for someone who wants to possess you.'

Despite such trials, Ani Fran adopts typically Germanic pragmatism in summing up the appeal of the Buddhist teachings, the dharma. 'It is so logical. That is what I love about it,' she says, her etched features softening into a smile. 'If you follow the path, you will get a result.' At this point a minibus pulls up in the car park in front of us, disgorging passengers for that afternoon's meditation session. Ani Fran signals that she must get back to work. I thank her, grateful for the brief insight she has given me, but I realize I have many more questions.

The 'result' Ani Fran referred to seems a mysterious thing. Regardless of its outer trappings and traditions, the Buddhist path, I come to understand, is essentially private and solitary. As one nun I met in Kathmandu put it, Buddhist practice is 'a personal activity that is hard to explain.' Adhering to its path, she said, is 'long and difficult, like following a stony, winding road on the edge of an abyss.'

3

BIRTHPLACE

Before leaving Nepal, I travel to the south of the country to the place where the Buddha's own journey through life began, in the small town now called Lumbini. This lies in the lush subtropical region of Terai, close to Nepal's border with India. I have no plans to speak with nuns in Lumbini, and will in any case encounter none. The purpose of my visit is more prosaic. There are clearly defined physical markers here that will help me make sense of the complex web of different Buddhist lineages to which the nuns I meet belong.

In my imagination, I picture Lumbini thronged with Buddhist pilgrims in the same way that Christians flock to Bethlehem. But this illusion is shattered the moment I arrive back at Kathmandu airport to catch the flight to Terai. While the queue of mountaineers and trekkers jostling to get to Pokhara, the northern gateway to the High Himalaya, snakes right through the airport terminal and out onto the pavement beyond, there is not a single passenger waiting to check in ahead of me for my flight south to Bhairahwa, on the plains of Terai.

At the time the Buddha was born, this region formed part of northern India, only falling within Nepal's borders when the present-day nation took shape in the eighteenth century. More than 2,000 years ago, this area would have been both forested and cultivated for crops. But the forests have long since been felled and on the drive from Bhairahwa airport I pass through only paddy fields and mango groves; the road is largely empty but for a few cyclists and ambling bullock carts. As in neighbouring India, the majority of Nepal's population today is Hindu, with less than twenty per cent now registered as Buddhist. So it is perhaps unsurprising that I pass only a few stupas and Buddhist shrines here, compared with many multi-coloured Hindu temples. Still, I am taken aback to find Lumbini quite so deserted.

While Buddhism once flourished in India, reaching its peak during the reign of the great Buddhist emperor Ashoka, more than 200 years before the birth of Christ, it slowly went into decline, first with the ascent of Hinduism and the strengthening of caste regulations and then, from the eleventh century, because of the Muslim conquest of much of the Indian subcontinent. For more than a millennium, all traces of the Buddha's connection with the area around Lumbini were erased, only to be rediscovered by archaeologists in the nineteenth century. But it was not until the 1960s, following the advocacy of U Thant, the Burmese United Nations secretary-general, a Buddhist, that Lumbini's heritage was both metaphorically and literally dusted off. With funds gathered from Buddhist countries in the East, a new road was built from Bhairahwa to Lumbini, and plans were drawn up for many new temples and shrines. The monastic zone that has grown up around the Buddha's birthplace has since been declared a UNESCO World Heritage Site and is now known by the rather drab name of the Lumbini Development Zone, or LDZ.

The morning heat is already intense as I pull into a dusty car park that serves as the public gateway to the LDZ. I had originally intended to walk from here. But on discovering the size of the site, I hire a rusty bicycle and bump along an uneven track to the precise location where the Buddha was born. This is now marked by the low, white, castellated Mayadevi Temple, built in honour of his mother, Queen Maha Maya. Beside it are the dark green waters of a sacred pond where she is said to have bathed before going into labour. Within a week of giving birth, she died, leaving the Buddha to be raised by her sister Maha Pajapati, who went on to marry his widowed father. Close to this temple lie the ruins of a stone pillar erected by Emperor Ashoka after making a pilgrimage here. Metal fencing surrounding the pillar is covered with colourful flags, but there is litter strewn about and the site seems to hold little interest for the handful of visitors I watch come and go.

Leading away from the Mayadevi Temple is a long waterway that holds the clue I have been looking for. Marked at the other end by a peace stupa, this waterway divides the LDZ into two distinct zones: an East Monastic Zone and a West Monastic Zone. The split reflects not so much a geographical divide as the doctrinal difference that developed in the way the Buddha's teachings came to be interpreted after his death.

Those who follow the tradition of temples located in Lumbini's East Monastic Zone, such as those of Myanmar (Burma), Thailand and Sri Lanka, practise a more austere, monastically inclined form of Buddhism known as Theravada, or the 'Doctrine of the Elders'. This relies on the first written records of the Buddha's original teachings, as transcribed, after centuries of oral transmission only, in extensive volumes known as the Pali canon. Those who follow the traditions in the West Monastic Zone, which houses temples in Tibetan style and includes those from Japan, Vietnam and several countries in Europe, adhere to a more populist form of Buddhism known as Mahayana. Mahayana Buddhism is a more devotional form of practice, observing much ritual and ceremony, in which the Buddha is transformed from the status of compassionate teacher to more of a 'celestial guru'. Within Mahayana fall such traditions as Tibetan Vajrayana Buddhism and Zen.

The journey I have planned through the East is to take me to places where both the Theravada and the Mahayana traditions are followed. And during the two days I spend in Lumbini, I wend my way between the various temples in the LDZ, beginning to soak up the atmosphere of these different traditions. I pass from the sweeping white gables of the Royal Thai Monastery to the graded golden steeple of the Myanmar Golden Temple, the red-winged roof of the Vietnamese Phat Quoc Tu and other lavish temples built by Buddhist followers in China, Japan, South Korea, Sri Lanka, and also France, Germany and Austria. Most of the temples I visit are virtually deserted, the silence, in some, broken only by the sound of cicadas and the flapping of birds that have found a way into the eves.

Lumbini itself is a place of little charm, too impoverished and removed from tourist routes to attract curious foreigners, and too inaccessible from Kathmandu to allow many devotees ease of access. But perhaps there is another reason for its failure to take off as a site of pilgrimage. Perhaps this lies in the nature of Buddhism itself, which does not encourage blind worship or idolatry. So much so that for the first 500 years after his death, the Buddha was represented only by images of an empty throne, a footprint and a bodhi tree.

There are those who believe the Buddha's teachings, far from being conceived as a religion, were intended as guidelines for moral conduct and a more compassionate society at a time when India was in the throes of violent internecine conflict. The Buddha certainly didn't consider himself a god, merely a monk, an ordinary man who had achieved enlightenment through perseverance on a path open to all. After this enlightenment in his mid-thirties, the Buddha spent more than four decades wandering the plains of northern India, giving teachings to devoted followers, before passing away in his early eighties.

After several centuries in which fewer and fewer in India chose to follow in the Buddha's footsteps, instead turning to Hinduism or Islam, in the last seventy years there has been a significant revival of interest in Buddhism in India, principally amongst Dalits, the nation's poorest population, the so-called untouchables. Given the dire circumstances of so many in this downtrodden class, the focus of the majority of India's Buddhists has been more on empowering women in a secular rather than a monastic context. As a result, it is in the Tibetan community in exile in India that some of the most flourishing nunneries are to be found.

As I prepare to leave Lumbini, cycling back past the green waters where the Buddha's mother is said to have bathed, I reflect on how this monastic path might never have been open to women but for the Buddha's willingness to break with social norms. Even so, it is said that the Buddha hesitated before agreeing that women could become nuns. According to legend, his aunt and stepmother, Maha Pajapati, wished to be admitted to the monastic life following the death of King Suddhodana. Initially the Buddha refused and Maha Pajapati cut off her hair, donned yellow-saffron robes and, together with a large number of her Sakyan kinswomen, walked barefoot for 150 miles from her palace to the place where the Buddha resided. Again, he refused her request, until his closest assistant, Ananda, asked him if women were capable of 'realizing the various stages of sainthood as nuns'.

'They are, Ananda,' the Buddha is said to have replied, after which he agreed that his aunt and her followers could be admitted to his monastic order on condition that they accepted a set of precepts in addition to those required of monks. These rules, some of which enshrined a nun's junior position relative to a monk, made the decision to allow women to adopt the monastic life more acceptable to wider society at the time. The authenticity of these rules has since been challenged.

Some Buddhist literature explains the Buddha's initial refusal to ordain women by referring to an often-disputed prophecy that the admission of nuns could bring about the collapse of Buddhism within 500 years. More than two millennia later, both the women I am meeting and the flourishing interest in Buddhism around the world belie this foretelling.

PART II

INDIA

4

BURNING FOR JUSTICE

My return to Dharamshala, 'Little Lhasa', is marred by frequent storms. The longest monsoon season in more than half a century is in its last throes. Torrential rain has lacerated the roads that snake through the foothills of the Himalayas in India's mountainous border state of Himachal Pradesh, far to the north of New Delhi and the plains of Punjab. For the final stretch of our journey, a thick fog descends and as my taxi driver veers past oncoming traffic on hairpin bends where this seems impossible we pass signs that do little to soothe the nerves. 'Speed thrills but kills,' says one; another, 'Dashing means danger.' Finally, rounding a wide curve, the fog lifts and our destination comes into view. In that moment Dharamshala, meaning 'sanctuary' or 'sacred dwelling', lives up to its name.

Perched like an eagle's nest at a height of nearly 7,000 feet in the Himalayan Dhauladhar mountains, the ramshackle settlement of thousands of refugees from Tibet encircles the home of the exiled Dalai Lama, regarded by many of his countrymen as a living God. But for a people used to the clear, crisp days of the Tibetan plateau, the precarious access to this mountain settlement and its frequently dank climate also causes many new arrivals hardship and severe health problems.

'To this day, His Holiness still jokes that the advisor who recommended he settle here himself chose to live elsewhere in India,' the Dalai Lama's sister-in-law, Rinchen Khando, confides with a wry smile as we sit drinking tea shortly after my arrival. Outside the window of her secluded hillside cottage, the thick mist all but obscures the spectacular backdrop of the snow-capped Himalayas.

Occasionally, I glimpse a curved-winged bird of prey slowly wheeling out of the gloom.

It is hard to believe now that the upper reaches of Dharamshala, known as McLeod Ganj, where the majority of refugees have settled, were once a thriving colonial enclave prized by officers of the British Raj as a summer retreat to escape the heat of the lowland plains. Fading sepia photographs on the walls of some of the oldest shops show elegant scenes of ladies in fine gowns promenading under avenues of pine trees that once stood at the heart of this Himalayan hill-station. Today, little from this era of questionable privilege remains. A massive earthquake in 1905 levelled most of the spacious bungalows built to house colonial families. The only trace of their presence is in the names and dates on headstones in the mossy cemetery of an almost deserted English church, aptly named St John in the Wilderness, which stands in a forest clearing away from the main square.

Following Indian independence in 1947, what remained of McLeod Ganj languished as little more than a ghost town until the late 1950s. Then, in the wake of the cataclysmic invasion of Tibet by Chinese communist forces, it once again stirred into life. When the Dalai Lama came under threat and fled over the Himalayas in 1959, under the cover of darkness, 100,000 traumatized Tibetans eventually followed in his wake. At first, they were housed in transit camps in Nepal and then in various provinces throughout India. But when it became clear more permanent homes were needed, at the suggestion of one of his advisers – the one who later settled elsewhere – the Dalai Lama accepted Prime Minister Nehru's offer to move with some of his people and repopulate McLeod Ganj.

Ever since the Dalai Lama was awarded the Nobel Peace Prize in 1989, McLeod Ganj has become a magnet for both the curious and the devout. What was once a forgotten backwater is now a busy tourist hub, with all the usual tat and hustle. When the Dalai Lama is not travelling abroad, he gives public teachings here and the narrow thoroughfares of McLeod Ganj fill with a sea of saffron- and maroon-robed monks and nuns and other Buddhist devotees.

The modest bungalow where the Dalai Lama has lived in exile for more than fifty years is shielded from view by lush gardens patrolled by Indian security forces. But, for many visitors who revere the Dalai Lama as a spiritual leader and a man of peace, the Tsuglagkhang Temple complex and monastery adjoining his private residence are the main focus of pilgrimage. The rocky track that winds through stands of deodar and pine trees around this complex has long been regarded as a *kora*, a sacred path for walking meditation by the devout. It was here, two years ago, that I first met Nyima, the former nun whose whispered account of years of torture suffered in a Chinese prison before escaping from Tibet planted the seed of my current journey.

So, on my return, I once again walk this sacred path. Alone this time and with no pressing appointment, I tread the path slowly, running my fingers along the rows of prayer wheels that line the track, as the sound of bells on the wheels echoes through the mist. It is a damp day and I pass few others. When I reach the place where Nyima and I sat and talked, I find moving testament to events that have unfolded since.

There, under a corrugated iron shelter erected as a place of rest for pilgrims, I come across a long wall of framed photographs, their glass reflecting the glimmer of flickering butter lamps. In total, there are more than 130 portraits of men and women, most of them young, most in monastic robes. Beneath each photograph a name and age are printed, with a date written below. This is the date when each of those pictured doused him- or herself in kerosene, then drank some of the liquid fuel before setting a match to their clothes, ending their lives in an agony of flames. This wall is a commemoration, a testimony to the desperation Tibetans now feel as their land, rich culture and right to religious freedom are ever more diminished under Chinese rule.

As I walk along the wall, I pick out the faces of seven nuns, amongst them the ruddy features of Palden Choetso, thirty-five, from the Kham region of eastern Tibet. A simple click on the internet instantly reveals the last moments of Palden Choetso's life. They are almost unbearable to watch. Less than twenty seconds of grainy video footage, captured on a mobile phone and smuggled out of Tibet, show her engulfed in flames in the middle of a busy street. It is just before noon, 3 November 2011. As horrified onlookers cry and scream, one laywoman calmly steps forward and tosses a white khata scarf, a traditional offering of respect, towards Palden Choetso as she crumples to the ground. It is a moment of quiet dignity in an otherwise appalling scene. For weeks following her death, the international media replayed the footage amid reports of growing unrest in Tibet.

Despite Chinese claims to the contrary, the Dalai Lama has spoken out repeatedly to discourage these self-immolations. As the numbers staging such painful protests continued to rise, he warned that a jaded world was paying less and less attention and that the beleaguered Tibetan people could not afford such a tragic loss of life. While Buddhist teachings proscribe any kind of violence, including self-harm, the altruistic motivation of the self-immolators is afforded deep respect and their passing officially mourned. Every time news reaches the exile community that there has been another self-immolation in Tibet, prayer services are held. Severe tightening of border controls by Chinese forces in recent years has meant few Tibetans are now prepared to risk the harrowing trek over the Himalayas as they face near-certain capture and imprisonment. But shortly after arriving in McLeod Ganj, I hear of one recently escaped exile, who was born in the same village as Palden Choetso. Hoping to piece together a little more about her life than her final moments, I go in search of him in the valley below Dharamshala, in the small village of Sidhpur.

The smell of open drains is almost overwhelming as I approach the crowded hostel for new arrivals, where I am told I will find him. The majority of Tibetan exiles in India live in grinding poverty. So I am touched at the care the young man appears to have taken with his appearance for our meeting. Jinpa looks handsome in a smart velvet jacket and fresh cotton shirt. But his features are sad and serious as he relates what he knows of the circumstances surrounding Palden Choetso's death.

In the weeks before she died, he explains, the nuns at her nunnery had been issued with papers they were told to sign by the Chinese authorities, denouncing the Dalai Lama as a 'splittist', the term the Chinese use to label as dangerous subversives those they accuse of seeking Tibetan independence. Even though the Dalai Lama's repeated stance has been to seek autonomy for his homeland within China, the Chinese government has branded him a 'wolf in sheep's clothing' and deemed it a criminal offence to display pictures of him or revere him in any way. Rather than sign the papers, many nuns ran away.

Few reliable figures exist for the number of monks or nuns left practising in Tibet. Before Chinese troops invaded in 1950, there were over 6,000 monasteries and nunneries in a country with a population of just under six million – little more than that of Scotland. In the immediate aftermath of the invasion, many were used as barracks by Red Army soldiers, who fed rare Buddhist texts to mules as fodder and smashed ancient Buddhist statues. A decade later, all but a handful of Tibet's monastic institutions lay in ruins. In an effort to break the Tibetan people's deep faith, tens of thousands of monks and nuns were amongst those killed or starved to death, and those who survived were forced to disrobe. Many were coerced into marrying each other, even to copulating in public. During the 1960s it is said that not a single robed figure was to be seen anywhere in Tibet.

Gradually, as Choying Khandro, the Tibetan Princess I met in Nepal, described, some of the destroyed monasteries and nunneries were rebuilt by the monks and nuns who once worshipped there. Although the exact number of nunneries today is unknown, some estimate that there are around 100,000 nuns, many dispersed in villages and remote areas of China and in what the Chinese call the Tibet Autonomous Region, or TAR. Despite this gradual revival of monasticism, repeated waves of prohibitions on religious activity still result in the periodic demolition of monastic institutions; one of the most disastrous in recent years was the near total destruction of the Serthar Institute, world renowned as a place of high scholarship, in what is now Sichuan province, in south-west China. As recently as the 1990s, this sprawling combined monastery and nunnery was home to 10,000 monks and nuns and 2,000 lay practitioners. But in 2001 several thousand Chinese soldiers and hired labourers moved in with bulldozers, and all but a few buildings were razed to the ground. The soldiers then held a lottery to determine who would be allowed to remain. Some nuns faced with eviction suffered mental breakdowns, a number committed suicide.

One young Serthar nun I meet describes going in search of a friend after the bulldozers moved in, only to find her body hanging from a tree.

Much of this is going through my mind as I sit speaking with Jinpa in the cramped room he shares with other recently arrived exiles. 'Let me show you something,' he says, rolling a broken chair close to where I sit, perched on the edge of a bed beside my young interpreter, Tselha. Scrolling through the pictures on his phone, he clicks on one, enlarges it and hands his phone to me. It is a photograph of Palden Choetso dressed in a thick maroon coat with a conical yellow cloth hat pulled down low to her eyes. There is a faint smile on her lips and, looking more closely, I feel a sudden chill; in the background I see the leaping flames of a stove where incense is ritually offered. The photograph was taken just a few hours before Palden Choetso took her own life, Jinpa tells me, before relating what he knows of the circumstances in which it was taken. That day she went for an early-morning walk with another nun, he says, in the mountains close to their nunnery in Kardze, in the historical eastern Tibetan region of Kham. He describes how, after offering incense, Palden Choetso asked her friend to take a picture of her.

'You are not so beautiful. Why should I do that?' the friend teased, before taking a snapshot.

'Soon, you will see, this picture will be useful,' Palden Choetso replied.

This last image is all the nun's parents now possess as a reminder of their daughter's love both for them and for Tibet's spiritual leaders. Hidden in Palden Choetso's yellow hat, says Jinpa, was a picture of the Dalai Lama with the Karmapa, the head of the Karma Kagyu school of Tibetan Buddhism to which her nunnery belonged. This is only known because when she collapsed, engulfed in flames, her hat toppled to the ground and the image was preserved, scorched at the edges, but otherwise intact.

The last words one onlooker heard her shout out before she succumbed to the inferno were: 'Long live the Dalai Lama! Let the Dalai Lama return to Tibet!'

The room falls silent as Jinpa finishes speaking. This is all he knows, he says. Emerging from the hostel, my interpreter and I sit quietly on a wall outside for a while. Before leaving the area, there is another nun I wish to speak to. But this will be another difficult meeting, and I need to collect my thoughts before we carry on. The woman I hope to meet has a close connection with Nyima, the first nun I met in Dharamshala, and she too knows well the brutal treatment meted out to monks and nuns who question their Chinese rulers.

Some time after my meeting with Nyima, I sought news of her via the London-based human-rights group International Campaign for Tibet. I was relieved to hear that supporters had helped her move to Brussels to start a new life with four other former nuns who had been imprisoned with her in Tibet's Prison Number One, the feared Drapchi jail, notorious for its treatment of political prisoners. The five women spent a combined total of forty-two years locked away for peacefully protesting for the right to religious freedom. They were part of a larger group who became known as 'Drapchi's Singing Nuns' after they sang songs in praise of the Dalai Lama from their cells; they were then placed in solitary confinement, with their original prison terms extended. They were also subjected to such severe torture that, rather than endure more abuse, five of the nuns, all young women in their twenties, are believed to have committed suicide. The young women's bodies were never released to their families. But those in prison at the same time reported that they had locked themselves in a storeroom within their cellblock and either hung or choked themselves by swallowing strips of material.

Eventually, the surviving 'Singing Nuns' were released and most fled into exile. Some were then granted asylum in Europe or the United States. But one nun also held in Drapchi, I am told, has been left behind in India, alone and struggling to survive without her friends as the chances of obtaining asylum abroad have steadily dwindled. So, after leaving Jinpa, I go in search of her in a huddle of hole-in-the-wall shops and lean-to shacks that serve hot meals to the small exiled Tibetan population in a community nearby.

I catch sight of Dhamchoe stooped low over a table at the back of one of these cafes, her slight frame dressed in a baggy pink T-shirt and loose trousers. She is serving steaming bowls of soup to packed tables of maroon-robed monks and nuns. The cafe lies close to several important monastic institutions. One is the home of the exiled Karmapa, Ogyen Trinley Dorje, another is an innovative seminary for nuns called Dolma Ling, where I have been invited to spend time. I had not expected to see Dhamchoe in nun's robes. From Nyima's account, I knew that many nuns who survived Drapchi were left too physically frail and emotionally traumatized to be able to re-enter holy orders after their release. But to see her now working as a servant still comes as a shock.

At first Dhamchoe is reluctant to speak. I sense it is because we are not alone and I take a seat with my interpreter Tselha in a far corner to drink tea until the last diners have gone. When the cafe finally empties, Dhamchoe comes to join us. Her small build, high forehead, rounded cheeks and shy smile give her the appearance of someone much younger than her thirty-eight years. Slowly, she begins to talk of her life in Tibet, explaining how she entered a nunnery when she was fifteen years old. Her mother had also once been a nun, she says, but had been forced to disrobe when her nunnery was destroyed during the Cultural Revolution.

Dhamchoe was twenty-two when she staged a brief protest on the streets of Lhasa in 1995, calling for the Dalai Lama to be allowed to return to Tibet. As a result, she was sentenced to six years in jail. Most of that time she was imprisoned in Drapchi, and suffered repeated torture. In a low voice she talks of being beaten with bamboo sticks, lengths of hose filled with sand, and the buckle end of military belts. Electric batons were thrust in her mouth, on her breasts and sexual organs and repeated shocks administered until she lost consciousness. Like Nyima, Dhamchoe speaks of how she and other nuns were forced to stand for hours in the prison's exercise yard in extreme summer heat, with newspapers stuck under their arms and between their legs and sometimes with cups of water balanced on their heads. Some had planks strapped to their legs to keep them upright. If the papers slipped or water spilt, the women would again be beaten.

When I ask her what she and the other nuns held in Drapchi had sung that so enraged their Chinese jailors, she begins singing softly, her eyes cast down out of shyness. The grimy cafe fills with a haunting melody. The lyrics of one song that incurred the jailers' wrath simply speaks of the nuns looking at the full moon through the bars of their cell windows and wishing it were the face of the Dalai Lama.

'O white crane,
Bring this message from us,
To have a quick audience with him is all we wish for.
Please relate this to him.

Our subtle consciousness is sent to Dharamshala.
But our bodies, a mixture of stone and earth,
Remain in Drapchi prison.'

After Dhamchoe was released from jail in 2001, she joined other Tibetans determined to flee into exile. The small group trekked for twenty-two days across the Himalayas to Nepal, trading items of clothing for food from villagers along the way. This meant crossing some of the highest passes with no coats, only thin shirts and trousers. Despite the agonies suffered by nuns like Dhamchoe and Nyima, the Dalai Lama continues to stress the Buddhist principle of compassion for all, including the women's Chinese jailers, because of the bad karma they create for themselves through their brutality.

When I ask Dhamchoe how she feels when she sees nuns walking past the cafe or coming in to drink tea, she lowers her gaze and for a few moments falls silent. Then, slowly, she raises her eyes to mine and speaks with such conviction that, for the first time, I glimpse a flicker of the inner steel she must have possessed to survive six years in a Chinese jail and the long journey into exile.

'As far as I'm concerned, I'm still a nun. I live the life of a nun in every way I can,' she says. 'I get up early to recite prayers and do the same when I finish work. His Holiness [the Dalai Lama] tells us that it's not the clothes you wear that make you a monk or a nun. It's the way you live, having a pure mind.'

'But still, don't you wish you could live together with other nuns, perhaps nearby at Dolma Ling?' I ask, aware the question might seem insensitive. Dhamchoe's forehead wrinkles into a frown.

'I would feel ashamed to be in the nunnery,' she says, speaking slowly so that her words are not lost in translation. 'I cannot have such a pure mind and heart as the nuns there. His Holiness teaches us that we should have compassion for our captors. But I don't feel compassionate towards them. I suffered a lot. I can't say I feel no hatred towards them. So I think my mind is not pure enough to share the same food that is offered to the nuns,' Dhamchoe admits, with a frankness that is heart-rending.

It is growing late, and it is clear Dhamchoe is tired. Her health is delicate and the cafe still needs to be cleaned. As we part, she ducks through a curtain at the rear and is gone. But her story, like Nyima's, stays with me long after we have left her.

5

ENTERING THE DEBATE

The route from Dhamchoe's cafe to Dolma Ling nunnery winds along dusty roads and narrow lanes bordered by low buildings and open fields. There is little physical distance between the two places, yet they seem separated by so much sadness. In the early-morning hush of the following day, I lie on my bed in the guest room I am graciously offered during my stay at the nunnery and my mind goes over the argument I have heard many times justifying China's takeover of Tibet.

From the point of view of Beijing, where celebrations have been held to mark the sixtieth anniversary of 'the peaceful liberation of Tibet', China brought 'democracy' to a benighted and backward nation of serfs, while at the same time providing the region with modernity and development through huge amounts of investment. Much to the frustration of those Tibetans who want complete independence for their homeland rather than autonomy within China, the Dalai Lama himself admits Tibet was in dire need of modernization and has benefited from Chinese investment. In the same breath, however, he accuses the Chinese communist regime of carrying out cultural genocide on his people. Fifty years of forced migration of Han Chinese into Tibet means that Tibetans now constitute an ethnic minority in the capital, Lhasa, and in large swathes of surrounding territory. The Tibetan language is banned in schools and the country's rich traditions, including an unprecedented wealth of Buddhist learning, are ruthlessly repressed. For centuries, Tibet's vast network of monasteries served as virtual universities, centres of educational excellence and Buddhist scholarship. When all but a handful of these monasteries were destroyed, the heart was ripped out of every community in Tibet.

Compared to the speed with which Buddhism is currently being eviscerated in Tibet, the process by which it became synonymous with the national psyche took almost 1,000 years. Following Buddha Sakyamuni's death in the fifth century BCE, Buddhism gradually spread beyond the borders of India, with monks and scholars travelling the Silk Roads of central Asia. Buddhist teachings reached early Tibetan kingdoms from the second century onwards but they did not immediately find a natural home amongst the deeply superstitious people of the high plateaux. It was only in the seventh century, when Tibet was unified under King Songtsen Gampo, two of whose wives, princesses from China and Nepal, were devout Buddhists, that Buddhism was introduced into the royal dynasty. It was then that Lhasa's sprawling Potala Palace and Jokhang Temple were built. But it would be more than 100 years before another king invited to Tibet the great Indian sage Padmasambhava, regarded by his followers as a second Buddha, and Buddhism began to take a firm hold on the nation, with the first Buddhist monasteries being built. With the arrival of the renowned Indian Buddhist master Atisha in the eleventh century, there was a flowering of scholarship and devotion. A widespread monastic system evolved and further monastic orders were established. All four of the major schools of Tibetan Buddhism – Gelugpa, Sakya, Kagyu and the older Nyingma lineage – trace their origins back to Indian masters, who gradually transferred a large part of Buddhist tradition, written and oral, to Tibet.

But even as Buddhism wove itself into the fabric of Tibetan society, with a third of the male population eventually becoming monks, back in India the religion was being systematically eradicated. The spread of Islam through India led to the mass destruction of monasteries, heralding Buddhism's decline in all but the most northern Himalayan states. Because Buddhism places such emphasis on the role of the teacher as guardian of the dharma, and because leading teachers throughout history have been monks, its spiritual practice has traditionally relied heavily on monasticism. The demise of monasteries, first in India, and then Tibet, has therefore dealt Buddhism a heavy blow.

While Buddhist monasteries have been revered historically as places of high scholarship, and some early nunneries established in India also aspired to this role, the nunneries founded later in Tibet were often set in remote areas, far from any centre of learning. As in most countries in the East where Buddhist cultures have flourished, women occupied a low status in traditional Tibetan society. The Tibetan word for woman – *lümen* or *kyemen* – literally means 'inferior being'. I had not realized initially that Tibetan Buddhism, along with some other Buddhist schools, still doesn't allow nuns to become fully ordained, and that the highest level of ordination for a nun in these traditions is that of a novice.

While the term ordination is commonly understood in the West as the act of conferring holy orders on religious clergy in order for them to take up some form of priestly office, in a Buddhist sense it is taken to mean the admission of a man or woman to a community of monks or nuns. Such a monastic community is known collectively as the sangha, though many also use this term to include laypeople who commit to following Buddhist teachings through 'taking refuge', or making a promise of trust, in what are referred to as the 'Three Jewels': the Buddha, the dharma and the sangha. Although the procedure for Buddhist monastic ordination is clearly laid out in a regulatory framework, the Vinaya, I come to understand that the number of vows or precepts taken by monks and nuns often varies according to the tradition to which they belong, as do the levels of monastic training to which they can aspire. As is the case in many religions or religious denominations, the question of how far women are permitted to progress along the ordination path has become a controversial issue in Buddhism in recent years. Just how controversial becomes clearer as my journey progresses.

But whereas ordaining women as priests is ruled out in the Roman Catholic Church, for instance, on the grounds that it would contravene divine law, the official reasons Buddhist monks give for objecting to women becoming fully ordained are more pragmatic. Few question that an order of fully ordained nuns existed in antiquity, after the Buddha agreed that his aunt could become one. But in some areas and lineages, for different historical reasons, this order died out. Conservatives argue that this makes it impossible to reintroduce it, since full ordination ceremonies for nuns require the presence of both fully ordained monks and fully ordained nuns. It is, in effect, a Catch-22.

Historically, Tibet's relative inaccessibility is said to have prevented a quorum of fully ordained women from reaching the region and so the nuns here were – and apparently still are – destined to remain as novices. Nonetheless, in the past couple of decades, life for Tibetan Buddhist nuns at Dolma Ling has started to change.

As the first glimmer of dawn creeps through the curtains, I lie listening to the soft footfall of nuns at Dolma Ling returning to their rooms from early-morning prayers. At the sound of a metal gong, I get up and follow a single file of maroon-robed figures as they make their way through the labyrinth of passageways and covered cloisters to a series of courtyards at the rear of the nunnery. Just as the sun breaks over the snow-tipped crest of the Himalayas in the distance, turning the highest glaciers into shimmering sheets of gold, I emerge into an open area to see hundreds of nuns converging from every direction.

At first the nuns, some barely out of childhood, sit cross-legged in rows on the floor, facing each other and reciting more prayers. They then break into small groups and scatter to separate corners of interlinked pavilions. Within minutes, the reverential sound of worship is replaced by ear-splitting claps and a chorus of nuns shouting out quick-fire questions. This unexpected cacophony signals the start of the many hours the nuns will spend engaged in fierce debate over the coming days and weeks. My stay at Dolma Ling coincides with the arrival of more than 200 nuns from nunneries all over India and Nepal who join the 200 permanently resident here for an annual month-long debating marathon. This festival, Jang Gonchoe, provides the women with a unique opportunity to hone their skills at an ancient form of Buddhist learning from which nuns were once strictly prohibited.

For centuries in Tibet, this form of intellectual jousting was practised solely by monks. While other Buddhist traditions have historically put more focus on meditation and devotional practices, Tibetan Buddhism, particularly that of the Gelug school headed by the Dalai Lama, relies heavily on rigorous intellectual enquiry. This tradition of debate is a key tool for refining the practice and theory of Buddhist philosophy and logic, sharpening the analytical capacity of students. Its central purpose is to defeat philosophical misconceptions and help those engaged in debate to understand, and later meditate on, central Buddhist teachings, rather than automatically accepting anything as a matter of doctrine. This principle is a fundamental tenet of all Buddhist practice.

In traditional Tibetan monastic education, this form of intellectual combat forms the crux of a lengthy study regime, which can last up to twenty years, ending with exams that lead to a degree known as a Geshe, roughly equivalent to a doctorate in Buddhist philosophy. In Tibet, it would have been inconceivable for a nun to follow this education programme. Throughout history, female monastics were expected to pray, cook for monks and leave studying to these men. But in the mid-1990s, centuries of tradition were overthrown by the nuns of Dolma Ling. With the Dalai Lama's blessing, growing numbers of determined women here began studying for the Geshe degree, which, when undertaken by a woman, is known as the Geshema. Unlike some other nunneries I visit, Dolma Ling is now first and foremost a centre of learning. The nuns' days revolve around a packed educational timetable, which grows progressively more demanding as they advance in years. Even the outline of some of the programme sounds daunting: seven years spent studying philosophy and 'perfecting wisdom' are followed by a further seven or eight years studying logic, reasoning and the so-called Middle Way of fundamental wisdom.

The animated faces of the nuns I watch debating on my first morning at Dolma Ling convey the joy they feel at being able to participate in this ancient tradition. The debating, following traditional guidelines dating back to its origins in the great monastic universities that once flourished on India's northern plains, has a very striking choreography, which is hypnotizing to watch. It involves elaborate movements of the hands and arms, mimicking the opening and closing of a crocodile's jaws, by the one posing the point of philosophy to be debated. This culminates with a clapping of hands, both to keep the attention of the one called on to take up the philosophical gauntlet, and to symbolize the way Buddhist teachings, if properly understood, extinguish suffering and confusion.

For the first time in the history of Tibet, nuns have recently been invited to debate in front of the Dalai Lama. As a result, in May 2013, ten nuns from Dolma Ling were deemed ready to embark on the lengthy programme of exams, which, if successfully completed, will see them awarded the Geshema degree. This group of ten includes a number of nuns who have been at Dolma Ling since its inception in the early 1990s, some of whom could barely read or write when they fled into exile.

Amongst these early arrivals from Tibet was a group of forty nuns who were instrumental in the building of Dolma Ling. The women came from a remote area of Tibet called Lithang, one of the highest inhabited places on the planet, truly the 'roof of the world', in what is now the western Chinese province of Sichuan, and their extraordinary pilgrimage from Lithang to Lhasa took them almost two years to complete. They travelled every inch of the way in accordance with the ancient spiritual custom of prostration: bowing full-length, face down on the ground, walking three steps to where the head has touched the earth, bowing again and so on – for 1,000 miles.

It is late evening when I arrange to meet Delek Yangdon in Dolma Ling's deserted dining hall. The forty-three-year-old nun has brought with her two photographs. She flicks on a strip light in a corner of the cavernous hall and lays out the photographs for me to inspect. The first snapshot is covered in plastic for protection; it is the only reminder she has of the family she left behind when she fled Tibet.

The second photograph is dog-eared and out of focus, but shows a group of smiling nuns and monks posed against a mountain backdrop. Delek Yangdon invites me to take a closer look. Shifting it towards the light, I see the blurred figures are wearing long brown aprons of battered leather over their monastic robes. Tracing her fingers over the photograph, Delek Yangdon then points out wooden blocks some have strapped to their palms and strips of rubber, salvaged from old tyres, tied over the front of flimsy shoes.

'This is how we were dressed when we set out for Lhasa,' she says.

Looking again at the smiles of those in the photograph, I sense their optimism as they embarked on the pilgrimage. None could have known what lay ahead. Delek Yangdon recounts how it began, her eyes glistening with nostalgia. Her family were reluctant for her ever to leave home, she says. The family was part of a nomadic community living in tents on the highland plateau close to the regional capital of Lithang. She was eighteen when she heard that a local lama was organizing a pilgrimage from Lithang to the Jokhang Temple in Lhasa and announced to her family she wanted to join it. At first, her brother forbade her from leaving, but after some gentle persuasion she was allowed to go.

Together with an older cousin, Delek Yangdon shaved her head and donned the robes of a novice. The group performing the pilgrimage was more than 100 strong. It included around sixty monks and forty nuns, the youngest just twelve years old. After loading basic food supplies on trolleys that the pilgrims would pull behind them as they moved, the group set off. It was early 1988. Delek Yangdon recalls the bitter cold of those winter mornings when the pilgrims would rise at dawn and inch painstakingly forwards on their hands and knees. Each evening was spent huddled around campfires, memorizing prayers and listening to teachings by their lama.

'You were young, but your body must have ached terribly. However did the young girls manage?' I ask, knowing, from having completed a yoga teacher training course, the pain that comes from repeating dozens of times the sequence of yoga postures, or asanas, known as *surya namaskar*, or sun salutations – the nearest physical parallel I can imagine to the prostrations the pilgrims were performing for many hours, day after day. But Delek Yangdon brushes aside my concern. 'It was hard in the beginning,' is all she will concede. 'Then we got used to it.'

For the pilgrims, the most painful experience was yet to come. When they finally reached Lhasa, they were stopped at a bridge on the outskirts of the city and prevented from going any further. Suspicious of their intentions, Chinese security forces bundled them into the backs of trucks and drove them to a police holding centre, where they were interrogated for hours. Exhausted and frightened that his flock would be further detained, their lama claimed the group's final destination was not Lhasa but 600 miles further west. Their goal, he said, was to reach Tibet's most holy mountain, Mount Kailash. Eventually they were released and the group went underground for several weeks. Some of the older monks and nuns became resigned to returning to Lithang. But the majority set off for Mount Kailash, riding part of the way in buses. Once there, they again took to circumambulating a rocky *kora* at the base of the sacred mountain by performing repeated prostrations.

Having come this far, their leader, Lama Yonten Phuntsok, was determined to press on even further. His intention was to reach Nepal and finally India, to be able to attend a rare teaching the Dalai Lama was to give in December 1990 in Sarnath, close to the north Indian city of Varanasi. This is a place of huge significance for Buddhists, celebrated as the site where the Buddha first taught the dharma. The pilgrims who had travelled so far vowed to continue. But while at Mount Kailash they once again came under Chinese surveillance. The area lies close to Tibet's border with Nepal and battalions of soldiers and border guards are constantly stationed here on the lookout for Tibetans wanting to escape into exile. In order to give themselves a head start, the monks and nuns stole away from their encampment under cover of darkness, leaving their tents standing on the shores of Lake Manasarovar, the vast freshwater lake, so that soldiers, stationed at a distance, would, for a time, be fooled into thinking they had not left. But this meant the pilgrims faced crossing the Himalayas with very few provisions.

Delek Yangdon's description of crossing the highest mountain range in the world has striking similarities with Dhamchoe Dolma's account. When their meagre supply of *tsampa* ran low, they too resorted to swapping items of warm clothing for food with those they passed along the way. Some lost fingers and toes to frostbite as a result, some became ill with altitude sickness and had to be carried on the backs of those still strong. Whenever they were in danger of being spotted by border patrols, they would spend the daylight hours concealed in rock crevasses and caves, only daring to move across the high mountain passes at night.

'Night-time was very difficult. We were very, very tired and it was so very high. Sometimes we got to top of mountain and we see how far still to go. It was so far,' Delek Yangdon says in halting English, lifting her hands from her lap with a soft laugh.

This last harrowing stretch of what had become an epic journey lasted twenty-eight days. When the group eventually made it to the Nepalese border, they were transported by bus to a reception centre in Kathmandu, where many fell sick with high fevers from contaminated water. And yet, they did get to Sarnath in time to fulfil a dream beyond the reach of most Tibetans. There they joined the ranks of around 100,000 Buddhist devotees taking part in one of the supreme rites of Tibetan Buddhism, a Kalachakra initiation dedicated to world peace.

'We sat many days listening to His Holiness. We not understand well as speak a different Tibetan language in Kham. But we sit close and every time he rings a bell, we look up and he smiles. Much joy in that,' she says with a broad smile. 'So much joy.'

What happened next I learn from the Dalai Lama's sister-in-law, Rinchen Khando, who had founded an organization called the Tibetan Nuns Project in the mid-1980s to assist refugee nuns arriving from Tibet, and who was also in Sarnath at the time. Married to the Dalai Lama's youngest brother, Rinchen Khando was once a minister of education in the Tibetan government-in-exile and became founding president of the Tibetan Women's Association and its sister organization, the Tibetan Nuns Project. She is an elegant woman of noble birth, but since fleeing her homeland lives a simple life, running the spacious bungalow where she raised her family as a small guesthouse.

It is here that she invites me to join her for tea and takes up the story of the Lithang nuns. When she met them in Sarnath, she says, 'most of them had health problems and trauma. All had fear-stricken thoughts from everything they had been through.' At first Rinchen Khando rented a small house for them adjacent to her bungalow. The house had no beds, few blankets and only a cold-water tap outdoors for washing. The nuns arrived with only the clothes they stood up in and so Rinchen Khando went from door to door asking others in the exile community to donate what they could spare. 'You should have seen the nuns walking around in high heels and coloured dresses,' she says with a wide toothy smile.

At the time, a plot of land had already been bought by the Tibetan Nuns Project with the aim of setting up Dolma Ling as an institute of higher learning to raise the standing and educational level of nuns fleeing into exile. With the arrival of the nuns from Lithang, however, the immediate priority was to build housing for them on the site. As the years passed the emphasis once again shifted to turning Dolma Ling into an educational institute, and today it is internationally renowned as a centre of excellence.

While the majority of those now living and studying at Dolma Ling are from Tibet and other Himalayan regions, at the time of my visit there are some nuns in residence who have been drawn here from much further afield. Amongst them is a Korean-born American with a PhD from Harvard, whom I first meet in passing in one of Dolma Ling's flower-lined corridors. While some of those I speak to volunteer the names by which they were known before becoming nuns, not all do, and I do not insist. So I know her only by her ordained name of Yeshe Chodron and, though she has not undergone the extreme physical hardship of the Lithang nuns, her journey from Harvard to this nunnery in the foothills of the Himalayas has been challenging emotionally.

Yeshe Chodron's Korean parents felt betrayed when she became a nun in her early thirties, she confides, and virtually disowned her. As first-generation immigrants to America, they made great sacrifices for their children's education. When their daughter graduated from UC Berkeley, embarked on a musical career that took her to Paris, and won critical acclaim as a composer, culminating in a Harvard doctorate, her achievements were lauded in the local newspaper and they felt their investment had paid off. She had a boyfriend and was leading a life that many might envy. But while at Harvard she began attending dharma talks at a local Buddhist centre. 'Slowly it dawned on me that my math had been wrong!' She laughs. 'Like everybody, I was looking for happiness but I hadn't really achieved it.'

The more she studied Buddhist teachings, she says, 'the more I came to see that if I followed the scientific path the Buddha taught for realizing happiness, that would be the greatest gift both for myself and for others I might also one day teach.' But when she told her parents of her intention to ordain, they accused her of 'driving nails into their heart' and said she was no longer part of their family. Although their attitude has gradually softened, whenever she goes home to see them in California, they hurry her from the car into the house 'so no one will see me with my shaven head,' she tells me. 'Even though traditionally it was those who were the most intelligent and spiritually inclined, those who could endure the difficulties of a monastic life, who became nuns and monks,' she continues, 'in my parents' eyes it was, "Why would someone like you become a nun? What is it that you're lacking?"'

There are many who might ask a similar question. But as I listen to her talking, calmly and with composure, it is clear she is simply someone who has the total courage of her convictions. Still, I ask whether it would not have been possible for her to follow the Buddhist path as a layperson. Her reply echoes that of other nuns I have asked. 'I have the sort of personality that if I decide to do something, I do it 100 per cent,' she says. As to what brought her from Harvard to the Himalayas, she explains it was 'the high level of scholarship at Dolma Ling'. Once her Tibetan becomes fluent enough, Yeshe Chodron's intention is to work towards achieving the Geshema degree.

But it is not just the doors of deepest Buddhist study that have been thrown open to nuns. A heated debate is now under way about them being permitted to progress from novice to fully ordained nun. While the Dalai Lama has given this his full backing, and even though he is invested with supreme power in most matters, such a fundamental change in the monastic order requires the consensus of all senior monks belonging to a council of elders. Some still prefer the status quo.

While these discussions continue, largely behind closed doors, the focus at Dolma Ling remains on nurturing nuns to realize their potential. 'I am very hopeful they will become very good teachers, doctors, nurses and even, if they want it, politicians,' says Rinchen Khando. The thought that nuns might one day go into politics seems unlikely. 'Has it ever happened in history?' I ask. 'I don't think so. But why not? They could set a good example of being truly guided by right and wrong,' she replies. 'I tell the nuns that when they go back home [to Tibet], and I believe we will go back, then they might not have diamonds or gold, but they will take their learning with them, and this will be my gift to Tibet,' she says as our meeting draws to a close. Before we part, she tips a bowl of dried apricots into a napkin and presses them into my hand for my onward journey.

6

OUT OF SILENCE

To understand more of the struggle for full female ordination, I travel to another nunnery, a couple of hours away from Dharamshala, to meet a slight Englishwoman who is something of a legend in Buddhist circles. Her name is Jetsunma Tenzin Palmo, *jetsunma* meaning 'venerable or reverend lady', a title rarely bestowed. Much of her renown stems from having spent twelve years meditating alone in a remote cave high in the Himalayas. While in the cave, she never lay down, sleeping just a few hours a night in a meditation box one metre square.

It has not been easy to arrange to meet with Tenzin Palmo, such is the demand for her on the international teaching circuit. Her talent for presenting ancient Buddhist teachings in a modern context pulls in packed audiences in both the East and the West. But part of the draw is also her extraordinary past, which came to prominence in the late 1990s in a book about her life, *Cave in the Snow*, by Vicki Mackenzie. When we eventually meet, I sense this spiritual stardom sits a little heavy on Tenzin Palmo's shoulders. By nature, she seems truly a hermit and, far from courting acclaim, her true calling is to tend to the needs of the seventy nuns in her care at the nunnery she has built from scratch with the help of donations and the proceeds of earnings from international teachings and books.

The road that leads to this nunnery dips sharply from Dharamshala and runs along the lush Kangra Valley, through tea plantations tended by women in brightly coloured saris, stooping low to pluck leaves. At frequent intervals along the route sprawling military barracks interrupt this tranquil scene, a stark reminder of the strategic importance of this northern tip of India, caught between the pincers of China, Pakistan and the disputed territory of Kashmir. As I pass one gunner station, I see, behind the barbed wire, the words 'Mob Attack Win' and 'Pure Aggression' daubed on a wall in giant letters. The contrast with the sentiments nurtured by those I am on my way to meet could hardly be more striking.

As my taxi takes a sharp left onto a narrow lane, the barbed wire gives way to a high stone wall draped with climbing roses. This is Dongyu Gatsal Ling, the nunnery Tenzin Palmo built. Her vision was for a nunnery that acts not only as a centre of learning and devotion but also as a haven where a unique lineage of female spiritual practitioners can gradually be revived. This rare tradition of nuns known as *togdenma*, distinguished by their total commitment to a lifetime spent in meditation, often in strict seclusion, was all but extinguished in Tibet by the Chinese during the Cultural Revolution. Only a few of their male counterparts survived and escaped into exile. Even before she undertook her own long period of retreat high in the Himalayas, Tenzin Palmo seems to have been drawn to the austere path chosen by such spiritual practitioners, though it is hard to trace the origins of this in a youth spent in London in the 1960s.

When I am finally ushered in to see her in her small study close to the nunnery's main entrance, I sense I am pulling her away from pressing matters. Her smile is warm and her manner welcoming, but the look in her piercing blue eyes seems a challenge not to waste time asking questions she has answered many times before. So, as we begin talking, I am conscious of not dwelling on well-documented territory.

I know already from her biography that Tenzin Palmo was born Diane Perry, the daughter of a fishmonger in London's East End; as a teenager she had long blonde curly hair, wore stilettos, loved jazz clubs, dancing and Elvis Presley; she had boyfriends, several marriage proposals and a personality described as 'bubbly'. But a photograph from this time, showing her dressed as a bridesmaid, her youthful face framed by a crown of flowers, already captures a wistful look. From a young age, she says, she knew she did not want to marry or become a mother. She wanted independence and felt a strong yearning to travel to the East. After meeting in London some of the first Tibetan lamas to come to the West, she resolved to travel to India where most were then settling in exile.

To earn the money for her sea passage to India, she worked as a librarian in Hackney. By 1964 she had saved enough to take up a post she had been offered at a temporary school set up in the Himalayan hill station of Dalhousie, teaching English to refugee Tibetan *tulkus* – young boys recognized by Tibetan lamas as reincarnations of previous spiritual masters. At the time, conditions for refugees were pitiful and her temporary accommodation there was plagued by giant rats. But shortly after arriving in Dalhousie, she met a high lama, the Eighth Khamtrul Rinpoche, with whom she felt an immediate and intense spiritual connection. Within a few hours of the meeting, she felt very clear that she wanted to become a nun.

At the time of her ordination as a novice, she was just twenty-one and only the second western woman to be ordained in the Tibetan Buddhist tradition (the first was another indomitable Englishwoman, Freda Bedi, founder of the Dalhousie school). Following her ordination, Tenzin Palmo went to work as Khamtrul Rinpoche's assistant and found herself the only woman living amongst 100 monks, all trained to keep their distance.

In addition to intense feelings of isolation and loneliness, she immediately hit a spiritual glass ceiling. Chauvinistic attitudes, which for so long in Tibet had reserved the heights of spiritual endeavour for monks and relegated nuns to subservient positions, continued to prevail in monastic communities in exile. The monks, though kind, said prayers that in her next life she would have the good fortune to be reborn a man. Despite her deep devotion to Khamtrul Rinpoche, after enduring years of such treatment, Tenzin Palmo became convinced her spiritual path lay in a different direction.

With his blessing, she undertook to become the first western woman to follow in the footsteps of male yogis, or spiritual practitioners who, through the ages, have retreated to remote caves for long periods of seclusion. Travelling by foot over a high Himalayan pass, she sought solitude in a remote corner of Himachal Pradesh called Lahaul, close to India's border with Tibet, an area renowned as a place conducive to meditation. Once there she eventually found a small cave perched at almost 4,000 metres – the height of some of the tallest peaks in the Alps – that would become her refuge for the next twelve years. The cave was little more than an indent in the mountains, a space she closed in with a simple brick wall, window and door, giving her a living area of approximately three by two metres.

During the twelve years she spent alone in this cave, Tenzin Palmo survived blizzards, avalanches, the attention of wolves, even a snow leopard, and temperatures plunging to −35°C in the winter months that lasted from November to May. On a small stove she cooked simple meals of rice, lentils and vegetables – supplies brought up to her occasionally by local villagers. Her days began at 3 a.m. and were divided into three-hour periods of intense meditation. During one stretch of three years, she neither saw nor spoke to a single soul. Tenzin Palmo was thirty-three years old when she entered her mountain retreat and forty-five when she was forced to emerge by a policeman who scrambled up to her eyrie to warn her that her visa had expired.

When I ask Tenzin Palmo about her time of solitude in the mountains, she deftly sidesteps the question. Talking about such an intimate spiritual experience is, she has argued, akin to a person discussing their sex life; some people like to talk about it, others don't.

Much of the discipline and forms of devotion she practised during those long years of solitude belong, in any case, to some of the more esoteric practices in Tibetan Buddhism known as Tantra, many of which remain largely secret to all but those who have advanced far enough along the path of practice to be able to truly comprehend their meaning. Even the Dalai Lama admits he hesitates to try to explain Tantric ritual and practice to those who do not have a deep understanding of Buddhism, as they are too often misunderstood. Some of this practice relies on complex visualizations during meditation to challenge fixed views of reality and the self. These visualizations are sometimes represented in intricate paintings.

I find myself wondering if Tenzin Palmo undertook such painting, though I can hardly imagine conditions in a damp mountain cave being conducive to the making of spiritual art. 'Have you any reminders from that time?' I ask, unsure what to expect. At this, Tenzin Palmo disappears into a side room and returns with a framed picture in her arms. I am taken aback both by its delicate beauty and by its graphic detail. The painting depicts a pubescent girl, entirely naked, with full breasts and vagina bared. She is wearing a necklace of human skulls and in one hand holds a cup overflowing with blood. Pressed under one foot is a small red figure, symbolizing the quashing of anger – and under the other a figure representing greed. I recognize it as a painting of Vajrayogini; often referred to as a female Buddha, she is an important meditational figure in Tibetan Buddhism. When I ask Tenzin Palmo again if she is able to talk a little about the spiritual practices she undertook in the cave, 'Those centred perhaps on this painting?' she declines again with a simple 'no', polite but firm. The painting is returned to its rather unceremonious place on top of a fridge in an adjoining room.

Some have described those who become masters of esoteric Tantric meditation as 'quantum physicists of inner reality', with a profound understanding of the nature of the mind and of consciousness. Realizing how little I would understand were I to ask a physicist to summarize the intricacies of quantum science, I let the matter rest.

Instead, I ask about a subject with which Tenzin Palmo clearly feels more at ease: how far nuns have come since the days when she first ordained. 'In the last twenty years there has been quite a revolution,' she begins. 'Not only are nuns now living in well-run nunneries, they are also being taken seriously.' The leading role she herself has played in changing traditional attitudes towards nuns is not to be underestimated. Before our meeting, I read moving accounts of how she had once reduced the Dalai Lama to tears when she spoke at a packed conference in the early 1990s about the plight of the Tibetan nuns and, in passing, mentioned her own unhappiness during her early years as a nun; she recalled how monks had told her that it wasn't 'too much' her fault that she had had 'an inferior rebirth in the female form'. By the time she finished speaking, the Dalai Lama had his head in his hands and was silently weeping. 'You are quite brave,' he said softly.

Following an outpouring of similar frustration by others attending this conference, Tenzin Palmo joined a small group of women lobbying for the right of Buddhist nuns to become fully ordained. It is a cause that she has continued to champion. Those who have resources to travel, like Tenzin Palmo, have been able to fully ordain abroad, in places such as Hong Kong, Taiwan, Vietnam or Korea, where traditions of full ordination have flourished for centuries, but this option is impossible for most novices, and progress towards full ordination within the Tibetan tradition has been painfully slow. At the time that I meet Tenzin Palmo, the consensus of senior monks needed to approve this is still out of sight.

'We need the lamas to fully support it, otherwise it looks like a bunch of western feminists interfering,' says Tenzin Palmo. When I ask what the main sticking point is, she answers with one word: 'Fear'. 'Some of those in the big monasteries are simply afraid of women becoming more powerful,' she says. 'In their mind it's like a cake, and if you get a bigger slice, I get less. Instead of recognizing that as women become more empowered it just adds to the general empowerment of humankind.'

In the light of the Dalai Lama repeatedly declaring his readiness to be reborn as a woman, I question how so many senior monks can still have their heels so firmly stuck in the mud, resisting equality. I then hear, not for the first time, the Dalai Lama's remark doused with weary scepticism. 'If he ever got reborn as a woman, they would never ever recognize him,' Tenzin Palmo says flatly. 'I'm sure that from his point of view he would be open to it. But he knows perfectly well that, the situation being what it is, if he were reborn in a female form, they simply wouldn't recognize him,' she repeats, referring to the complicated way successive Dalai Lamas are traditionally identified through a mysterious process of prayer and divination led by a chosen handful of senior lamas.

In recent years officials of the Chinese Communist Party have stated, without any apparent trace of irony, that all reincarnations of senior religious figures, including the Dalai Lama, would have to win prior approval from the government's religious affairs bureau before being reborn. To avoid the prospect of a 'duel of the Dalai Lamas', with one appointed by Beijing and another by his followers, Tenzin Gyatso has raised the prospect that he might personally name an adult successor before he dies. This would also solve the problem of an interregnum in leadership while a reincarnated child undergoes decades of spiritual preparation.

Should the matter rest in the hands of senior lamas as is customary, however, I question how men who are highly realized spiritually can perpetuate such antiquated attitudes to women. Tenzin Palmo says it's also due to simple blindness on the issue. 'It's very interesting how little they recognize the inequities in the system, the patriarchal structure. They just don't see it, because that's the way it always was in Tibet, and since everything in Tibet was perfect,' she says, her voice lifting with a note of irony, 'if you change that, it's considered a degeneration. That's why it's so very important for nuns to lift themselves up.'

By now, Tenzin Palmo is fully into her stride and talks of how the seventy nuns in her care are not only educated to a high level but also encouraged to cultivate self-confidence. While they do not engage in kung fu like the nuns at Gawa Khilwa in Nepal, they instead practise yoga – fully dressed in monastic robes. One morning, shortly after dawn prayers, I join them and am touched by the sight of young novices furiously tucking yards of maroon cloth between their legs to maintain decorum as they roll themselves up into inverted postures. Later the same day, I attend a teambuilding workshop designed to help the nuns develop leadership skills.

What strikes me is the women's clear enjoyment of life here, despite their arduous schedule. One day I follow this programme, beginning long before dawn with meditation and chanting sutras, followed by a full academic day, then more chanting late into the evening, and find my eyes quickly closing as I sit cross-legged on a cushion at the back of the meditation hall. By contrast, the nuns appear alert and enthralled; when the power cuts out and the hall is plunged into darkness, a handful of nuns quietly light storm lanterns as the majority continue chanting without missing a beat.

In my final hours at Dongyu Gatsal Ling, Tenzin Palmo takes me on a guided tour of the nunnery. As we set out I can see that she is tired and ask if she plans to go once more into retreat. She rolls her large blue eyes and lifts her hands upwards in supplication. 'Who knows?' she says, with a shrug. I sense that the spiritual stardom and frequent teaching tours have taken their toll on a woman whose nature is more suited to quiet reflection and journeying inward. But I also sense in her an understandable feeling of deep accomplishment at having created such a centre of devotion for future generations. As we pass through the nunnery's immaculate modern classrooms, library, sleeping quarters, dining hall and temples, young nuns gently bow and smile greetings. Tenzin Palmo is clearly much loved, and the high standards she expects of her charges seem to be met.

Before we part, Tenzin Palmo expresses her heartfelt conviction that living as a Buddhist nun is as relevant today as it was 2,500 years ago. One of the unfortunate characteristics of the growing interest in Buddhism in the West, she argues, is the decreasing focus on monasticism. 'The whole emphasis of Buddhism in the West is on the lay community. As a result of this growing secularization, there is a lot of understanding of Buddhism on an intellectual level, but very little joy and devotion.

'I think the reason we get so much support for our nunnery is that people see how happy our nuns are,' she continues. 'They are so relieved to see that there are girls in their teens and women in their twenties and thirties totally immersed in studying the dharma, leading disciplined lives based on abstinence, who are happy.'

'This life is not for everyone,' she concedes. 'But knowing that there are groups of monastics who are happy being monastics gives people a sense of proportion,' she concludes. 'I think it's very important to have a group of people who are living a life based on contentment with little, who live the example that genuine joy comes from within, from a sense of leading a life well lived.'

Tenzin Palmo takes my two hands in hers with genuine warmth and wishes me well before hitching up her robe and climbing the steps back to her private quarters. For all her kindness and generosity with her time, I can't help feeling her sense of relief at being able to retreat once again, however briefly, into solitude.

By contrast, Tenzin Palmo's assistant, an ebullient Irish-born nun named Aileen, seems glad of the brief company of a fellow English-speaker. But as she walks me to the nunnery's main gate she too voices concern about the increasing secularization of Buddhism in the West and leaves me with a powerful image: 'Sometimes I feel we nuns are like icebergs that are melting away,' she says in a soft Irish lilt. 'The significance of this will not be realized until we are gone.'

On my last evening before leaving Dharamshala I arrange to meet a Tibetan poet and political activist I know there, intending simply to catch up on developments within the exile community. But when our conversation turns to the reason for my visit, he asks if I have met a Bollywood actress who has recently been ordained as a nun. Curiosity piqued, I ask where she is, and later that evening hail a taxi on the main thoroughfare of McLeod Ganj to take me further up the mountain, along a narrow winding track, to an isolated meditation centre called Tushita. On opening the door to a small reception office here, I see two nuns relaxed in conversation, one so striking that, even before I ask, I feel sure she must be the woman I have come to meet.

Gyalten Samten has large eyes, voluptuous lips and a stunning smile. The images that abound on the internet of Barkha Madan, as she was before she was ordained, show a sophisticated beauty dressed in tight-fitting satin to reveal curves that once saw her chosen as a Miss India finalist. After a successful career as a model, she became an actress and rose through the Bollywood ranks to become a popular film and television star, with enough wealth and fame to be able to pick her roles.

It is less than a year since she shaved off her long dark hair and donned monastic robes; she is still in her thirties. When I ask if she has time to talk to me, she readily agrees and together we walk to a small temple building, where she curls up on a cushion on the floor, her knees to her chin, and opens her eyes wide in anticipation. When I ask why a beautiful woman, who apparently has it all, would make the choice she has, her face again breaks into a broad smile. 'Yes, I was successful, making a lot of money, doing these great things. But I wasn't happy,' she says. 'I had boyfriends and they were very nice. But I never saw myself becoming domesticated with kids. I kept thinking, there must be more to life than this.'

Over two hours, her story pours out. She talks of how she was 'bored out of her wits' modelling in a size-zero fashion culture where models were reduced to taking drugs to stay thin and dying from overdoses and anorexia. People accused her of committing professional suicide when she gave up modelling in her mid-twenties, then her acting career took off, bringing her a glamorous lifestyle and a sumptuous apartment in the plushest quarter of Mumbai. But she was never much interested in the trappings of wealth, she says. Though she was raised in a Hindu culture, she began attending Buddhist teachings when time allowed.

'When I was a child I kept asking my mother so many questions. I have a very analytical mind,' she continues. 'I wanted to know the reason behind all the Hindu rituals and she'd say, "That's just the way it's done." But I wanted to know, if there is a God, why is there so much suffering in the world? Then I heard His Holiness the Dalai Lama speak and he said, "There is no God . . . If you want to stop anything, you have to change your karma, transform yourself,"' she says, putting on a gruff male voice to imitate his. The more she heard of Buddhist teachings the more they made sense to her, and gradually her priorities changed.

When I press her again to explain her reason for being ordained, rather than continuing on the lay path, she puts her decision down to 'karma ripening very fast'. When she first expressed her wish to a lama, she said simply, 'Can you make me a nun?' She laughs as she recalls his response: 'He immediately said, "Did you have a fight with your boyfriend? Did you run away?" When I said, "No," he told me, "A nun's life is very tough, very difficult, and if you really want to take that path, you must study. You must get to know more."' So she spent the next decade doing just that and finally, in November 2012, her wish was granted and she was ordained at a ceremony in southern India. A few weeks later she called an old friend in the fashion industry to give him the news. 'I told him I'd ordained and he thought I said I'd OD'd!' she says, erupting into laughter.

It is still so soon after her ordination when we meet that *Surkhaab,* the last film in which she starred, and which she also produced, has yet to go on general release. With the permission of her teacher, Lama Zopa Rinpoche, she has continued promoting it at film festivals around the world. This has meant walking the red carpet in her monastic robes. 'People kept looking behind me. They kept asking where the star of the film was. When I said, "She's right here!" they didn't believe me,' she tells me.

I ask Gyalten Samten how she feels now about her new life. 'I have never been happier,' she says, her face glowing. Conditions at Tushita, where she is helping to run meditation courses, are basic and a far cry from Bollywood. So, as she walks me back along the mountain path to my waiting taxi, I ask if there is anything she misses about her old life. After wrestling with the thought a minute, she blurts out her answer with more laughter: 'My own private bathroom!' She admits that she has yet to experience the Buddhist virtue of equanimity in the face of adversity while getting fully dressed in monastic robes in order to trudge to a distant shared bathroom when nature calls in the middle of the night.

This last evening of Gyalten Samten's lively company is a counterpoint to the many hours spent speaking with nuns whose lives have been marked by tragedy. The lights of Dharamshala flicker far below as my taxi winds its way down the mountainside and I reflect on this chance encounter. It feels somehow fitting that my last meeting before leaving should be with an Indian nun, albeit one ordained in the Tibetan tradition. Nearly 1,000 years after the demise of the last Indian dynasty supportive of Buddhism, I wonder if Gyalten Samten's experience might signal a wider renewed interest in Buddhism in the land where the Buddha taught for more than forty years until his death. The former actress thought so: 'People are questioning now,' she told me. 'They are more aware, better educated and don't want to rely on empty ritual and taking things on faith. There is a very strong degeneration in faith otherwise.'

As I take my leave of India I am aware that all the nuns I have met so far here, and in Nepal, belong to the more devotional Mahayana tradition, carried north from India to China, Tibet and beyond by travelling monks and merchants. I have yet to encounter those who follow the older Theravada tradition, sometimes referred to as the Southern School since it is the dominant form of Buddhism in South East Asia, where my journey leads me next.

PART III

BURMA

7

GOLDEN SPIRES

The lost Buddhist civilization of Bagan shimmers like a mirage in the half-light. Whispers of mist curl across the landscape until dawn breaks and early shafts of sunlight capture an almost unearthly silhouette. A vast plain stretches out in all directions and from it arise the remains of more than 2,000 temples, some with spires still gilded in gold and elaborate white plaster carvings, others worn back to bare terracotta brick by almost 1,000 years of flash floods, dust storms and earthquakes.

Before travelling to Burma, I had heard it said that were all the medieval cathedrals of Europe to have been built in one place, it would look something like Bagan. It had seemed an impossible parallel. But now, gazing out on the ruins of this ancient kingdom, I see some truth in the analogy. Built on the banks of the immense Irrawaddy River, more than 500 miles south of its source in the melting glaciers of the Himalayas, there seems barely a stretch of skyline unbroken by the contours of sacred pinnacles.

In the distance, beyond the morning chorus of birdsong, I hear faint strains of monastic chanting. Unlike the chanted Buddhist sutras that have accompanied me on my journey so far, the words of these rhythmical recitations that echo across Burma day and night are not Sanskrit, but Pali, the original scriptural language of Theravada Buddhism. It is an early indication that I have entered different liturgical terrain.

For over two centuries, from the turn of the last millennium, Bagan was a thriving hub of Theravada Buddhism. To its adherents, the Theravada tradition is regarded as the purest form of Buddhism, or at least that which tries to remain as close as possible to the form practised by the Buddha. In the third century BCE its conservative teachings were brought to the river delta regions of contemporary Burma, Thailand, Cambodia and Laos by emissaries of Ashoka, the great Indian emperor and devout Buddhist convert. Setting sail from the far south of his kingdom, modern-day Sri Lanka, they arrived on the shores of what was once known collectively as the Golden Land.

It was not until the reign of the first king to unify Burma in the eleventh century, however, that the country became united in following Theravada Buddhism. Before this, native animist worship and Mahayana and Tantric traditions were practised in the north of the country bordering Tibet. Then, in 1047, King Anawrahta ordered these practices be excised and, both as a proclamation of power and as a way of earning religious merit, called for the building of countless monasteries and temples at the crux of his empire in Bagan. More than 10,000 temples, monasteries and pagodas were subsequently built within an area of around sixteen square miles. When Marco Polo came upon the site in the late thirteenth century, he wrote of it as 'a gilded city, alive with tinkling bells and the swishing of monks' robes'.

But the frenzy of construction had unintended consequences. For more than 200 years, kilns for making bricks were fired with wood from local trees. As these were cut down, the plain was gradually exposed to the elements, eventually turning it into a waterless desert. By the fourteenth century Bagan had been all but abandoned after repeated Mongol invasions saw the country collapse into fragmented warring states. Fast forward more than half a millennium and a renewed era of destruction unfolded. For nearly half a century from 1962, Burma was in effect a giant prison, its people brutalized by a succession of generals who looted the country and ran it as a repressive police state. In search of hard currency, this opportunistic military regime came to view Bagan as a potential cash cow. Oblivious to the site's unique archaeological worth, and heedless of the local community that remained, it attempted to turn it into an international tourist destination. In the 1990s, a botched restoration programme of some its monuments began. Bulldozers moved in to raze the homes of those who lived close to the temples, and a paved highway was built through the site, together with a golf course, luxury hotels and a concrete observation platform sixty metres high. I can just make out the outline of the platform in the distance; emerging from the morning mist, it looks more like a giant prison watchtower.

During the decades of military rule, most tourists stayed away at the urging of Burma's Nobel peace laureate, Aung San Suu Kyi. But following nominally free elections in 2010, international economic sanctions on the pariah state were eased and Aung San Suu Kyi asked that visitors use their freedom to promote that of her own people. The tourist floodgates opened and, as the sun begins to climb from the horizon, I hear the result approaching from the distance. Looking back from the river, I see dust clouds churned up in the wake of the morning's first wave of sightseeing coaches.

As a historical marker of Burma's extraordinary Buddhist heritage, Bagan is an important place of pilgrimage. But as a contemporary crucible of devotion and monastic practice, it holds little interest. For this I must travel onwards to a place that still feels untouched by time. My destination lies upriver from the country's last royal capital of Mandalay, on the opposite bank of the Irrawaddy. It is an area known as Sagaing and, in all of Burma, this stretch of rolling hills and secluded valleys is the one place that still carries an echo of what Bagan must once have been.

Here, within the space of just a few square miles, shimmering with the golden spires and turrets of countless temples and pagodas, live 6,000 Buddhist monks and 6,000 nuns. It is one of the greatest concentrations of monasticism anywhere in the world. More than 200 nunneries are nestled in the folds of these hills, a verdant expanse that some have called the Kingdom of Nuns.

I had wanted to travel to Sagaing by boat, but the water level is unusually low, with ferries regularly running aground. This is due not only to the dry season, but also to a controversial mega-dam being built by the Chinese at the headwaters of the Irrawaddy, channelling electricity back to China and leaving devastation in its wake downriver. While the West for decades turned its back on Burma in protest at the horrors of the regime, the Burmese military was busy striking lucrative deals with Chinese companies, encouraging a steady influx of Chinese immigrants into the north of the country.

'If the country hadn't opened up and economic sanctions been lifted, who knows what would have happened here. Burma was, and still is, well on the way to being stripped bare of resources by the Chinese in the same way as Tibet,' remarks one weary observer, as we leave Mandalay airport and our shared car skirts the banks of the Irrawaddy, en route to Sagaing. Despite the allure of its name, Mandalay is a place of limited charm. There is barely a trace of the romanticism conjured up by colonial cheerleader Rudyard Kipling in his poem 'On the Road to Mandalay'. Least of all in Mandalay airport's neon-lit Kipling Cafe, with little but pallid Swiss roll on display. In the heart of the city, at the gates of Burma's last royal palace, which was ransacked by British troops at the time Kipling was writing, a large banner carries an eerie reminder that Burma is not yet out of the grip of its armed forces, the feared Tatmadaw. 'TATMADAW AND THE PEOPLE COOPERATE AND CRUSH ALL

THOSE HARMING THE UNION' it reads, both in English, for the benefit of tourists, and in Burmese. Over the past half century, much of Mandalay has morphed into a fume-choked concrete jungle. Almost half of its population is now Chinese.

But travel south-west from the city and take the iron cantilever Ava Bridge to reach Sagaing and a different picture unfolds. In many ways, life here remains untouched by the modern world. As an ornate golden sign near the riverbank proclaims: 'Welcome to Sagaing Hills: The Abode of Noble Sage Recluses.'

On the day of my arrival in Sagaing I am invited to lunch at the Sakyadhita Thilashin Nunnery School, which is tucked away on a quiet dusty lane beyond the bustle of the town's central market. Sakyadhita, meaning Buddha's Daughters, is one of the newest nunneries in Sagaing and one of the most disciplined and highly regarded in Burma. *Thilashin,* which translates literally as 'Keeper of Moral Virtue', is the Burmese term for a female novice or renunciant. As in the Tibetan tradition, the full ordination of nuns has yet to be recognized in many countries adhering to Theravada Buddhism. And few places resist this change as stiffly as Burma.

It is shortly before 11 a.m. as I enter the nunnery gates and I am in time to see the young nuns line up in silence in the shade of a giant tree before entering the dining hall. Unlike the nuns I have encountered so far in Nepal and India, whose principally maroon robes mark them out as followers of the Mahayana Buddhist tradition, those lined up before me are swathed in delicate pink cloth with light brown shawls neatly folded across one shoulder. As they stand waiting for the signal to proceed, a light breeze catches the thin fabric of their long tunics, causing it to flutter like ruffled feathers. The pink and orange of their robes match the colour of flamingos and as they stand quite still, it is almost as if a flock of exotic birds has momentarily come to rest in the morning sun.

Out of sight, a signal is given for them to move forward and they do so with the precision of a choreographed ballet. The dining hall is up a few steps, which the student nuns climb, in single file, in order of height, a handful of those at the end barely into their teens. Before they enter the hall, the nuns slip off their flip-flop sandals, each placing her shoes equidistant from the other pairs. The pattern of so many black sandals against the white tile floor has the precision of a chessboard.

Inside the dining hall I am beckoned to a low table at the back. The nuns are eating in silence, their freshly shaven heads bowed. I have been invited to lunch by the abbess of Sakyadhita, Daw Zanaka, and her patron Dr Hiroko Kawanami, a Japanese social anthropologist and Buddhist scholar, who now lives in the UK and works as a senior lecturer at Lancaster University. The nunnery, established in 1998, was founded and largely funded initially by Hiroko, who, together with her Burmese husband U San, continues to work to raise funds for the nunnery's maintenance.

After the nuns have filed from the hall, Hiroko tells me how she first met Daw Zanaka when she came to Burma in the 1980s to research a doctoral thesis and temporarily became a nun. To aid her doctoral research, Hiroko lived as a *thilashin* for sixteen months in Burma, and some of that time was spent in a nunnery in Yangon, where Daw Zanaka then lived with her daughter Ma Kusalawati, 'Ma Ku'.

As a silent nun sets before us a saucer of pickled tea leaves, a traditional Burmese culinary delicacy, I broach the confusing matter of whether to use the name Burma or Myanmar and whether to refer to its one-time capital as Rangoon or Yangon. All four names are recognized internationally, though in the past, to use the name Myanmar was sometimes seen as a sign of being soft on the military regime. The ruling generals changed the English version of the country's name from Burma to Myanmar in 1989, following the suppression of a popular uprising that left thousands dead, after which Aung San Suu Kyi insisted for some time that Burma continue to be used, on the grounds that the name change had no legitimacy. 'But the name of the country in the Burmese language has always been Myanmar,' Hiroko points out. Many Burmese continue to use both, however, so I decide to stick with what is most familiar, a combination of old and new: Burma and Yangon.

It is not yet midday when the remnants of lunch are cleared away. The nuns, I know, will eat nothing from now until the following sunrise. It is a strict tenet of the Theravada tradition that monks and nuns should not eat after noon, a ruling that harks back to the Buddha's day, when monastics were strictly reliant on alms and ate their main meal after returning from collecting food given by donors on their morning alms round. After lunch, I am ushered into a spacious room to meet Daw Zanaka.

Daw Zanaka, *Daw* being a Burmese honorific used for women, is in her mid-sixties and sits bolt upright in a heavy wooden chair, her hands resting on her knees, as we speak. In Burmese Buddhist terminology I learn that Daw Zanaka is a *tàwdwet,* or 'one who has left for the forest', meaning a nun (or monk) who was previously married or widowed and has chosen to leave home to ordain. Buddhist nuns in Burma are generally categorized as either *tàwdwet* or *ngebyu,* the latter meaning 'ones who are young and pure'. *Ngebyu* nuns are those who ordain while young and sexually inexperienced and who train to become professional nuns by vocation. Having studied the scriptures from a young age, virgin nuns are widely regarded as having had a better Buddhist education and as being more spiritually accomplished than those who ordain later in life, and so command greater respect from the lay congregation. In general, *tàwdwet* renunciants like Daw Zanaka occupy less significant positions within monastic hierarchies than *ngebyu*, as they have had less time to study Buddhist texts and often focus their practice primarily on meditation, so her role as abbess and the high regard in which she is held make her an exception.

The circumstances of her becoming a nun are also unusual. Daw Zanaka was twenty-nine and mother to two children – a ten-year-old son and a younger daughter, Ma Ku – when both she and her husband and their two children decided, en masse, to dissolve the familial bonds and embrace the monastic life. 'We were a typical middle-class family. We had a good life. Our salaries were small. But everything was cheap in those days,' Daw Zanaka begins to explain. She and her husband both worked as civil servants with the Port Authority in Yangon during the early years of their marriage in the late 1950s and 1960s. But these were years of political tumult in Burma. After the military took control of the country in a coup d'état in 1962, a xenophobic dictatorship went on to rule for nearly half a century. Initially this took the form of an aberrant Soviet-style socialism. Later, following the 1988 anti-government uprising, it evolved into the chaotic paranoia of the eccentrically named State Law and Order Restoration Council or SLORC. Throughout these years, Burma was cut off from the world and descended into misery. A country with immense natural resources, once a rice bowl for the world, became one of the poorest nations on earth, its people suffering severe starvation and deprivation of personal freedom.

Like many, Daw Zanaka and her husband sought refuge in their

Buddhist faith, often attending religious festivals with their children. Ma Ku was just eight years old when she became the first in the family to announce that she wanted to become a nun. As with the nuns I've met from Nepal, India and Tibet, in Burma an early sense of vocation is often viewed as karma ripening at a young age, a kind of cosmic reward for having lived well in a previous life. But this does not mean that such proclamations are always accepted without question. While Daw Zanaka and her husband appreciated the calling their daughter expressed, permitting her to ordain temporarily as a novice during the summer holidays, they encouraged her to then return to school. The practice of temporary initiation, whether it be for just a few weeks, or for months or years, is common in the Theravada tradition, and nowhere more so than in Burma, where it has long been the custom for every boy between the ages of seven and thirteen to shave his head and enter a monastery for a period of a few weeks or a month.

When Ma Ku insisted she wanted to remain in the nunnery rather than continue with regular schooling, the young girl's wish was respected, and it inspired her parents to believe the whole family might follow the same path. First Ma Ku's brother ordained as a novice monk. A few weeks later the children's father did the same and shortly afterwards Daw Zanaka ordained as a nun.

'In the beginning, people said we were crazy. But now everyone understands,' she says. While her son chose to return to lay life when he reached adulthood, and subsequently married and had children, Daw Zanaka, her husband and daughter have continued on the monastic path. The equanimity the couple found in meditation eased their separation, she says. 'We rarely see each other now unless there is something important to discuss, and then we meet more as brother and sister.'

As we sit talking, a light breeze lifts the curtains and I turn to see a nun enter the room clutching a pink towel at her neck. Many of the young nuns wear pink towels across their shoulders or wrapped around their heads, as if they have just washed their hair, except that they have none. When the head is shaved, I am told, even the slightest breeze is keenly felt. The woman who has come to join us is Ma Ku. I am puzzled at first that mother and daughter should still live together, since monastic life requires the dissolution of close familial bonds. Yet Ma Ku, who was quickly recognized as having considerable academic flair, is here in her role as head teacher. When I question Daw Zanaka about this, she explains that their lives and their attachment to each other are now totally different. 'I do not see myself as Ma Ku's mother, nor she as my daughter,' she says. 'I am abbess. I look after everyone equally.'

Taking a seat beside her mother, Ma Ku, now in her early forties, smiles broadly and nods her head in agreement. 'We do not interfere in each other's business,' she says, with a sideways look and slight tilt of the head that suggests this might, on occasion, be challenging. But their duties at the nunnery are quite separate: while Daw Zanaka oversees every aspect of the ongoing construction of the nunnery, now home to around 200 student nuns, Ma Ku guides their education, and, although the nunnery has only been established for fifteen years, her charges regularly top the national league of state-sponsored Buddhist exams.

Hiroko's role in ensuring that the formidable talents of both mother and daughter are combined then becomes apparent. It was Hiroko who bought the first plot of land for Sakyadhita, in the hope of founding a Buddhist seminary close to the site of the country's first recorded independent nunnery school. As a young anthropologist studying at the London School of Economics in the 1980s,

Hiroko had been spurred to research the position of women in Burmese Buddhism after reading a Burmese proverb which held that 'Buddhist nuns are those women whose sons are dead, who are widowed, bankrupt, in debt, and broken-hearted.' She wanted to know if this stereotype, which might have been true in the past, was still the case in modern society. It was during this time that she temporarily ordained and came to know Daw Zanaka and Ma Ku well. 'To my pleasant surprise I found few nuns who fitted the profile of the old proverb,' she says. 'The programme of scriptural study in most nunneries is so rigorous that unless a girl or young woman has a strong sense of calling, it's a very hard life that they're unlikely to stick with.'

Far from harbouring unhappy social outcasts, Burmese Buddhist nunneries today are seen as places where many girls and women can fulfil both their spiritual and their educational potential and go on to make an active contribution to society. Over the last three decades, Hiroko estimates, there has been a thirty per cent increase in the number of Buddhist nuns in Burma. Around 50,000 are now officially registered, though there may be some who do not carry the government-issued monastic passport. This is dwarfed by the number of monks in the country – estimated to exceed half a million in more than 50,000 monasteries – but it still represents one of the highest concentrations of Buddhist nuns per head of population anywhere in the world.

The majority enter a nunnery in their late teens, and while many come from families in rural areas financially comfortable enough to support their daughters' decision to take up the monastic life, others come from all walks of life. Many girls see becoming a nun as an appealing alternative to a life of reproduction and domesticity. 'There is a still a prejudice, especially amongst the intellectual, middle-class urban population, not only here but also in the West, about nuns being poor or ugly or women whose lovers have left them,' says Hiroko. 'But look around! They're all beautiful. They're smiling. None of them are girls with broken hearts.

'It's as if women who abstain from sex and are in complete control of their body somehow offend men,' Hiroko continues. 'After all, women are supposed to bear children and look after the family, and when they renounce that prerogative, some see it as quite threatening,' she says. 'I think this is one of the reasons nuns are sometimes ridiculed by society.'

But in Burma, the reason so many girls have been choosing either a temporary or a permanent monastic vocation is also tied up with the country's turbulent politics. 'During the years of the military regime, parents saw nunneries as safe places for their daughters when they were not at school,' says Hiroko, explaining that from the late 1970s teenage girls started to spend time in nunneries during school holidays. 'By the 1980s this was becoming very popular and today it's fashionable, almost a custom,' she says.

'You make nunneries here sound like summer camps for girls,' I say.

'That's right,' Hiroko replies, explaining that the profile of nuns in Burma is also being raised with the increasing popularity of Buddhist magazines.

'Some women's magazines today even feature a Nun of the Month,' she tells me.

In Burma, however, those who follow a monastic calling have traditionally fulfilled the role not only of spiritual guide but also of social conscience. Monks have long given voice to their people's suffering, sometimes acting as catalysts for popular unrest. As the country descended further into chaos in the wake of the 1988 popular uprising that ended in a bloody coup, hundreds of thousands of monks joined lay protesters in taking to the streets, just as they did in 2007, in what became known as the Saffron Revolution, sparked by a 500 per cent rise in fuel prices. Although nuns have traditionally been more cautious, flashes of pink were seen amidst the sea of saffron and crimson robes that streamed through the streets on that occasion, and there were reports of nuns jailed or 'disappeared' in the weeks and months that followed.

Amongst the *thilashin* of Sakyadhita is one nun whose father was a senior military officer during the fateful events of the Saffron Revolution. It takes some days to arrange a meeting with her, as the nuns' daily schedule is gruelling; they rise at 4 a.m. for an hour of morning prayer before breakfast, followed by rigorous studies morning, afternoon and evening, before retiring at 10.30 p.m. But, forgoing her brief rest period late one afternoon, the officer's daughter, Wimalar, sits down to speak to me. Wimalar is in her early thirties, though she looks younger, with dimpled cheeks and a clear, open face. She is poised and calm as she begins to talk of her upbringing as the twin daughter of a colonel in the Burmese military.

Wimalar was nineteen and had just begun to study as an architect when a friend proposed she join a meditation retreat. Once there, a monk suggested she become initiated as a *thilashin*, she explains. 'I was happy because I believed it meant he recognized some inner potential in me,' she says. Her intention was to become a temporary nun. 'But I never disrobed. I was very happy and I still am,' she says, beaming. Her father was less so. 'When we were young, my father used to tease us by saying, "If you don't study hard, you'll have to become a nun."' Wimalar admits she became a nun quickly so her family had no time to object.

Wimalar begins to lace and unlace her fingers as she speaks of what followed, several years later, during the 2007 uprising. 'I've never been interested in politics,' she says. 'But when I saw what was happening, I called my father frequently on the phone and pleaded with him: "Please don't attack the monks. Please don't kill the monks." I believe, because I was a nun, this had some impact on him. I know that he used to tell the monks that his daughter is a nun,' she says, then deftly changes the subject. When I guide our conversation back to her father, Wimalar says her grandfather too had been in the army and the family had never been particularly religious. But since her father has retired, he has begun asking her questions about Buddhism. 'My father has completely changed. Now he is happy I am leading a good life. He even says if I ever disrobe, I would not be welcome back home.'

As we speak the light begins to fade and I take my leave of the nunnery until the following morning. Wimalar's hesitance in discussing the bloody events of the Saffron Revolution is fresh in my mind on the journey back to my small hotel; as if in passing, another passenger in the car points to the derelict hulk of what was once the only cinema in Sagaing. 'Here, right here in front of the cinema, the military shot many people,' he says. Checking later, I find it was the site of a massacre carried out in the 1988 uprising in which hundreds of civilians were killed. For many in Burma, the suffering continues. Despite the fanfare surrounding the release of dozens of political prisoners during the time I am in the country, many are quietly re-arrested shortly afterwards. Human-rights activists report that gang rape by soldiers in ethnic areas continues, as does extortion and forced labour by military-linked enterprises. Striking up a conversation one day with a young father in Yangon, I ask, 'How different is this government from what went before?'

'The military just took off their uniforms,' he says with a shrug.

*

The next morning, the hotel staff are still asleep, huddled under blankets on the floor of the small lobby, as I slip out in the early hours to return to the nunnery. There is a chill in the air and the headlamp of my tuk-tuk casts a thin light through the mist. On either side of the narrow lanes weaving through the centre of Sagaing there passes a stream of monks with crimson outer robes wrapped tight around their shoulders. Their bare feet pound softly on the mud track, and behind monastery walls small bells ring out. This tableau unfolds every morning in Buddhist cultures where monks follow the Theravada tradition of daily alms rounds. The cooked food slipped by devotees into the monks' alms bowls provides their sustenance for the rest of the day.

Rules regarding nuns collecting alms have traditionally been more restrictive, partly out of concern for their safety. But in Burma many aspects of monastic discipline are also overseen by the state. As in many traditionally Buddhist countries, over the centuries monarchs and rulers have both supported and sought to control the monastic community as a means of legitimizing and strengthening their own regime. In Burma, where monks have played a leading role in fighting for freedom in the past, the military junta attempted to curtail their involvement in non-religious affairs by creating a handpicked council of high-ranking monks in 1980, known as the State Sangha Maha Nayaka Committee, or SSMNC. The SSMNC has the power to disrobe those it wishes to sanction, a prerogative it exercised during the Saffron Revolution by ordering a number of prominent monks be disrobed and imprisoned.

As for alms, regulations dictate that nuns may only conduct alms rounds roughly every eight days and according to the lunar calendar, on the days before a full moon, a new moon and half moons. While monks receive only cooked food, nuns collect uncooked rice and are also permitted to receive monetary donations. Unlike fully ordained monks in the Theravada tradition, who have to observe more than 200 monastic rules, including not handling money, full ordination is not offered to Burmese *thilashin*. The majority, who observe eight precepts, are seen as a bridge between the lay and the fully ordained monastic communities. Belonging to neither community gives the *thilashin* more freedom, but it also means some are assigned to cooking and caring for monks or doing routine chores in monastery administrations rather than being able to further their spiritual development as they might wish.

The distress this position of monastic limbo causes some nuns unfolds gradually as my journey continues. But on this crisp winter morning, amidst the hills of Sagaing, I witness only communal harmony and a rare generosity of spirit. Daw Zanaka and Ma Ku wave a greeting at the entrance to Sakyadhita nunnery as I clamber out of the back of the tuk-tuk. A long line of young nuns is already lined up at the gates waiting to depart on their alms round. After a senior nun passes down the line, instructing some of the younger students to straighten their robes and adjust the tin alms bowls tucked in the crook of their arms or parasols held in their hands, a signal is given for them to move off. As they file swiftly into the dim lane beyond, I have to run at times to keep up. Unlike monks, who travel barefoot, the nuns tread lightly and quickly in flimsy flip-flops.

After walking for some time, the nuns turn off the main road and enter the first of many narrow tracks lined with tumbledown shacks and small houses. At the sound of their approaching footfall, the occupants of these modest homes step out into the lane with pots or small plastic bags in their hands. As the novices begin to chant a blessing in unison, one by one they offer up their alms bowls, into which spoonfuls of uncooked rice or small denominations of money are placed by their lay benefactors, most of them women. Over the course of the next few hours, this ritual is repeated again and again as the nuns weave their way through a network of back streets. When the sun climbs towards noon, the young nuns are invited to rest in the porch of a simple home where a young mother sets out a table of plates piled high with lentil fritters and cups of green tea.

As the smallest novices huddle together on a swinging garden seat to tuck into the homemade snacks, they giggle and tease each other, kicking their heels to keep the seat in motion. It is the first time I have seen the girls relax like the children they are. But their playfulness and broad smiles suggest they are at ease with the life they have chosen, or that has been chosen for them. While most of the novices have made their own application to join the nunnery in their mid-teens, the younger girls are sent by families keen for them to receive both a good spiritual education and often a better grounding in the Burmese language. All novices are free to return to lay life at any time. Disrobing carries no stigma in the Burmese tradition, being respected as an individual's choice and personal karma. But few, I am told, choose to leave.

By the time the coral-robed procession reassembles, the heat of the sun has begun to burn. At a signal given by a senior nun, her charges unfurl their burgundy parasols and proceed in line, continuing from one house to another. I feel I am witnessing a ritual that has remained unchanged for 1,000 years. It is humbling to see householders, clearly struggling to feed themselves, spooning grains of rice into the bowls of those who might have lived more materially privileged lives but who have taken vows of poverty. 'The role of monks and nuns is to receive in order to provide others with the opportunity to give. Both play an equally important part,' Hiroko explains as we eventually make our way back to the nunnery. 'This symbiosis of the monastic and lay community is crucial to the way Buddhism here is woven into society.'

The following day I have another opportunity to witness the culture of giving that puts our more western habit of self-interest to shame. Through friends of Hiroko I am invited to join the monks of a monastery in Sagaing for their midday meal. Today it is a special meal paid for by the villagers of a remote farming community in Burma's northern Shan highlands. The village has saved all year to be able to make this offering, and has sent a delegation to witness it being received. While the monks eat in silence, concentrating on each mouthful, the members of the small delegation kneel on mats at the back of the dining hall, dressed for the occasion in the colourful costumes of the Palaung people to whom they belong. Some clasp their hands in prayer as the monks finish the meal and file from the hall. When the last of the monks has left, the villagers invite me to join them at a low trestle table, laughing and joking as they eat what is left. To record the day, for those not able to make the journey, they pose for pictures on the steps of the monastery.

'Please can I have my picture taken with you?' one young woman whispers shyly for U San to translate, looping her arm through mine, before clambering into the back of an open truck for the long road trip home.

Through the open door of a workshop on a side street that afternoon I watch a weaver operating an antiquated loom. As she throws a giant bobbin back and forth to create the weft, sunlight catches a glint of golden thread running through the fabric, bringing the rest of the colours alive. When I reflect on the oppression endured by the Burmese people over the centuries, it seems as if the tradition of Buddhism in Burma has formed a thread of resilience and generosity that illuminates the fundamental kindness of the human spirit.

8

PEACE AND PERSECUTION

After taking my leave of Hiroko, her husband U San and the nuns of Sakyadhita Thilashin Nunnery School, I make my way to another nunnery in Sagaing run along more traditional lines. Apart from the outstanding academic achievements of its nuns, Sakyadhita is unusual in that all there live and eat communally. The Mauka Thiwon Chaung nunnery is one of many older nunneries in Burma operating on a 'separate pot' basis, in which the community of nuns come together for prayer and worship, but live and eat in detached dwellings – sometimes housing a small number of nuns loosely connected by kinship – within a walled compound.

I am here to meet one of Burma's most outgoing senior nuns. Venerable Molini is the first Burmese nun to have left the country to study for a PhD, and my communication with her before reaching Burma prepares me for a generous spirit. But the woman who greets me now is positively ebullient.

'Come, come, sister, Christine,' she booms into a microphone, laughing and beckoning me to hurry as she spots me walking up the lane to the nunnery in pre-dawn darkness.

I have been invited that morning to join another celebration of giving. Daw Molini no longer lives in Sagaing, though this is where she spent some of her earliest years as a novice and she returns regularly to visit her teachers here. Much of her time is now spent in Nepal, where she runs a project providing shelter and education to young Nepalese girls at risk of falling into the hands of people traffickers who would sell them to brothels in India. Although it is little spoken of in Burma, a similar problem of girls being trafficked from the country's border regions to Thailand and China is on the increase.

In recent years Daw Molini has also established a nunnery in Yangon, part of which will provide similar protection for vulnerable girls. Her intention is that the nunnery will evolve into an international Buddhist education centre with facilities for western lay practitioners. However, the day we meet Daw Molini's focus is not on the young but on the old. She has returned this time to honour the eldest in this 'Kingdom of Nuns'. She has drawn up a list of nearly 100 nuns here who are in their eighties and nineties with a few over 100 years old. She has been collecting donations to be able to provide each of them with a warm fleece jacket, a blanket, packages of food and simple toiletries, all now carefully wrapped and awaiting collection. By the time I arrive, shortly after 5 a.m., there are around eighty elderly women sitting cross-legged or kneeling at low tables in a large communal room finishing breakfast.

In the dim light and with the confusion of age, one mistakes me for Daw Molini and clutches at my legs, thanking me again and again for offering her warm clothes. As the women finish their meal and get slowly to their feet, helped by the younger nun assistants most have brought with them, three very young novices scurry about readying shoes for the older women to step into. Unlike the nuns of Sakyadhita, who wrap pink towels around their heads for warmth, these young girls, who must be less than ten years old, wear knitted, tea-cosy-style caps that make them look like small pink pixies. When the girls catch me watching them, their smiling faces turn suddenly serious and they start correcting the alignment of the shoes, making sure each pair is evenly placed, glancing up to see if I notice.

Then I hear Daw Molini outside, tapping on a microphone before her booming voice begins a devotional roll call. One by one she calls out the names of the elderly nuns, followed by their age.

Eighty-three years old! Eighty-seven years old! Ninety-two years old! Ninety-eight years old! Each time she calls out their age, the tone of her voice rises with an air of incredulity and respect. As each elderly woman hears her name, she steps forward and passes slowly between two lines of tables piled high with bags full of comforts. Some of the nuns walk with difficulty, using sticks, their backs stooped. Others lean on the arms of their assistants. Despite their advanced years, few apparently suffer from dementia, partly, I am told, because their minds have been kept active by years of memorizing and chanting Buddhist sutras. As the sun rises, the old women begin to make their way back to their nunneries, treading gingerly, bundles of blankets tucked under their arms, the sunlight turning their robes into billowing pink clouds.

When all have gone, the microphone is put away and I retire to a quiet room with Daw Molini, keen to understand the source of her fierce devotion and energy. From a brief meeting in Yangon, I already know that the religious life was not her first calling. As a child she dreamt of becoming a lawyer, and went on to study law at university before starting work in legal chambers in Yangon. So why, I wonder, had she not continued? Daw Molini is not a woman to mince her words. 'I saw how corrupt the lawyers were and I wanted nothing to do with them,' she says, tossing her shawl across her shoulder.

Though she makes the decision seem simple, turning her back on the chance of a career that would secure her future cannot have been easy, given the hardship of her upbringing. She was born the sixth of ten children in the northern Shan hills; her father was a junior army soldier with a meagre salary barely able to support the family, while her mother suffered repeated bouts of mental illness and was frequently hospitalized, sometimes jailed, for her erratic behaviour.

The family sold much of its furniture to pay for her treatment, which included electroshock therapy. But it was of little use.

'I saw very early how hard life is,' says Daw Molini. 'I became very withdrawn as a child and retreated into books. I understood education was very important and wanted to earn money to help care for my mum.' The ambition to study law came after her brother was imprisoned for taking part in student demonstrations. These were the years when the highly superstitious and ruthless military commander Ne Win ruled Burma with an iron rod and the country sank into the torment of his 'Burmese Road to Socialism'. Even though her family suffered at the hands of the military regime, she recalls how she used to overcome her shyness as a teenager by borrowing one of her father's army shirts, because, she says, 'It made me feel braver.'

After resigning from law, she began working as a schoolteacher, saving what money she could in a milk-powder tin to send home to her family. When she was knocked off her bike, badly injured and unable to continue teaching, she sank into despair. 'I remember at that time reading a book called *After the Storm* in which it was written "after the storm the breeze will come". But I felt my life had been one long storm. A breeze never came.' While at university she had occasionally attended meditation sessions, and after her accident, her interest in Buddhist teachings deepened. She was particularly drawn to those on the nature of karma, the connection between cause and effect. 'Finally I realized I could not blame other people for my life any more. This was a great lesson. Slowly I understood I needed to learn more about the dharma,' she says, reasoning that becoming a nun would allow her to make this her sole focus. After selling her few possessions and giving the money to her family, she travelled to Sagaing to enter the nunnery where we sit talking.

Then came an invitation to study abroad, first in Nepal and then in India. The invitations were a result of her standing up for a prominent Nepalese nun who, while visiting Burma, was bullied by one of President Ne Win's bodyguards. She describes how she confronted him, saying, 'What is a bodyguard? A bodyguard is nothing!' Considering the brutality of Ne Win's regime, it is astonishing she suffered no retribution.

Now in her late fifties, Daw Molini's energy seems undiminished and she is determined to instil in the young nuns here the same spirit of confidence to engage with the world beyond the walls of the nunnery. Her ambition is that the novices at her nunnery in Yangon will have a high level of spiritual education and schooling in secular subjects, such as English, so that they will eventually be able to offer Buddhist teachings abroad. As I take my leave of Daw Molini, I am struck once again by how the religious calling of the nuns I am meeting is matched by a dynamism and a determination to make a difference. These are not women who have chosen to ordain as a way of running away from the world.

My time in the Sagaing Hills is nearly over, so I take one last stroll through its narrow lanes. For the first time I notice a number of young men wearing Muslim *kufi* skullcaps. The wearing of *kufis* was less common in the past, I am told. Their increasing use in public is taken by some as a mark of growing divisions between Burma's Buddhist majority and the Muslim minority, which has been the target of violent attacks in recent years.

Although my need to feel uplifted in the wake of grief has drawn me to the inspiring aspects of the lives of the women I meet, I cannot ignore the fact that acts of ideological and violent zealotry are committed in the name of Buddhism as they are in other faiths.

Hundreds of Muslim homes were burnt to the ground in the greater Sagaing region in the summer of 2013. In the previous twelve months, more than 200 people, mostly Muslims, were killed. Many more were displaced after conflict between the two communities spread to towns across the country from the western state of Rakhine, with its large Rohingya population – descendants of Muslim migrants from neighbouring Bangladesh. In one attack, twenty Muslim boys were hauled from a madrassa school, hacked to death, their bodies soaked in petrol and set alight.

Many blamed the controversial Buddhist monk Shin Wirathu for stoking the flames of ethnic tension by calling on Buddhists to boycott Muslim-owned businesses and marry within their own religion. In 2003 Wirathu was jailed by the military junta for seven years on charges of inciting anti-Muslim violence and, after tensions flared in 2013, his picture appeared on the cover of *Time* magazine under the headline 'The Face of Buddhist Terror'. Some nuns I speak to voice a concern, shared by other Burmese, that military thugs had dressed in monks' clothes and become agitators, using unrest to justify the need for a strong military presence, and to deflect attention from the military's shadowy grip on the economy. On my way back through Mandalay, before returning to Yangon, I call in at Wirathu's Masoeyein monastery to get some sense of the man and other monks there.

It is early evening and the paths that connect Masoeyein's many buildings are crowded with monks on their way to evening prayer. Wirathu is not amongst them. I am told by young monks gathered outside his quarters that he is away from Mandalay. As we speak my eyes are drawn to a series of graphic posters pinned to the wall behind them. 'Stop Killing Monks' and 'Don't Rape', reads a banner above pictures of monks with their heads cut open and the mutilated bodies of women with spilt guts. When I question the monks, they say attacks against Muslims were sparked by these acts of violence. It seems pointless to argue.

Back in Yangon, I want to understand the extent to which the religious fanaticism of some of Burma's senior monks affects the lives of the country's burgeoning community of nuns. I have heard of a particularly disturbing case involving a nun called Saccavadi. More details about this emerge as I accompany her elder sister, Daw Sucinti, also a nun, on a visit to Burma's most sacred Buddhist site, Yangon's breathtaking Shwedagon Pagoda.

Daw Sucinti's slight figure is dwarfed by the towering splendour of Shwedagon as she kneels on its marble floor, hands clasped. As she prays I take in the scale of this place of pilgrimage. Rising before me is a complex of temples and stupas clad in so many tonnes of gold – more, it is said, than is held in the vaults of the Bank of England – that all those who climb within its walls seem to glow with reflected light. At the pinnacle of the tallest spire is a giant golden orb, beneath it a jewel-encrusted weather vane, both studded with rubies, sapphires, rare emeralds and more than 5,000 diamonds, the largest weighing seventy-six carats. According to legend, the central temple contains eight strands of the Buddha's hair.

On the evening I am there, Shwedagon is thronged with pilgrims, who weave around Daw Sucinti's pink-robed figure, some bowing their heads respectfully towards her. Daw Sucinti is in her mid-fifties and has been a *thilashin* since she was twenty-six. Though she lives in a township to the north of Yangon, she comes often to Shwedagon to pray. Her favourite place in this vast complex is a corner known as Aung Myay, or the Victory Ground, where kings and generals traditionally came to pray for success. More recently, this corner of the temple grounds has been the site from which student activists launched anti-government rallies. There are military surveillance cameras everywhere, constantly scanning the crowd. Daw Sucinti's sister, Saccavadi, has suffered the consequences of a different kind of scrutiny, which led to her being put on trial and then imprisoned in Burma's most notorious jail. Her punishment was meted out not by the military, however, but rather by a council of the country's most senior monks.

From Daw Sucinti I learn that the two sisters took the decision to ordain while they were both still young women. It was not a life their parents encouraged. 'Our mother used to say, "Nuns are so poor!" She didn't want that life for us,' Sucinti recalls. As children their family was not wealthy, but lived comfortably in a rural area of Shan state in north-east Burma. Their father was a junior army officer and both parents, as devout Buddhists, regularly took their six children to ceremonies at a nearby monastery. As the youngest in the family, Saccavadi was spoilt as a child. When her siblings stood in line to be chastised, their mother always held back from punishing Saccavadi because she was so little.

Although Sucinti had thoughts of becoming a nun from a young age, she says, she was mindful of their mother's objections and studied instead to become an engineer. But when their mother died suddenly in her forties, Sucinti followed her heart and ordained. Saccavadi had just finished university and the following year, when she was twenty-one, she took the same step. 'Sacca wanted to be like me,' her elder sister says, by way of explanation. After the two sisters became nuns, their father retired from the army and he too ordained, remaining a monk until shortly before his death.

The more I speak with Sucinti, however, the greater her hesitation in talking about more recent events. Reluctant to push her beyond what she is comfortable discussing, I fill in the gaps of what happened to Saccavadi by establishing contact with her directly. Saccavadi now lives in a remote corner of southern California desert; unable to travel there myself to meet her, I call on the help of two generous friends who offer to make a twenty-hour round trip from their home in San Francisco to hear her account. They are Sandra Cate, an anthropologist at San José State University and author of a book on Buddhist art and culture, and her husband Robert Gumpert, a dedicated photographer and colleague from my work as a foreign correspondent. What follows are the interwoven recollections of both sisters, drawn from my meeting with Sucinti and their conversation with Saccavadi.

My friends describe to me how Saccavadi, whose name means 'truth speaker', struggles at times to express herself, her hands dancing while she talks. She is now in her late forties and she sits perched on the end of a daybed, knees tucked under her, with a photograph album on her lap, as her bitter tale unfolds. The photos of her as a nun show her constantly smiling. But Saccavadi no longer wears monastic robes, dressing instead in simple, homemade sarong-style skirts and T-shirts. Her head is no longer shaved and her thick black hair is chopped into an uneven bob. Her skin is burnt the colour of dark chocolate from seeking solace in long walks through the sculpted granite landscape, dotted with scrub oak, juniper and Joshua trees on the edge of the Mojave Desert.

When she was young, Saccavadi was a tomboy, preferring to hike and fish rather than spend time on schoolwork, she says. But after she ordained, her dedication to her spiritual studies saw her excel. She regularly came top in state-sponsored Buddhist exams and was regarded as one of the most promising monastics of her generation. In late 1998, when Saccavadi had been a *thilashin* for sixteen years, she took the decision to study for a further degree in Buddhist Literature at a university in Sri Lanka, long a cradle of Theravada Buddhism. While in Sri Lanka, she was surprised to find nuns wearing the same saffron-coloured robes as fully ordained monks.

In Sri Lanka an order of fully ordained nuns, known as *bhikkhuni* in the Theravada tradition, existed for more than 1,000 years, until in the eleventh century invaders from southern India entrenched the caste laws of Hinduism, which relegated women to subordinate roles. As Buddhism went into decline the island's order of monks dwindled. It was later revived, but the *bhikkhuni* order was not restored until the 1990s, when the full ordination of a small number of Sinhalese nuns took place as part of historic ceremonies held at Sarnath and Bodh Gaya in India. Since then a vibrant *bhikkhuni* community has flourished in Sri Lanka. Though some conservative monks dispute this, there is evidence that Burma too had a flourishing order of *bhikkhunis* until around the thirteen century, when it is thought to have died out. But in Burma resistance to reviving full female ordination is deeply entrenched, as Saccavadi was to discover.

Seeing the Sri Lankan *bhikkhuni* nuns inspired her to want to follow the same path. But when she sought the advice of Burmese monks living in Sri Lanka, she was told full ordination was not possible for women. The monks did not leave it there. They filed a complaint about her request with the council of senior monks appointed by the Burmese government, the State Sangha Maha Nayaka Committee, in Yangon. Despite then receiving written objections from the SSMNC, Saccavadi, together with another Burmese *thilashin* named Gunasari, proceeded to ordain as a *bhikkhuni*. It was 2003 and they were the first Burmese novices in modern times to receive higher ordination in Sri Lanka.

Two years later, when Saccavadi received news that her father was gravely ill, she returned to Yangon and events took a darker turn. After learning of her return to the country, the SSMNC opened a formal investigation into her *bhikkhuni* ordination. Shortly after her father died, Saccavadi was summoned by the SSMNC's senior monks to explain herself. 'They kept wanting to know what is my point [in taking full ordination],' Saccavadi says. In May 2005 she was ordered to appear before a council of senior monks at a religious court hearing held at Kaba Aye Pagoda in Yangon, a temple where monks traditionally have close links to the government. The charge she was called to answer was, in effect, one of 'impersonating a monk'.

'It was a huge hall, a Buddhist courtroom, and it was full, maybe 400 people there,' Saccavadi recalls. 'A row of senior monks seated up on a platform, me below, alone, in front of everybody. Staff from the department of religious affairs came to watch. There were old monks, some nuns and young monks too. I could see the old monks didn't want any dispute. They want peace. They sat there very upset.

'I close my eyes and meditate. I think of the Buddha,' Saccavadi says, in a quieter voice, switching to speaking in the present tense, as if transported back to the courtroom.

'It is dead quiet. I am calm. I feel what I am doing is not just for me, but for all Burma,' she continues.

'Then I hear the monks clear their throats loudly, "Huhhumm!" like that. Like I must show respect. Then they start to read their demands over a loudspeaker.'

The demands were, first, that Saccavadi bow three times to them. Second, that she remove her saffron *bhikkhuni* robes and replace them with the pink robes of a *thilashin*. Third, they demanded that she sign a document admitting she was foolish and wrong to have become fully ordained and, fourth, that she read this admission out loud.

'I was alone. My father had died. There was no one to help me answer their questions. The monks were saying how stupid I was. Everyone was scared. It all happened quickly,' says Saccavadi.

The account of what happened next differs according to whom you speak to. But Saccavadi is quite clear in her recollection.

First, she says, she bowed to the monks three times, as they demanded. She was then presented with two sets of clothes. 'I was forced to change,' she says. 'They laid out the pink *thilashin* dress and also lay dress. I chose the lay dress.' Reverting to wearing a novice robe was simply too galling. According to Saccavadi she stepped behind a privacy screen to swap her clothes. She then signed a document given to her admitting she had been wrong to take full ordination. But she could not bring herself to read it aloud and ask for forgiveness.

Instead, she says, she turned and addressed the lay people present in the courtroom. 'Please forgive me if I have abused your support. I have accepted your alms food not as a beggar but as a female monastic who has tried to follow the teachings of the Buddha.'

Again, the senior monks asked her to read her admission of guilt aloud. Again, she refused. Indignant at the affront, the monks promptly sentenced her to five years in prison.

'I was taken to a police car. Bam, bam, bam, very quick,' she says.

First Saccavadi was taken to a local jail close to the temple. Shortly afterwards she was transferred to Burma's infamous Insein prison, a place that more than lives up to its name. Insein is internationally renowned for its inhumane treatment of inmates, many of them political dissidents and prisoners of conscience. It was here that Nobel laureate Aung San Suu Kyi was twice imprisoned. Accounts of the mental and physical torture detainees are regularly subjected to are repeatedly highlighted in human-rights reports.

'When I first ordained in a forest nunnery in southern Burma and went on alms rounds, I used to see groups of prisoners tied together, working in chain gangs, picking up rocks by the side of the road. I used to look at their faces and think, "How fortunate that I'm a nun,"' Saccavadi says. 'Then when I went to prison I thought, "My God! Now I am one of them."'

It was the beginning of Yangon's rainy season when Saccavadi was incarcerated at Insein. Threats of rape and beatings were common. Sanitation was almost non-existent. Prisoners were plagued by mosquitoes and rats. Saccavadi was locked in a large hall-like cell with hundreds of other female inmates. They slept on the floor, huddled together 'like sandwiches,' she says, crouching down to demonstrate. 'Everything very dirty. Many prisoners with skin diseases.'

No family visits were allowed inside the prison. Instead, Saccavadi was taken several times to a holding area nearby, where her sister Sucinti was able to meet her. 'I was very sad to see her,' Sucinti says of those visits. 'She was full of skin problems. Everywhere I went, especially at night, I used to think of her. I could hardly eat.'

Saccavadi does not speak of it, but Sucinti describes the way her sister also fell victim to a malicious whispering campaign. 'They called her an enemy of Buddhism, an enemy of her country. They even said she was an American spy.'

Worst of all, in the eyes of the monastic community, Saccavadi was said to have committed blasphemy. It was rumoured that while in the courtroom she had shouted at the monks, screwed up papers and thrown them at the presiding council. It was said she had written letters denouncing the senior monks and pointing out their faults. Most damaging of all in the eyes of monks and nuns I speak to afterwards, it was rumoured that, rather than go behind a screen to change out of her *bhikkhuni* robes, Saccavadi had stripped off in front of the monks.

In the background Sucinti was doing everything she could to secure her sister's release. Two of the sisters' brothers had become soldiers, one a captain, the other a major, while a brother-in-law was a lieutenant colonel. Using these connections, Sucinti began a letter-writing campaign. 'I wrote letters to everyone I could and sent copies to the top generals. I said my sister is not guilty. She loves Myanmar. She is a good person.'

But by then Saccavadi could take no more. 'I met a lady doctor at Insein who had been elected to represent Aung San Suu Kyi's party. She had been there for seven years already. I looked at her and I freaked out. I had reached my limit. I had a choice, either stay in jail for five years or apologize.'

After seventy-six days in prison, Saccavadi agreed to do as the monks had demanded: admit in public that she was guilty and ask their forgiveness. 'Some people have the determination to stay in jail for many years. But for me seventy-six days was plenty, plenty,' she says. Hearing of her contrition, the monks convened another hearing. 'I bowed down. I sat in front of a microphone and read out what I was told to say clear and loud. I said, "Yes, I am stupid. I am foolish." I said what they wanted and thought "Whatever,"' she says, with the air of a diffident teenager masking the wounding she felt.

'I believe that robes support your practice. But if they don't, then what's the point?' she goes on, in a more sombre tone. 'What's important is what's in your mind and heart.'

After her release from jail the monks made it clear Saccavadi was no longer welcome in Burma. She was driven to the airport and put on a plane back to Sri Lanka. There she was told by one senior nun that, because she had been in prison, she was dirty, stained, and must re-ordain.

'I said I was already clean, that I had been through hardship in prison. I had been through enough already. I didn't accept what she was saying. I didn't have the energy,' she says. 'Sometimes you need to know your life. For me Buddhism is something we practise together. It is about the heart and mind. I knew I could continue with my practice in my own way.'

So in 2007 Saccavadi flew to the United States to be reunited with Gunasari, the other nun who had become fully ordained in Sri Lanka. Together they lived a simple monastic life with a small group of nuns in a monastery near Pioneertown, in southern California's San Bernardino County. But the trauma of what she had been through remained with Saccavadi. Some time later she went for a period of quiet retreat to a cabin in the desert and there fell in love with its owner. When she failed to return to the monastery, her fellow nuns came looking for her. As they drove her away she broke down in the car and demanded that they take her back to the cabin. The couple married shortly afterwards.

Saccavadi describes how she made her own white wedding dress the day before the ceremony. 'She was a beautiful bride,' says her husband Dave, a devout Buddhist, who hovers protectively close by as she relates her story. When her tale is told, Saccavadi says she has spoken of what happened to her for the last time. 'Now I will delete it from my mind,' she concludes, rising from her seat to loop her slender arms around her husband's waist.

The private sense of loss both Saccavadi and her sister Sucinti feel is evident, but there are more public repercussions too. In Burma, when I raise the subject of Saccavadi's trial with some Burmese monks, their attitude is unforgiving. They repeat the rumour that she had committed blasphemy by stripping off in the courtroom, before leaving the country and getting married. Among the community of *thilashins*, there is some criticism too. Following her trial, the country's senior monks issued an edict banning any further discussion of full ordination for Burmese nuns. While many show little interest in the issue of full ordination, and some argue the subject has become entangled in gender politics irrelevant to monastic life, for those who wish it were possible, what happened to Saccavadi is a source of regret. 'Her case has set the cause back many years. It's no longer permitted to even speak of *bhikkhuni* ordination,' says one senior nun.

The treatment of Saccavadi is a dismal chapter in Burmese Buddhism. At the end of my time in Yangon a ceremony is held during which the steady rhythm of chanting from monasteries across the city echoes across the rooftops all day long and throughout the night. The chants are ancient blessings to protect all those who hear them, incanted continuously by relays of monks. Nowhere else that I visit do I feel Buddhism so interwoven into the fabric of a country's soul. That those whose beliefs are so deeply rooted in an ethos of compassion should treat others with such inhumanity seems almost incomprehensible. But, after reporting on conflicts in the Middle East and the Balkans, where I encounter unspeakable atrocities carried out in the name of one faith or another, it is further confirmation that the curse of all organized religion is to become corrupted when power comes into play. From this Buddhism is not immune.

Before leaving Burma, I take a walk east of the Shwedagon Pagoda and skirt the shores of a small lake that acts as a watery mirror to the golden temple shimmering at sunset. Beyond a small enclave of heavily guarded embassy compounds, I turn into a narrow street that leads to a secluded meditation centre. Here I am ushered to sit in one of the meditation cells that surround a large hall. It is early Sunday morning and around me are Burmese men and women of all ages, kneeling or sitting cross-legged in private contemplation.

In the silence, the different threads I have followed in search of Burma's Buddhist nuns slowly slip from my mind. I bring my focus to the breath, observing thoughts as they come and go, gradually settling. My own path to a regular meditation practice came through many years of yoga, which I had originally been drawn to out of desperation for pain relief following a car accident in my twenties that fractured my spine. But the more I have practised yoga, the more I have come to appreciate how its physical discipline was originally devised partly as a way of getting the body healthy enough to be able to sit comfortably still in meditation. Though this traditional aspect has now been largely swamped by the keep-fit cult that has turned yoga into a global business, I am grateful for the ability the practice has given me to begin to feel more physically at ease as I sit in stillness.

An hour passes. A bell rings and all tread quietly from the hall, making their way across a wooden footbridge to the street beyond. The centre, surrounded by a lily-choked pond, is a haven of tranquillity amidst the bustle of a rapidly expanding city. I am the only westerner at that morning's sitting. But I am aware that beyond a roped-off area are those who have come from all over the world for a ten-day period of silent meditation in a tradition for which Burma is now globally renowned.

Those who come here follow a rigorous regime of meditation devised by the Burmese-born businessman Satya Narayan Goenka, who turned to meditation initially to relieve the pain and distress of severe migraines. Drawing on the ancient Buddhist meditation technique called Vipassana, or insight meditation, S. N. Goenka was so inspired by the positive effects regular practice had on his life that he abandoned his successful business and dedicated himself to developing and teaching a programme of meditation designed specifically for lay practitioners. Returning to the roots of Buddhism in India, he spent much of the rest of his life teaching there.

After Goenka passed away in the autumn of 2013 his ashes were returned to his homeland to be scattered in the Irrawaddy. Goenka's legacy is a worldwide network of retreat centres where every year more than 100,000 people follow courses taught according to his strict criteria of ten days spent in silent contemplation, focusing principally on the breath and the body's constantly changing physical sensations. Goenka stressed that his courses, although rooted in Buddhist practice, were a non-sectarian technique to provide practitioners with 'a set of tools for upgrading and optimizing the mind' in order to live life more fully.

Some of those taught by Goenka and other Burmese meditation masters, both lay and monastic, have gone on to establish meditation techniques better suited to the lives of those in the modern world. Throughout the history of Buddhism, there have been movements to return the focus of practitioners to the most fundamental teachings of the Buddha on meditation. And nowhere is this more evident than in Japan, where meditation is the very meaning of Zen.

PART IV

JAPAN

MIRROR ZEN

Petals of fading cherry blossom float on the wind as I arrive in Japan in mid-April. A warm spell has brought the flowers into bloom early and although the air is still tinged with fragrance, it is already past the peak of the ritual flower-viewing season, the *hanami,* celebrated as a national festival as it sweeps across the Japanese archipelago every spring.

Since ancient times the Japanese have cultivated an awareness of transient beauty, which sees the ephemeral nature of reality as a vital element. With the rise of the samurai in medieval times, the sudden burst of colour in the cherry blossom season came to be viewed as an allegory for the often brief life of the warrior. From this came a saying, 'The cherry is among flowers as the samurai is among men.' Aside from the centuries of clan warfare that brought the samurai to prominence, this nation of islands has, throughout history, grappled with vulnerability to natural disasters.

Nearly every day an earth tremor of some magnitude is felt somewhere in Japan. Memories of the March 2011 earthquake, tsunami and nuclear meltdown at Fukushima are still raw and I quickly get an insight into the caution this imbues. In the early hours of my first night, I am woken by the buzzing of an 'Emergency Alert!!' message flashing across the screen of my mobile phone. In a fog of jetlag, I turn the phone face down and continue dozing. The following morning I learn such alerts signal an imminent earthquake. The quake that night was sizeable, 6.3 in magnitude. It struck twenty miles offshore, causing little damage, but my sense of unease lingers.

Since an awareness of impermanence lies at the heart of

Buddhism, it seems natural that such teachings should have sunk deep roots here, eventually leading to the evolution of a distinct Buddhist tradition that became known as Zen. Today Japan is a largely secular society, but for more than 1,500 years Buddhism was a key influence shaping its history. To understand the pivotal role nuns played, I travel to Japan's former capital, the coastal town of Kamakura, an hour's train-ride south-west of Tokyo.

For mile after mile there is little but urban sprawl as we pull away from the metropolitan hub of skyscrapers that seem to dwarf the human spirit. But gradually the scenery changes, the landscape unfurls into a carpet of rice paddies. Then, as we draw close to the sea, a sudden lushness of vegetation erupts and it is clear we are entering a different environment. A large sign on the platform of the peaceful suburb of Kitakamakura welcomes visitors to 'The Home of the Samurai'. These days Kamakura is a popular coastal resort and dormitory community favoured by affluent Tokyo commuters. But from the twelfth to the fourteenth centuries, when the samurai rose to power, replacing the imperial court as a ruling military class, it served as the seat of Japan's military commanders, the shoguns. A short walk from the station, through a tunnel of tall pine trees and flowering azaleas, is a former nunnery called Tokeiji that for more than 600 years was renowned throughout Japan.

From early in Japan's pre-modern history, women played an important role in propagating the spread of Buddhism in the country. The first ordained Buddhist in the Land of the Rising Sun was female, just a girl when her parents sent her to Korea for instruction in the new religion that travelling monks and merchants had recently brought there from China. On her return to Japan in 590 CE, Zenshin-ni and two followers established the country's first Buddhist temple. In the years that followed, many more pilgrims, both men and women, travelled to China and Korea to learn of a distinct school of Buddhism that was emerging there, which in China was known as Chan, in Korea as Soen and, once it transferred to Japan, became Zen, a term derived from the Sanskrit word *dhyana*, meaning meditation. At the heart of this tradition, amongst the most well known in the West, is the belief that enlightenment is not some far-off goal that may or may not eventually be reached through spiritual study, ritual or repeated rebirths. Zen Buddhism holds that enlightenment is within reach of us all and its key lies in the rigorous practice of meditation.

At first this strict emphasis on meditation was regarded as an obscure movement practised in remote mountain areas, which was one of the reasons Chan survived the persecution of Buddhist followers in China from the ninth century onwards. But in Japan the stringent practice required in Zen was of great appeal to the emerging class of samurai, with their focus on self-discipline and ethical behaviour. As Zen took hold in Japan various schools within this tradition evolved alongside more devotional forms of Buddhist practice, such as Pure Land Buddhism, with its greater emphasis on prayer. Over the course of Japanese history both forms of Buddhism were adopted at the highest levels of society.

As power fluctuated through the centuries between shoguns and imperial rule, thirty-six emperors, seventy-four empresses, two-hundred-and-thirty-three imperial princes and sixty-seven princesses were ordained as Buddhist monks or nuns. Many ordained after the death of their spouse, others when they became ill, or as a way of surviving the continual clan warfare, believing that the power of the Buddha would protect them. As a result a significant network of nunneries and monasteries carrying the imperial seal was established. Such powerful patronage and lavish state support ensured that

Buddhist orders, including those of Buddhist nuns, prospered throughout long periods of Japanese history.

The nunnery I have come to visit in Kitakamakura enjoyed unique protection from its inception in 1285 CE, since its first abbess and founder, Kakuzan Shido, was the widow of a powerful shogun. From the fourteenth century, when power returned briefly to the emperor, the nuns of Tokeiji wore purple habits, at a time when purple robes were reserved for members of the royal household. The secret to the special role played by Tokeiji lies in the name by which it became known throughout Japan: the 'Divorce Temple'. For almost 600 years after it was founded, this nunnery was the only place in Japan where women were able to obtain a divorce, a right otherwise reserved exclusively for men until the late nineteenth century.

Climbing a steep flight of steps set back from the road that leads up to Tokeiji's main temple building, I pass through a thatched gateway and enter an extraordinarily beautiful garden. Tucked in a winding fold in the mountains that surround Kamakura, it is an oasis of butterflies and spring flowers, a place of almost otherworldly peace punctuated now and then by birdsong. Such tranquillity seems far removed from the time when Tokeiji was besieged as a sanctuary for battered and abused women. But its protection was once in such demand that three inns were opened at its gates to house all those attempting to enter. Angry husbands would try to prevent their wives passing through Tokeiji's gates, so a system was developed whereby it was enough for a woman to throw her shoes over the nunnery's perimeter fence to secure asylum. The women who found refuge here then had to live as a nun for three years before being granted a legal divorce, which allowed them to survive as a single woman or remarry.

To the rear of the grounds of Tokeiji lies a cemetery with the graves of the women who championed this pre-modern claim to women's liberation. Beneath one rocky overhang, in a shady cavern half-overgrown with moss, are the remains of its founding abbess Kakuzan, beside her those of its fifth abbess, an imperial princess named Yodo. A little further on is a more prominent seventeenth-century monument to its twentieth abbess, Tenshu, granddaughter of a powerful shogun, who was granted one wish after her entire family was slaughtered. Tenshu begged that Tokeiji remain as a place of asylum for women indefinitely. It did so until Japan's laws changed in 1873 granting women the same rights as men to divorce.

In the nunnery's small temple, barely visible in darkened recesses, are seated statues of these three abbesses, with replicas of their tiny shoes neatly placed in front of them. The delicacy of these figures belies their enormous influence. In addition to the power they wielded in granting divorce, Kakuzan and Yodo also introduced a potent tool for meditation. While most monks and nuns were encouraged to face a wall or cast their gaze on a point on the floor in front of them when meditating, the nuns of Tokeiji were also taught to meditate in front of a mirror.

This form of meditation, known as 'mirror Zen', sought to help women see through feelings about their appearance, whether positive or negative, and so deconstruct attachment to physical form, recognizing instead their own true nature. Generations of nuns would practise meditation in front of the nunnery's great mirror, concentrating on the question, 'Where is a single feeling, a single thought, in the mirror image at which I gaze?' Each abbess of Tokeiji would write a verse following the practice of mirror Zen. The enigmatic words of Princess Yodo still survive:

'Heart unclouded, heart clouded;
Standing or falling, it is still the same body.'

Mirror Zen was also a way of teaching the Buddhist concept of *sunyata*, the profound principle of interconnectedness between all beings, which stresses the essential emptiness of a separate self. Gradually the practice of mirror meditation died out, however, and at the turn of the twentieth the nunnery itself declined. Following the change to Japan's divorce laws, Tokeiji came under the administration of a neighbouring monastery, and these days it is viewed as something of a curiosity, a fall from grace, which in some ways reflects the fate of Buddhism in Japan, too.

In the latter half of the nineteenth century Japan began to emerge from more than 200 years of self-imposed isolation, during which it was illegal both to leave the country and for a foreigner to enter. This key period of opening up to the world, known as the Meiji Restoration, marked the demise of control by successive shoguns and their samurai and the re-emergence of the imperial court. In order to strengthen loyalty to the emperor, Japan's ancient native Shinto faith, a mixed animistic, polytheistic spiritual tradition, was reinstated as the state religion.

As Japan continued to struggle with the aftermath of centuries of isolation and then rushed to modernize as a way of shaking off the ignominy of defeat in the wake of the Second World War, Buddhism went into slow decline. While three-quarters of Japan's population of 127 million may now profess to be Buddhists, the only formal contact most will have with a Buddhist priest is to make the final arrangements for a departed relative. In Japan today it is common practice for families to take newborns to be blessed at a Shinto temple. Many then choose to get married in a Christian chapel, though this is often a mock ceremony staged for the photo opportunity offered by a traditional western-style white wedding. Only at the end of life will most turn to a Buddhist temple, leading many these days to disparage the faith as '*soshiki bukkyo*' or 'funeral Buddhism'.

Even as interest in Buddhism was waning in the 1960s and 1970s, however, one of Japan's most prominent and controversial figures stunned the country by choosing to ordain as a Buddhist nun. Jakucho Setouchi is a prize-winning novelist who once scandalized society with a series of sexually explicit novels that have sold millions of copies. At first I hold out little hope of meeting with 'Jakucho san'; now in her nineties, she is still in such demand that lotteries are held for tickets to attend the monthly talks she gives at the small temple she has built in a quiet northern suburb of Kyoto. But after some persuasion, a meeting is agreed.

On a rainy afternoon, together with Hisako, the kind retired physician and friend who has offered to act as my interpreter, I take a taxi to the leafy residential district of Sagano, where Jakucho lives. There Hisako and I are ushered into an airy, feminine salon in a spacious pavilion overlooking lush gardens in the temple grounds. My eye is immediately drawn to a framed print on the wall: a seductive drawing by the French Expressionist Marc Chagall of a couple lying side by side, the man with his hand on the woman's breast.

Jakucho does not keep us waiting. Even before we have sat down, she sweeps into the room in a deep purple robe, with gold brocade trim, worn over a white kimono. Wrapped around her fingers is a string of crystal meditation beads, on her feet the white split-toed socks associated with her vocation. With the customary bow of introduction, she flashes a warm and friendly smile. By some accounts, Jakucho Setouchi is the most instantly recognizable figure in Japan after the members of the imperial family. As the story of her life unfolds, over tea served with dainty bean-paste tarts, I begin to appreciate why.

'Ask me anything you like. Don't hold back!' Jakucho declares, with a raucous laugh and the energy of a woman decades younger. As she talks I am mesmerized by her expressive pencil-thin eyebrows that dance close to the former hairline of her shaven head. From reading other accounts of meetings with Jakucho, I understand she is weary of being asked why she became a nun.

This did not happen until she was fifty-one years old. By then she was already a bestselling author, having won Japan's top award for women writers for one of her early novels, *Natsu no Owan* [*The End of Summer*], which sold over a million copies when it was published in the 1960s and has recently been made into a feature film. At the time, many in Japan's literary establishment denounced the novel as obscene. Jakucho's early novels are unashamedly autobiographical, often drawing on her tangled relationships with men. Another book, *Joshidaisei Qu Ailing* [*Female College Student Qu Ailing*], about a woman who abandons her husband and child for a series of unconventional affairs, also won a prize. The novel's sexually explicit scenes led conservative critics to accuse her of writing the book while masturbating, to which she retorted that the reviewers must be impotent and their wives frigid. For five years Jakucho was shunned by Japan's male-dominated publishing houses, which accused her of penning pornography.

Since ordaining as a nun in 1973, Jakucho has continued writing novels and other books of non-fiction, 400 in total, many on Buddhist themes. Her literary career has now spanned seven decades, so I start by asking Jakucho about her writing. She beams approval and slides towards me a printed sheet with all the literary distinctions she was won, listed in chronological order, attesting to her success in many genres. In her seventies she embarked on translating into contemporary Japanese the country's eleventh-century tale of romance, *The Tale of Genji*, which runs to more than 2,000 pages. 'The publishers even asked me if I would live long enough to finish it. It was a gamble,' she admits. But her version of the epic tale sold over two million copies. Her honours include one of Japan's most prestigious literary awards, the Tanizaki Prize, given in 1992 for her novel *Hana ni Toe* [*Ask the Blossoms*], and in 2006 she received Japan's highest cultural accolade, the imperial Order of Culture, for her lifetime contribution to Japanese literature.

Jakucho continues to write nearly every day, in longhand, with a fountain pen, in traditional Japanese vertical style. Some of the novellas she still writes are erotic fiction. 'In fact some people have remarked that what I write now is even more romantic than what I wrote when I was younger,' she says. By romantic, I am not sure if she means graphic. But certainly, her understanding of the worldly aspects of life seems as acute as ever. In addition to novels and non-fiction, she also contributes regular newspaper columns dispensing pithy, modern agony-aunt advice on affairs of the heart. This has won her a keen following among the young.

Occasionally, when she was spotted strolling through the streets of Kyoto in her monastic robes, teenage girls will call out to her, greeting her as 'Jakky'. Of an evening, she sometimes dines in Kyoto's downtown restaurants at the invitation of devotees. She eats meat, drinks alcohol and appears the picture of health when we meet, her rounded face surprisingly smooth. When I ask her the secret of her energy and unlined features, she puts it down to the ability to 'fall asleep anywhere anytime'. Her eyebrows then curl mischievously as she adds, 'When I'm very stressed I drink sake. This helps me feel relaxed.'

Given her openness, I have no hesitation asking from where she continues to derive the inspiration for such sexually charged writing, since she chose to take a vow of celibacy when she became a nun forty years ago. Hisako raises an eyebrow as I ask her to transmit the question, but Jakucho throws her head back with a throaty laugh before replying that she has a good memory. 'What people do now is not that different from what they did fifty years ago, and I have had enough experience,' she says, still laughing.

While addressing a packed audience she once admitted, 'Usually people who do bad things make good writers. I did a lot of bad things, which is why my novels are interesting.' The biographical details of Jakucho's life are well documented. Born Harumi Setouchi to a family that ran a business selling Buddhist artefacts, by her mid-twenties Jakucho was already married and the mother of a young child. After starting an affair with one of her husband's students, she walked out of her marriage and, with no means to support herself or her child, was forced to leave her three-year-old daughter with her husband's family. When she tells me this during the hours that we sit talking, it is the only moment that her animated features fall.

In the years that followed, in addition to her relationship with her younger lover, Jakucho embarked on a lengthy affair with a married man. In her early forties, after the publication of *The End of Summer*, based largely on her adulterous affair, her writing career flourished. 'I was very popular. Whatever I wrote, I made money. I had a lot of jewellery, beautiful clothes and kimonos.' For a decade she continued writing and had a string of further relationships. 'But gradually it all began to seem empty,' she says. Despite having won awards for her novels, she began to doubt her talent as a writer. 'I felt bad because I aspired to writing of a higher quality. I had had enough.' When her passion for writing faltered, so, it seems, did her passion for life. 'I had many affairs. But I was getting tired of those things. After my divorce, maybe I hurt other people because of my strong interest in writing. But writing was my life, so when I became tired of writing, I became tired of living,' she explains.

It was this existential crisis that set Jakucho on a search for a deeper meaning to her life. Despite her family's connections with Buddhism, she initially turned to Catholicism and began avidly reading the Bible. 'When I didn't find answers in Catholicism, I finally felt I should start paying attention to Buddhism, and very soon I knew I wanted to become a nun.' Jakucho says this as if the life-changing decision were a natural progression. The depth of her anguish during this period only becomes clear when I press her to explain. 'If I hadn't become a nun, I probably would have committed suicide,' she confesses. 'For me, to become a nun is to erase the past. To start life anew.'

Although Jakucho attributes such desperation to her loss of zeal for writing, a possible connection to the life she once led gradually emerges. Even after she had made the decision to become a nun, she admits she had trouble finding a Buddhist order willing to ordain her. 'I approached various temples, but they didn't take me seriously.' It was not until she asked for help from a fellow writer named Kon Toko, who was also a priest in the Tendai Buddhist tradition, that her wish was treated with respect. Tendai, a form of Buddhist practice especially prevalent in the area around Kyoto, does not belong to any Zen lineage but traces its origins back to an ancient school of Chinese Mahayana Buddhism. 'Kon Toko knew what my intention was without me even having to tell him –

perhaps there was something different in my demeanour,' Jakucho continues. 'When he suggested a date for my ordination, I got rid of all my personal belongings. I gave everything away.' Kon Toko performed her ordination ceremony in the autumn of 1973.

'At first I didn't want people to know what I was about to do. When I told a few of those close to me, some cried,' she says. Despite Jakucho's attempts to keep news of her ordination secret, details were somehow leaked to the press and the ceremony 'turned into a media circus', she says. It was only through a news report that her daughter then learnt that her mother had become a nun. 'My daughter was out of the country on her honeymoon,' Jakucho explains. 'When she returned, she asked me if my becoming a nun had anything to do with her. Maybe she thought I had become a nun as a way of asking for forgiveness because she had been abandoned,' she says, her eyebrows knitting into a deep furrow. 'I told her, no, it was not the reason. But when I look into my own heart, maybe, just possibly, there is a grain of truth in that. Looking back on my life, I have no regrets except that I could not take my daughter with me,' she continues. 'But my husband's family would not let me. When I tried to go back for her, when she was about four years old, she told me, "My mother is dead," and I realized this is what she had been told. I knew it was no use.'

An air of sadness fills the room. When I listen back later to my interpreter Hisako translating Jakucho's words, I hear the softness in her voice as she transmits my questions and am grateful for her sensitivity.

Rallying her spirits, Jakucho returns to talk of her ordination, describing how her friend Kon Toko advised her that she should continue writing. 'He knew how important it was to me. He told me to carry on writing until I die, and this is what I have been doing,' she says. Jakucho then recalls how Kon Toko also told her it was not necessary to cut off her long hair if she needed more time to adapt to being ordained. 'But I told him I wanted to change on the outside as well as the inside, so he could go ahead and shave my head.' Kon Toko then asked her what she was going to do about 'the lower part of her body'. There is some delay in Hisako translating this, as she is not clear at first what Jakucho means. 'He wanted to know what I was going to do about sex!' Jakucho explains bluntly, and all three of us burst out laughing. 'He said, you don't have to give it up right away. You don't have to stop completely. You can give it up gradually.' More laughter.

Japanese Buddhism is the only Buddhist monastic tradition I encounter where there is no requirement of celibacy. Rules concerning monastic celibacy were changed in Japan, principally for political reasons, when imperial rule was reasserted during the Meiji Restoration and Shinto was re-established as the state religion. In order to diminish the influence of Buddhism, which had flourished under successive shogunates, it was thought that making Buddhist monks and nuns more like lay people would lessen the regard in which they were held, so new regulations were introduced in the late nineteenth century allowing them to grow their hair, wear lay clothing, eat meat and marry.

This historical quirk has left monks and nuns following Japanese Buddhist schools with far greater flexibility in interpreting monastic tradition. It also means there is still no requirement of celibacy, but rather one of abstinence from 'sexual misconduct'. After the rules were changed, most monks chose to get married and a tradition of fathers passing on temples to sons, who in turn became monks, was born. Most nuns, however, preferred not to marry, though this, I discover, is now changing.

When it came to her own decision, Jakucho says she did not hesitate. 'I told Kon Toko I would stop having sexual relations. I told him I was getting tired of it, so I would stop completely.' But Jakucho admits it was still a struggle to adopt celibacy. 'Sex is a very strong desire, a human instinct. To be celibate is hard.' While she is sometimes 'a little loose with some of the other precepts,' she says with a laugh, 'I chose to stick to celibacy because it is a very important practice. It is the practice of the original Buddha after enlightenment.' For millennia the tradition of celibacy earned Buddhist monks and nuns great respect 'because they were doing something that other people would have great difficulty with,' she says. 'So I was determined to abstain because this vow came from the Buddha.'

Despite Jakucho's certainty, many in Japan appear to have been sceptical about whether she could stick to this vow. 'Because of my reputation for liking men, there was a lot of speculation about how long I would last. Some even placed bets that I would only last three or six months,' she says, with such a sweet smile it is hard to imagine a time when the elderly nun seated in front of me with such poise was renowned for her freewheeling private life.

These days Jakucho is better known for the high-profile stand she takes on a range of political issues, including the death sentence: after a hiatus of several years Japan resumed hanging in 2012. She has also protested against the reopening of Japan's nuclear facilities following the Fukushima disaster and, much to the concern of her assistants, in May 2012 she joined a public hunger strike on the streets of Tokyo, sitting from dawn to dusk outside a government building with the message 'No to Reactivation!' pinned to her nun's robes.

Her energy seems boundless. Yet when I start to ask her about the situation of other Buddhist nuns in Japan today, she grows visibly weary. She recalls the period, following her ordination, when she was one of just four nuns amidst fifty monks undergoing training at the same time. All were considerably younger and would sometimes come to her for motherly advice. But still, when it came to bath time, Jakucho and the other nuns were expected to get up at 2 a.m. to fetch water in buckets for the monastery's customary Japanese communal bath. They then had to wait until the monks had finished bathing before taking their turn in the same water. When Jakucho enquired if she and the other nuns might be allowed to bathe first, she was told it was 'out of the question'.

I ask if the situation has now improved, with nuns being treated equally, but Jakucho retorts, 'Not at all!' Her own privileged position and high public profile seem largely due to the success she has enjoyed as a writer, both before ordaining and since. I ask if she has seen any positive developments in the lives of nuns compared with the past. 'I'd better not talk about that, as I might have little good to say.' She sighs, reaching out to touch her prayer beads. As our meeting draws to a close Jakucho slips from the room, then returns to present Hisako and me with signed copies of two of her books.

Later that evening, as we sit, jostled by tired commuters, on a train pulling away from Kyoto station, I ask Hisako to translate for me the first lines of one of the books we have been given. It is a fictionalized account of the Buddha's last days and is written from the perspective of the Buddha's cousin and close attendant, Ananda, champion of the cause to allow women to become ordained.

The book opens with the line, 'I came back from the brothel in the middle of the rain. The Buddha was sleeping in a small bed in the bamboo grove . . .'

Even when writing on Buddhist themes, it seems Jakucho has a talent for making a story gripping from the start.

STILLNESS

Less than 100 miles to the east of Kyoto lies a training temple and nunnery where, despite Jakucho's pessimism about younger nuns in Japan, there are signs that a significant change is under way. The nunnery of Aichi Senmon Nisodo is one of just a handful of places left in the country where women can now train to become Buddhist nuns. Tucked away in a quiet suburb of the bustling industrial city of Nagoya on the Pacific coast, Nisodo belongs to the Soto school of Zen Buddhism, now the largest of Japan's three main Zen traditions.

The first of these traditions to become firmly established in Japan, in the twelfth century, was the influential school of Rinzai, which emphasizes the use of *koans*, or enigmatic questions such as the famed riddle, 'What is the sound of one hand clapping?' as a central means of meditation practice. These inscrutable puzzles are intended to bypass our habitual rational mind, with its over-reliance on intellect and reason, in order to trigger insight and awakening through deep intuition. At the time Rinzai was becoming established, Japan was in the grip of a major power struggle between the samurai and the seat of aristocracy in Kyoto. When power was wrested from the imperial court and the Kamakura Shogunate was born, the enormous social upheaval involved led to a demand for a spiritual practice more attuned to the frustrations of ordinary people and the newly emergent warrior class; it was then that Soto Zen started to evolve.

The Soto Zen school followed the teachings of a monk named Eihei Dogen. Inspired by his Chinese Zen master, Dogen placed great importance upon *zazen*, simply sitting in meditation as an expression of enlightenment. The rigour, yet simplicity, of the practice of *zazen*, with its emphasis on physical posture while meditating, was particularly suited to the way of life of the samurai, as it developed in practitioners the ability to act in a spontaneous, intuitive way. Throughout the many centuries that Japan was ruled by military shoguns, Soto Zen flourished and tens of thousands of temples and training monasteries were built, some 15,000 of which still survive today.

Nagoya is not the loveliest of Japan's cities. It is a busy port and industrial powerhouse, which some have described as the nation's 'stalwart brother' to Kyoto's 'gracious geisha' and Tokyo's 'preening teen'. There is certainly little sign of grace or glamour when I open my hotel curtains on my first morning in the city: steel and concrete stretch as far as the eye can see. It is not until I take a taxi from the drab grey chaos of the city centre to a wealthy eastern suburb called Chikusa that the scenery changes to a more traditional patchwork of family homes with carefully tended gardens. As we turn uphill into a quiet lane, the entrance to Nisodo comes into view. A stone arch is set back from the road and a winding path leads through a garden lush with flowering shrubs and moss-covered stones. From the moment I shut the taxi door and walk into the temple compound, I feel as if I am entering a world somehow frozen in time.

To the right of the main path is a worship hall with traditional curved eaves, sliding doors and windows faced with translucent rice paper. To the left is an open-sided bell tower and a meditation hall, or *sodo*. Close to this I glimpse a low structure draped in a cloak of pale blue wisteria. This is a tea pavilion, where nuns are given many hours of meticulous instruction in how to perform with spiritual elegance the tea ceremony that is one of the pillars of traditional Japanese culture. Beyond these separate buildings is the main fabric of the nunnery, housing dormitories, a kitchen, classrooms and other facilities.

Despite many communications by phone and email to arrange my stay at Nisodo, the nun who first opens the door of the main building seems surprised to see me on the doorstep. She is even more surprised when I say that I will be staying a week. But after some discussion, I am shown to an upstairs storeroom, one corner of which is cleared to allow a futon to be rolled onto a rice-straw tatami mat as my bed. This will be my home for seven days and I am grateful to have been given this small space. Privacy, I discover, is in as short supply here as it is in all the nunneries I visit.

Only one condition is placed on my staying at Nisodo and this is that I spend the first three days participating in a strict regime of meditation known as a *sesshin*, which is followed once a month by all the nuns. Each of these days will start at 4 a.m. and involve five periods of *zazen* sitting meditation lasting fifty minutes, interspersed with other forms of meditative practice. These include formal meals, served in ritualistic fashion in the meditation hall, the chanting of sutras in the non-tonal style typical of Zen, and also attending dharma talks given twice daily by Nisodo's abbess, Shundo Aoyama, known as Aoyama Roshi – *roshi* meaning 'teacher'. Any free time is to be spent in one of four work divisions, which take care of the kitchen, office, temple and visitor relations. It is a demanding programme and I face it with some apprehension.

Before leaving for Japan, I had watched film footage showing how, during *zazen* practice, a nun paces around the meditation hall with a wooden stick ready to administer a blow to the shoulders of any meditator who requests it to help ease tension in the shoulders and keep her from dozing or slumping out of posture. I also know, from my yoga practice, that sitting repeatedly for long periods of time in a cross-legged position can be downright painful. The only guidance then, as in most forms of meditation, is to become aware of thoughts arising, including an awareness of pain, without reacting. This means neither getting carried away by a thought, nor repressing it, but rather observing and letting it pass, another lesson in transience. This is not simple.

While some forms of meditation suggest a focus, such as concentrating on the breath or particular visualizations, *zazen* emphasizes only attention to posture. The idea is that sitting will become comfortable enough to allow an awareness of what is happening in the mind and so quieten its incessant mental chatter and give space and time to be truly present. Paying close attention to what is really going on inside my head for three whole days is a daunting prospect. But my appointment with the *sodo* is fixed.

The night before the *sesshin* is to start, Nisodo is a hive of activity. As is customary, all the nuns have their heads freshly shaved in preparation. This is considered a sacred practice and is done sitting at a long tin sink close to the *sodo* while reciting mantras. Long into the evening, the nuns also take it in turns to bathe. Baths are taken every four days in the communal bathhouse, which nuns enter in groups of four. Each small group first washes using bowls on the floor before sinking into a large rectangular communal tin bath for a soak. The order in which the nuns take their bath is strictly hierarchical and is determined by how long they have been at Nisodo. As the newcomer, I am last in line.

When a wake-up bell is rung at 4 a.m. the following morning, it feels as if I have just fallen asleep. Bleary-eyed, I file into the *sodo* wrapped in a shawl against the morning chill. Walking ahead of me, barefoot but for loose flapping sandals, are Nisodo's eighteen nuns. All have swapped their working clothes of wide baggy trousers and wrap-around jackets for formal monastic attire. The inner layer is a white kimono, the outer garment, a wide-sleeved black over-robe, or *kolomo,* held in place by an intricately tied cord. Over both of these is the traditional cloak worn by all Buddhist monastics, the *kesa,* which in traditional Zen is generally brown or black and is fastened across one shoulder.

Slipping off our shoes, we step up onto a raised wooden platform running around the inside of the *sodo,* and take our places on low circular cushions, or *zafus.* One by one we swivel to face the wall, eyes half open, as is customary in *zazen* practice, in order to lessen the likelihood of drowsiness or daydreams. For the next three days, I will come to know every grain of wood in the panel in front of me. As silence descends I become conscious of the slightest movement of those around me; the easing of shoulders, the shifting of weight, even the creaking of bones as a spine is straightened. Knowing the other women will be distracted by any slight sound I make, I try to remain perfectly still. In the beginning, it is agony.

But almost as difficult as these long hours of sitting are the formal mealtimes held in the *sodo,* which take the form of a highly choreographed ritual known as *oryoki.* These ceremonies require meticulous attention to detail, by those who serve and are served; the practice of giving, receiving and appreciation is symbolized in small gestures such as nods and hand movements. Each meal is eaten from a set of nesting lacquer bowls carried to and from the *sodo* in napkins elaborately tied in the shape of a lotus and placed in front of the meditation cushions. Every movement concerning the way the bowls are handled is governed by strict protocol. Everything that is served has to be eaten to ensure there is no waste. Breakfast consists of thin rice porridge, served with ground sesame, salt, dried seaweed and pickled plums. Lunch is boiled rice with vegetables, and supper, which thankfully is slightly more relaxed as it is not served in the *sodo*, is invariably noodle soup accompanied by more cooked vegetables and occasionally dried fish.

After eating, still seated in the meditation position, I am shown how to clean the lacquer bowls by rubbing them with a pickled radish and weak tea. I then have to swallow this combination of radish and tea, which in the early morning has me gagging, before wiping the bowls dry and folding them back in a carefully arranged napkin. The whole process requires skill and speed and the nuns eat quickly. To avoid the repeated ignominy of fumbling to clean and wrap my bowls long after the nuns have finished, having to sit patiently waiting for me, and also to ensure I eat everything I am served in the evenings, I opt out of lunch after the first day. I retire to my room for a few moments alone, suddenly aware what a rare privilege this can be.

As the three-day *sesshin* draws to a close, I feel exhausted from the lack of sleep and the non-stop routine. But in the last hour on the last day that I sit in *zazen*, I sense a subtle shift in consciousness. The hours of silence and growing awareness of thoughts that come and go, with brief flashes of mental quiet in between, lead to a growing appreciation of the relief offered by observing rather than constantly reacting to the thinking process. It is a wake-up call to realizing how much of our time is spent literally 'lost' in thought. It is a lesson in being truly present. The realization is fleeting, but its effects stay with me.

On the evening the *sesshin* ends, a nun ushers me into Aoyama Roshi's private quarters. Throughout the long hours of ceremony over the previous days, I have watched her serious features sometimes break into a broad, slightly lop-sided, toothy smile. It lights up her face and radiates warmth, reflecting equanimity acquired through more than seven decades spent following the Buddhist path. It is this smile that greets me as I kneel opposite her at low wooden table.

Apart from Jakucho Setouchi, Aoyama Roshi is probably the most well-known nun in Japan. She is a revered teacher and the nun of highest standing within the hierarchy of Soto Zen. Every month, when fifty of Japan's most senior Soto teachers gather for discussion, Aoyama Roshi is the only woman invited to attend. In theory, regulations governing the Soto Zen order now offer nuns equality with monks. But as I knew from my conversation with Jakucho, the deeply hierarchical and patriarchal nature of Japanese society has, for centuries, kept nuns in most orders in positions subservient to monks.

One of the most significant outcomes of the ruling of the Meiji Restoration enabling monks and nuns to marry was to turn the majority of the country's Buddhist temples into virtual family businesses. When the majority of monks married and had children, the custom of fathers passing stewardship of temples to their sons was born and has continued for generations. As a result, less than five per cent of the thousands of Soto Zen temples in Japan are now run by nuns. This hereditary practice also led, in some instances, to a dilution of the monks' dedication to the dharma. The drunkenness and adulterous affairs of some monks became common gossip and public respect dwindled.

While in the past it was mandatory for families to be registered with a local Buddhist temple, to which they paid regular dues, this custom has waned. As a result, the income of many temples has virtually dried up and many now stand empty. As far as many 'temple sons' are concerned, Japan's affluent and consumerist secular society offers more interesting opportunities than following in their fathers' footsteps. The marked change in recent years, however, is that growing numbers of 'temple daughters' are choosing to take their place. In the absence of sons wanting to become monks to take over the running of family temples, daughters are increasingly becoming nuns to take up these leadership roles. 'This is a significant shift and a clear-cut difference from when I was young,' Aoyama Roshi explains.

Aoyama Roshi is eighty years old at the time of our meeting and began her monastic training at the age of five. At the request of her parents, an aunt who was a nun became her teacher and took her to live in an unheated temple high in the snowy mountains of the Japanese Alps in Nagano. The choice of whether she would want to continue on the monastic path when older was left to her, but she had few doubts. Her mother hoped she would delay the decision until she was in her twenties, even sewing her daughter a bridal kimono in case she should want to marry. But when she was fifteen, Aoyama chose to ordain. The silk-brocade bridal kimono her mother sewed was long ago refashioned into altar hangings that now decorate Nisodo's worship hall.

When Aoyama Roshi ordained in the 1940s, it was impossible for a nun either to perform an ordination ceremony or to become a teacher with her own disciples. Slowly, these rules were changed and today Nisodo regularly fills with laypeople, both men and women, who come to listen to her monthly dharma talks.

Another significant change Aoyama Roshi points to is that the average age of nuns who now come for training at Nisodo has fallen considerably in recent years. When she took over as Nisodo's abbess in 1970, many of the 100 or so nuns undergoing training at any one time had ordained later in life, most after having had careers and some having had families. All were looking for a deeper meaning to their lives. By the 1990s, the average age of newly ordained nuns was forty-three, with many older than that. Today, though there are fewer women entering the nunnery, their average age is just thirty-five, with many still in their twenties. At the time of my visit, the eighteen nuns in residence range in age from nineteen to sixty-six years old. Most are Japanese, but one is from South Korea and four have come from the West – from Germany, Latin America and the United States. Despite the dwindling numbers of nuns in her care, and the fact that there are estimated to be fewer than 2,000 across the whole of Japan, Aoyama Roshi is hopeful about the future.

'While I see quite clearly that many monks who are temple sons show little conviction and view it as a job, I am more optimistic about the future of nuns,' she says. Compared with the sometimes perfunctory preparation monks receive, she is determined that nuns who come to Nisodo should undergo intensive monastic training. While nuns in most other traditions go through an initial period as a novice, in which they take a limited number of vows, gradually taking more as their training progresses, those ordained in most of Japan's Zen lineages undergo training immediately after taking their initial vows. These initial vows also adhere to a greatly reduced number of precepts, sixteen in all, which are the same for both monks and nuns.

If fully observed, these sixteen precepts are said to encompass the essence of Buddhist monastic practice. They include the ten fundamental vows not to kill, steal, lie, become intoxicated, engage in sexual misconduct, talk ill of others, elevate the self, become angry, be stingy, or denigrate the dharma, the sangha or the Buddha. But since these vows are essentially the same as those taken by many lay practitioners committed to following the Buddhist path, some outside Japan question whether Japanese Buddhists can really be considered monks and nuns, preferring instead to refer to them as Zen priests, with similar pastoral duties to parish vicars in Christian communities.

As far as Aoyama Roshi is concerned, however, the women who enter Nisodo are dedicated to the monastic life. All come on the personal recommendation of their own teachers and receive rigorous instruction for periods that can last from six months to several years. But unlike other monastic traditions, where nuns or monks often continue living in fellowship, those in the Zen tradition return to their own communities, once their training has finished, to teach and run, or help run, temples there. The training that the nuns at Nisodo undergo, in addition to regular *zazen* practice, consists of a strict regime of study of Buddhist texts and extensive schooling in ancient temple traditions, including the arts of calligraphy, ikebana flower arranging, and the tea ceremony. All of this takes place within days that stretch from 4 a.m. to 10 or 11 p.m., sometimes midnight, punctuated throughout by the sound of different gongs and bells indicating which practice is to come. Many of the nuns look pale from exhaustion during much of the time I spend with them.

Once the *sesshin* has ended, some speak to me about what brought them to Nisodo, and a wide diversity of stories emerges. One of those with whom I speak is Myokyo, the tall young nun who circles the meditation hall during *zazen* wielding the posture correction stick, which I never see her use. She seems rarely to smile or laugh, unlike many of the other nuns, and I find her serious features a little intimidating. But as she settles beside me on the tatami mat in my temporary bedroom and starts to explain her background, I realize her stern appearance stems partly from shyness. She is twenty-nine and has been a nun for the past four years, she explains.

She is one of the 'temple daughters' Aoyama Roshi mentioned. Her father is a monk and runs a Soto Zen temple in Japan's northern Iwate prefecture. Growing up with two sisters in that temple, Myokyo recalls how difficult she found it waking up and finding strangers, worshippers, wandering around her home. 'I always felt scared there. The building was old and dark and we rarely left it as a family,' she says. 'My father was always working and my mother helped him, and I used to think, "What kind of life is that?"'

After Myokyo finished school, she moved to Tokyo to study art at university; she learnt from her tutors that what she chose to paint would always be influenced by her past. She started to look at the life of her parents through different eyes. 'I saw how dedicated my father was. How he attended to every detail and chanted sutras in the temple, even when there was no one there. I gradually became interested in why he did that.' As an artist, Myokyo says she was particularly struck by the simplicity and beauty of her father's black lacquer *oryoki* bowls. 'I began to question my direction in life, its deeper meaning, and for the first time started to consider whether I might lead a temple life too.' In order to give herself time to think, Myokyo went to work as a waitress in a busy restaurant in Tokyo. After a year she had made up her mind and asked her father to ordain her. 'My father was very surprised and a little concerned. We come from a very conservative part of Japan. He was worried that, as a nun, I would never be accepted as the leader of a temple. But I have never doubted I did the right thing.'

When Myokyo returns to her hometown, people there regard her as 'a rare species', she says. 'The older generation feels threatened seeing a nun carrying out temple duties. But gradually things are changing. Those of my own age are more liberal.' Myokyo is not certain yet if she will want to take over the running of her father's temple one day, or whether she will marry and have children. She does not rule either out. As the average age of nuns at Nisodo has fallen, with many now coming from temple backgrounds, so attitudes to celibacy and the prospect of having a family are also changing.

When I ask Aoyama Roshi how necessary she feels celibacy is for a nun, she says it is 'not essential, but preferable'. Once a woman becomes a mother, she says, her focus inevitably changes. The exception to this, she argues, is if a woman chooses to ordain later in life, once her children are grown. Helping me translate this discussion with Aoyama Roshi and the other Japanese nuns at Nisodo is a nun named Yusho, whose own experience seems proof that coming to ordination later in life, after having children and while still remaining married, can work.

Yusho tells me that before becoming a nun in her early fifties, she spent many years working as an investment banker in the City of London, first for Lehman Brothers and then for a Tokyo bank. Though born in Japan, she had moved to Paris in her twenties to study, before settling in London, marrying and having two children. Both she and her British husband practised *zazen* meditation for many years, she explains, before she tired of the financial world and gradually her interest in Buddhist teachings deepened. Once her children were grown, she and her husband returned to Japan to live for a year in the temple of one of her husband's first meditation teachers. It was then that she began to consider ordaining. 'Personally, it did not make a big difference to me whether I ordained or not,' she says. But she felt drawn to teach and for this she wanted to follow the monastic path.

'My husband was very understanding. He was one of the first generation in the West to become interested in *zazen*. He said it was up to me what I wanted to do with my life,' she says. For much of the year, Yusho still lives with her husband, who moved with her to Nagoya so that she could train with Aoyama Roshi to become a senior teacher, known as a *shike*, in the Soto lineage. The couple rent an apartment close to Nisodo and, when Yusho's four-year training has finished, they plan to return to Europe so she can continue teaching in the West, where the number of women ordaining in different Zen traditions is steadily growing. While few reliable figures exist, Yusho estimates that in the Unites States alone there are now between 750 and 1,000 Zen nuns, or priests, as they are often called in the West, with a further 400 or so in Europe.

Given the blurred lines between Buddhism and family business in Japan, Yusho reflects a commonly held view that the true spirit of Japanese Zen Buddhism is now more frequently found abroad. 'That is why I am more interested in teaching outside Japan, because it is a more pure form there,' she says. Women in the West certainly do not become nuns to ensure their financial security. All accept that they face an uncertain future, as I discover when I begin speaking to some of the western women at Nisodo.

Of all the faces I study during the many hours of *sesshin*, the one I sense masks the most boisterous character is that of a stocky nun with dark-framed glasses named Zentchu. With many of the younger nuns I notice she can be stern, but there seems a warmth beneath this serious veneer. As I struggle to wrap my *oryoki* bowls quickly at the end of meals, often sending chopsticks clattering to the floor, she catches my eye and smiles. When I wander into the kitchen to take photographs of the work division there, Zentchu leaps into a pose, making peace signs with both hands. I recognize her natural exuberance from many years spent in Latin America. Zentchu is originally from Venezuela.

There is much laughter as her story unfolds. Especially when she talks of her childhood in Caracas, where, she says, she had no intention of becoming a nun. Born Diana and brought up by her father after her mother left, she tells me she received 'a good Catholic convent education', but was never faintly tempted to follow the example of the women who taught her. 'The sisters used to say to us, "When God calls you to be a nun, you have to answer," and I'd lie in bed at night with my fingers in my ears because I didn't want to hear God calling,' she recalls, mimicking the action with her eyes shut tight. After discovering her talent for the piano, she travelled to Warsaw to study music for four years before moving to Brazil to work as a piano teacher. A chance meeting on the streets of São Paulo with a Buddhist nun, who was out walking her dogs, first brought her into contact with Buddhism.

'When I started talking to her, I became curious and asked if I could listen to her teaching. When I did, I knew very quickly that this was what I wanted. Three years later I requested to become a nun,' she says. Her teacher, Coen Sensei, advised her to wait before taking that decision and invited her to work as an assistant in a Buddhist temple in São Paulo. The experience only strengthened her conviction. In 2008 she was ordained in Brazil by Coen Sensei, who three years later sent Zentchu to Nisodo, the nunnery where she had also trained. 'My teacher warned me that I was going into hell, and the first year I spent here was the worst year of my life,' Zentchu recalls. 'The emotional part was the hardest,' she says. 'It was a mincing of my ego. But that has been a very positive thing. We all need our ego to function. But if it runs your life, then your view of the world is so much more limited.'

Zentchu likens the demands of daily life at Nisodo, and the difficulties of living at such close quarters with other women dealing with similar pressures, to the gradual smoothing of a pebble, or the polishing of a jewel. 'I came to understand the wisdom of Aoyama Roshi's teaching that, in life, we need to be flexible and fluid like water. Not rigid like ice.' Now Zentchu describes herself as 'a gypsy nun'. When she leaves Nisodo, she will go wherever she is needed, she says. She is not sure if this will mean returning to Brazil. With more than a million people of Japanese descent now living there, as a result of mass immigration to work on Brazil's coffee plantations, Buddhism has traditionally had a strong presence in the country. But interest is often superficial, says Zentchu. 'People take Buddhism as some kind of medicine to make them happy. But when they realize it is about finding out who you are, very deeply, they get scared and run away.' While Zen has been associated with everything from motorcycle maintenance to pebble gardens and a simple black-and-white aesthetic, the commitment of a true practitioner to constantly keep an open mind, a 'beginner's mind', and see every aspect of life as a question is seldom appreciated.

Apart from her mentor, there are still few Buddhist nuns in Brazil. When Zentchu walked the streets of São Paulo in her monastic work clothes of loose jacket and wide trousers, many would mistake her for a kung fu teacher, she tells me, or think her bald head was the result of undergoing chemotherapy. 'But as my teacher told me, a nun is someone who understands and is not understood, who is solitary and has little time to sleep.' Zentchu laughs. With none of the formal infrastructure that underpins Buddhist practice in the East, Zentchu also speaks of how nuns returning to the West face the challenge of how to support themselves financially. While she can continue to give piano lessons and work part-time in a temple as a teacher, that is not the full-time monastic life she envisages.

Such challenges and financial dilemmas face most western nuns once they return to their own countries.

Of the four western nuns I speak to at Nisodo, one of the first expecting to return to her home is a gentle-faced nun named Seishin, from Wiesbaden in Germany. In contrast to the more benign confusion over the reasons for her shaven head that Zentchu encountered in Brazil, Seishin has found herself mistaken for a neo-Nazi by her compatriots. Once, when she was travelling on a tram, she describes how a fellow passenger muttered under his breath how he couldn't stand her miserable presence and moved to the other side of the carriage. 'I find I have to justify myself all the time, and this is not easy,' she says in a soft voice. 'I can't answer the usual questions that people ask. I have no address, no job, no money.' The only thing she now possesses when she returns to visit her parents is a pair of sturdy shoes. Apart from this she has two pairs of traditional wooden monastic shoes, one of which she sweetly offers to me as a gift.

Born Claudia, to a conventional middle-class family, Seishin became a linguist and worked as a translator in Munich, where she spent many years attending Zen meditation sessions before her interest in Buddhism brought her to Japan, where she ordained in her mid-forties. Her family are concerned about how she will support herself as she grows old and she knows it will be a challenge. 'But every day here at Nisodo I have to find great inner strength to be able to carry on. Here you come up against your limits all the time,' she says. So, with the fortitude this has instilled, she trusts she will find her way once she returns to Europe.

Some western nuns do have a clearer idea of what they will do when they return, as Kaikyo, another nun originally from Venezuela, explains. Like some other nuns I meet, Kaikyo's dedication to the Buddhist path followed a devastating bereavement. Born Sara, to a Venezuelan mother and American father, she trained as a ballet dancer in her youth. In her early twenties, she moved to Paris to work as a choreographer for four years before returning to Caracas. Kaikyo jokes that she 'became a Buddhist without knowing it' when she was just a girl. An early childhood illness left her bald and from the age of ten she refused to wear a wig to disguise it. Kaikyo has striking features and compelling grey-brown eyes, but as a young woman she was convinced her baldness made her unattractive. 'It was a defence mechanism,' she says. She was fearful and guarded in relationships. She eventually fell in love with a man who helped her overcome these fears. It was an intense relationship, but he was killed two years later in a car accident. 'The earth just opened up,' she says. 'His death was a profound experience in impermanence.'

Some time before her partner's death, a friend had introduced Kaikyo to Zen meditation. 'I knew so little about it, the first time I went I turned up in my leotard!' She laughs. After losing her partner, however, she turned to *zazen* for comfort. 'It was a wonderful way to deal with grief, facing the wall in silence, with no one telling you it was going to get better.' After returning to Paris to work, she regularly attended Zen practice centres there and gradually started to consider ordination. 'It just seemed the right fit for me, like Cinderella finding the right shoe,' she says. At the same time as preparing for ordination, Kaikyo also spent many years undergoing psychoanalysis. She eventually trained as a psychoanalyst in the school of the French psychiatrist Jacques Lacan. By the time she moved to Florida in the late 1990s, Kaikyo was both ordained and qualified. She worked for more than a decade in the United States as a psychoanalyst and also as a non-denominational 'spiritual companion' to the dying.

With the encouragement of her Zen teachers in the United States, Kaikyo has come to Nisodo to be schooled in the more ceremonial aspects of Soto Zen practice, which she says are often lacking in the West. But when her training is finished, she intends to return to Florida and eventually Europe, to work in end-of-life care and psychoanalysis, sharing *zazen* and the Buddhist teachings. I imagine her as a uniquely calming presence in the face of death.

Many of the nuns in Nisodo run from one task to another so no moment is lost, but Kaikyo takes a slower pace. Her childhood frailty has begun to take its toll, weakening her bones now she is in her early sixties. But whenever we pass in the corridors, she smiles broadly and the depth of her commitment to her chosen path seems to shine from her. While Kaikyo is mature enough to be certain of her way forward, others are young enough for the confidence of youth to dispel doubts about the future.

One afternoon I accompany the nuns to the tea pavilion, where I watch a senior nun give instructions in the correct way to fold a napkin, prepare tea and then serve it with elegance. Initially I wonder what relevance such an ancient tradition can have to the future of Buddhism. But as I watch a young American nun's deep concentration at every step I realize how this seemingly simple ritual designed to inspire patience is turned into a meditation on simplicity and presence. Afterwards, the young nun, Gesshin, tells me that she is twenty-six and has already been at Nisodo for nearly two years. Born Claire, in San Francisco, she says it was when she started suffering academic pressure as a student at the prestigious Wellesley College, in Massachusetts, that she turned to different forms of meditation. After finishing college, she travelled briefly in Japan and then spent six months living in Hawaii with her boyfriend. She was, she says, living a seemingly perfect life.

'I went to the beach, I cooked, wrote part of a novel, had everything I wanted. But I was so unhappy,' she says. 'I realized then there were no positive conditions that were going to do it for me and this is just what the Buddha realized when he was surrounded by luxury in his palace.' After a period spent travelling in India, she decided to return to Japan to study Zen and when she was twenty-four was ordained in a temple in Okayama. Her move to Nisodo shortly afterwards was partly fuelled by a wish to practise in an all-female environment, 'away from temptation', she says. 'This is my way of turning the light inwards, answering questions about what it means to be alive. Now I can't imagine living any other life. My life is not about me any more. It is about something bigger,' she says, then quotes the teaching of Soto Zen Master Dogen:

'To study the Buddha Way is to study the self,
to study the self is to forget the self,
and to forget the self is to be enlightened by ten thousand things.'

The hours I spend watching the nuns of Nisodo prepare and serve to one another the pungent powdered green tea used in formal tea ceremonies are my last in this traditional Zen training nunnery.

Looking out through the open windows and doors of Nisodo's tea pavilion, I take in the tranquil scene in the Zen garden beyond. The way the late-afternoon sun glistens on the surface of the water of a low stone bowl. The minimalist beauty of single stems of delicate yellow daisies that have been laced around the bamboo pipe running into the bowl; the flowers are so fresh they must have been placed there simply to delight the nuns as they rinse their hands before entering the pavilion. The row of white-strapped wooden sandals lined up against the front step, half in the sunlight, half in the shade. To one side stands a crooked tree supported by wooden poles, with a carefully arranged circle of straw matting at its base and more straw woven around its trunk like a golden sleeve to ensure it flourishes. It seems symbolic of the precision and care with which the nuns here are being prepared for a new life.

Despite my struggles through the long days of *sesshin,* I leave Nisodo with a sense of regret, a feeling of having witnessed a disappearing world. As my taxi drops back down the hill towards the bustle of Nagoya I look at those we pass in a different light. I watch a mother pushing a pram uphill, arguing with her husband. I see a woman in her twenties teetering on improbable heels, her hair up in pigtails, in thrall to the trend for cuteness, *kawaii,* which dominates so much of Japanese culture today.

Rather than viewing the nunnery I am leaving as an anachronism, my perspective has shifted. I see those of us who live beyond it as somehow stuck in time, playing out patterns determined by remembered pasts or projected futures, while the nuns of Nisodo are trained to be truly present in each and every moment.

Back in London, on nights when I cannot sleep, I sometimes imagine myself transported once again to the peace of the meditation hall and the tea pavilion at Nisodo, or to the green spaciousness of the gardens of Tokeiji. A feeling of ease and calm descends.

I remember a far corner of the grounds at Tokeiji surrounded by maples with such delicate foliage that the sky seems woven with pale green lace. Here the remains of one of the most influential figures in Buddhism in recent years lie at rest. This is the grave of the prolific Japanese author Daisetz Teitaro Suzuki, whose writings have been so significant in spreading Zen Buddhism internationally.

D. T. Suzuki was not a monk, but he underwent rigorous monastic training in Kamakura. He then travelled extensively in Europe, living for many years in the United States, before returning to Japan, where he died in 1966. Some of his books, such as *An Introduction to Zen Buddhism,* with its lengthy foreword by psychiatrist Carl Jung, laid the groundwork for a great flowering of interest in Zen in the West.

With a small stretch of the imagination, I picture the headstone of D. T. Suzuki's grave facing out to sea. Beyond the harbour of Kamakura is the vast expanse of the Pacific Ocean, on its far shore the western coast of the United States. It is here that Buddhism sank some of its earliest and deepest roots in the West and it is here that I travel to next.

WEST

PART V

NORTH AMERICA

11

ROUTE 101

The entrance to 125 Waverly Place, in the bustling heart of San Francisco's Chinatown, is a narrow brown metal door. The faint drone of Laundromat washing machines can be heard to one side and from the other comes the chatter of customers jostling in a bakery. At first I wonder if I have mistaken the address. But then, stepping back into the road, I crane my neck upwards and there, beyond the zigzag of fire-escape ladders snaking up the front of the building, I see a sign tied to the railings of the top-floor balcony that confirms I am in the right place. At first glance this doesn't seem the most auspicious place to begin my journey on the path that Buddhism travelled in the West. But this is Tien Hau Temple, the first and oldest Buddhist temple in the United States.

Climbing five flights of stairs, I cross the threshold and enter a musty space that feels more like a museum than a place of devotion or worship. There is a crowded altar, crooked piles of crimson and gold paper offerings, several makeshift donation boxes and a ceiling festooned with dangling prayer flags that shrink the small, cramped room even further. Unsure quite what to make of this top-floor temple, I slip a note in one of the boxes and am about to leave when a young man emerges from a back room and, speaking little English, hands me a sheet of pink paper.

Printed on it is an explanation that Tien Hau was both a Taoist and Buddhist deity 'worshipped high and low, through all dynasties, as Goddess of the Sea'. I read that when the first Chinese immigrants came to the United States in the mid-nineteenth century with the California Gold Rush, they settled in San Francisco and built a temple in her honour, for guiding them across the Pacific Ocean 'after braving the most treacherous storm on earth in primitive wooden sailing boats'. By the turn of century it was one of 400 Buddhist temples along the West Coast, catering first to the spiritual needs of tens of thousands of Chinese and later to those of Japanese immigrants allowed to travel once the restrictions of Japan's Meiji government were lifted. Many temples were housed on the top floors of buildings so that no one could be higher than the sacred altars they enshrined.

As gold prices dwindled and anti-immigrant sentiments grew in the second half of the nineteenth century, some temples were burnt to the ground by vigilantes, who dubbed them 'joss houses', denouncing them for heathen practices carried out amid clouds of incense smoke. Few buildings in San Francisco escaped unscathed from the devastating 1906 earthquake, which left half the city's population homeless after fires raged out of control. The original Tien Hau Temple was one of those buildings razed. These days the relocated temple serves as something of a tourist trap, cashing in on the current booming interest in Buddhism in the United States and throughout the West.

To meet the true spiritual descendants of one of the most influential Chinese Buddhists to have brought the dharma to America, I take a short walk around the corner from Waverly Place. On the first and second floor at 800 Sacramento Street is the 'Gold Mountain Sagely Monastery', Gold Mountain being the name by which America was known to early Chinese immigrants. At the top of the wide staircase leading up from the main entrance, I find a display of books by Chan (Zen) Master Hsuan Hua, who founded the Sino-American Buddhist Association in 1959. It was here, thirteen years later, in this converted mattress factory, that Master Hua conducted the first Buddhist ordination of three western monks and two nuns. According to tradition, Buddhism is only said to have taken root in a country once native-born sons and daughters are ordained in their own land by their countrymen, so it might be claimed that Buddhism did not become firmly established in America until 1972.

In the narrow corridors of this urban monastery I come across a trio of nuns, one American and two from Taiwan, who ordained more recently. They have travelled here from a sprawling monastic complex called the City of Ten Thousand Buddhas, established later by Master Hua in a converted mental hospital several hours north of San Francisco. Above the din of traffic and hawkers selling their wares in the street below, the three women outline the rhythm of their daily life: they rise before 4 a.m., eat only one meal a day and, sometimes, as Tenzin Palmo did for years in a cave in the Himalayas, sleep sitting up in meditation posture. 'Bitter practice, sweet mind,' Master Hua said of such austerities.

Strolling on through Chinatown, I pass a throbbing dive called the Buddha Bar and rows of trinket shops selling Buddha statues for all budgets, and turn into a narrow passageway, lined with brightly painted murals, called Jack Kerouac Alley. The name offers some clue as to why such a rigorous practice as Buddhism has become lodged in the popular imagination of many in the West as an easy-to-drop 'happy pill', an effortless panacea often debased into New Age narcissism, to which the presence of Buddha heads in many beauty salons attests. Embedded in the concrete paving of this short alleyway is a circular brass plaque engraved with the following words:

'The air was soft, the stars so fine, the promise of every cobbled alley so great . . .'

The words come from Kerouac's 1957 novel *On the Road*, which cemented San Francisco as a hub for writers and poets of the 1950s Beat Generation, many of them with an interest in eastern philosophy and religion. A year later *The Dharma Bums*, Kerouac's follow-up cult classic, was published and Buddhism, in particular Zen, burst into a wider public consciousness. Some, like the British-born writer and philosopher Alan Watts, dismissed Kerouac's lyrical novel as 'Beat Zen', too self-conscious and subjective to reflect the true spirit of Zen. But by then the fire was lit.

On the corner of Jack Kerouac Alley sits the City Lights bookshop, which once championed the work of other Beat writers such as Allen Ginsberg and William S. Burroughs and poets like Philip Whalen and Gary Snyder, who spent years training as a Zen monk. Settling into an old wooden rocking chair on the first floor, I leaf through a posthumously published collection of Kerouac's letters to Ginsberg, in which he predicts that *The Dharma Bums* 'will crash open [the] whole scene to [a] sudden Buddhism boom ... '58 is going to be dharma year in America,' he writes, 'everybody's reading Suzuki on Madison Avenue.'

Kerouac and Ginsberg had met D. T. Suzuki briefly in New York in 1957 on their way to a book party to celebrate the release of *On the Road*. While Suzuki, then lecturing on Buddhist meditation at Harvard University and elsewhere in the United States, recognized that the two writers and others of the Beat Generation were not a 'passing phenomenon to be lightly put aside as insignificant', he believed their struggle against bourgeois conformity and their interest in Zen were superficial. But as the Beat movement gathered pace, so did an interest in Buddhism. By the following year, Suzuki's name was being widely dropped in fashionable circles. When articles on 'Zen style' began appearing in magazines such as *Vogue* and

Mademoiselle, it seemed the cosmopolitan elite might be embracing Zen Buddhism as a passing fad. But in the years that followed, numerous artists, performers and musicians followed D. T. Suzuki's teachings, as did prominent thinkers such as the psychoanalyst Carl Jung, who recognized that Zen and psychotherapy shared a common concern of 'making whole'.

While D. T. Suzuki was filling auditoriums in New York and on the East Coast, by the early 1960s San Francisco had embraced another Zen teacher by the name of Suzuki: Soto Zen monk Shunryu Suzuki, whose seminal book *Zen Mind, Beginner's Mind* would still be hailed as life-changing decades later by creative thinkers such as Steve Jobs. The cavernous downtown headquarters of the San Francisco Zen Centre Shunryu Suzuki founded was once a former shelter for single Jewish women close to the district known as The Haight. Arriving here without an appointment, I am led along the centre's polished corridors on a quick tour before the meditation hall in the basement starts to fill for that evening's sitting. In the quiet of the near-empty building I reflect on the time this district became the hub of the counterculture movement that saw different forms of Buddhism emerging in the West.

The Haight was where tens of thousands of hippies flocked in 1967 for the flower-power explosion of sex, drugs and music in the Summer of Love. While the Beats, adopting Zen as their credo, dressed in existential black, exuberant hippies wore beads and feathers and embraced religion of all kinds with unabashed devotion. Growing numbers made overland journeys to Nepal and India, intrigued by Hinduism and the more mystical form of Buddhism being brought across the Himalayas by fleeing Tibetan refugees, with its psychedelic imagery and portrayals of deities in ritual intercourse. Some travelled further east to Thailand and

Burma to sit at the feet of meditation masters in the Theravada tradition. When these wanderers returned, they brought with them an appetite for continuing these newly discovered Buddhist practices in the West.

A flow of spiritual seekers heading east has continued ever since, as has a smaller stream of Buddhist teachers in all traditions journeying in the opposite direction. From the earliest days of this East–West exchange, there have been men and women from the West who have chosen to take their devotion to the dharma one step further by ordaining as monks and nuns. Some have stayed in the countries in which their teachers live or from which they came. Others have returned home to establish their own communities. Some of these communities founded by nuns are now making history, forging a unique path for others to follow.

My meetings with the women at the forefront of this monastic revolution take months to organize. They are women with a mission and it takes them all over the world. They teach and travel tirelessly, meeting students and followers in far-flung corners of the globe. Though they come from different Buddhist traditions – Theravada, Tibetan, Zen – at a certain level of seniority, many know each other and meet occasionally when time allows. Some agree to share their experiences with me, but the places where they are making their mark are far from the heart of San Francisco. So I hire a car and head north.

The Pacific Coast Highway that winds north of San Francisco, through northern California, Oregon and Washington State, passes through such spectacular coastal scenery that sections of it are designated one of the USA's 'All American Roads', a coveted status giving it some environmental protection. The rocky cliffs, sheltered bays and pounding surf stretch for nearly 1,000 miles to the Canadian border. For much of its length, the highway is known as Route 101, rivalled only by Route 66 as the inspiration for countless road trips, movies and pop songs.

But in places where Route 101 cuts travelling time by dipping inland, the road that continues to hug the coastline becomes Highway 1, as it does shortly after crossing San Francisco's Golden Gate Bridge. This is not the quickest route to get me where I am going but it is the most spectacular. There was a time when much of the coastline from central California to southern Oregon was densely forested by giant coast redwoods, a species of sequoia that thrived here for millennia, with some trees surviving for more than 1,000 years and reaching heights of over 100 metres. These trees are the tallest living things on earth. Over the past 150 years, however, so many have been felled that parts of the coastline have been left denuded.

When I make a brief stop at a place called Bodega Bay, sixty miles north of San Francisco, I discover it was the setting for Alfred Hitchcock's thriller *The Birds*. One of the reasons the director chose this location was that its barren headlands reminded him of the Cornish coastline where Daphne du Maurier set the novella on which his film is based. Less than half an hour further along Highway 1, I cross Russian River and then turn inland. From here onwards, I am asked not to disclose the details and driving instructions I am given by the nuns I am to meet. My destination is a hermitage named Aranya Bodhi, and the nuns who live here prefer to keep it a place of quiet seclusion. There are other reasons for them wanting to maintain their privacy: in some circles abroad, the nature of the monastic renaissance they are fostering has caused considerable discord.

I wind my way deeper into a canyon where dense stands of redwood cast ever darker shadows; at a point where the dirt track becomes deeply rutted, I pull my car into a passing point and spot a dilapidated four-wheel drive parked in the shade with a shaven-headed nun snoozing at the wheel. At the sound of my approaching engine, she pulls herself upright and steps out of the vehicle to greet me with a wave and slight bow. Her full-length saffron robe marks her out immediately as belonging to Theravada, the oldest of the three main schools of Buddhism I have encountered in the East. I clamber into the passenger seat of her jeep and she drives me along the final twists in the track to a clearing in the woods that the nuns here have named the Awakening Forest.

The significance of this name becomes clear later that day as I stroll through the forest to join the small community of nuns for their evening meditation practice. To either side of the dirt track lie the stumps of redwoods that once towered over this rugged landscape, their enormous circumference suggesting they might have flourished for 1,000 years. Most of the sequoia trees in this area were logged long before the hermitage was founded, but in the years since then, the roots of some of the felled trees have put out suckers that are slowly growing into mature woodland.

The nuns of Aranya Bodhi are at the forefront of reviving an ancient tradition that flourished for more than a millennium, like the primeval trees that once thrived here, before dying out nearly 1,000 years ago. This is the practice established by the Buddha of fully ordaining women as *bhikkhunis* to take their place alongside *bhikkhus* as equal members of the four-fold sangha of male and female monastics, laymen and laywomen. The founder of Aranya Bodhi has been one of the leading proponents and engineers of this ongoing restoration.

I first catch sight of Ayya Tathaaloka sitting cross-legged on a straw mat, her hands resting in her lap amid the folds of her saffron robe. Her eyes are closed and a beatific smile lights up her striking features. She is in her mid-forties, with full red lips, long eyelashes and a delicate nose. Around her are gathered a handful of nuns, three older, two younger. All are seated beside a simple stone stupa erected in a high alpine meadow, part of more than forty hectares of land donated for their use by a well-wisher. The fading sun throws dappled light across their faces. At first I am unsure if it is the play of sunlight on Ayya Tathaaloka's head that creates a small white circle in her closely shaven hair. It gives the impression that this charismatic nun has a miniature halo on the crown of her head.

When the silent portion of the evening's meditation practice ends and Ayya Tathaaloka begins to speak, she moves her head and I see that the pale circle, the size of a tea-light candle, stays in place. The origin of this extraordinary mark emerges when we settle down to speak.

It is early evening when I join Ayya Tathaaloka in the small hut in which she is staying; she perches on a simple chair, while I take a cushion on the floor close to the window so I can take notes by the last of the daylight. The hut has neither electricity nor running water. Roughly three metres by two and a half, it is nestled in the forest some distance from similar huts that serve as meditation shelters for the other nuns and lay stewards. The huts, referred to as *kutis*, are modelled on the traditional meditation huts established by Buddhist monastics in forests in the East. The members of t his small community of nuns rely on solar camping showers and rudimentary cooking facilities. Their resources are limited, but they are determined to make a go of establishing the first Theravada *bhikkhuni* hermitage in the West, here in northern California.

With her knees drawn up to her chest, Ayya Tathaaloka sketches the details of her upbringing. Born Heather Buske in 1968 in Washington, DC, she was the eldest of three sisters. Her father was a forensic physicist, her mother a botanist, and she describes her childhood as one in which 'investigative enquiry' was encouraged. At the age of fifteen, however, her life very nearly ended before it had properly begun. As the result of a tick bite, she developed the potentially lethal Rocky Mountain spotted fever and, because of late diagnosis, almost died. Following three weeks of dangerously high fever, Ayya Tathaaloka says she had an out-of-body experience in which she felt she was floating above her own sick bed. 'When you are under that much physical stress, your consciousness and perception can detach from your body,' she says. She remembers a feeling of calm: 'I felt so peaceful and light and beautiful above my body. I no longer felt delirious, but rather a great sense of clarity.' Some time before this happened, she remembers having hallucinations in which all the members of her family appeared before her and she said goodbye to each one. Then she heard her sister calling her name in anguish, thinking she had died, and remembers the feeling of being pulled back into her body. 'There was a sensation that felt very much like a belly flop into a pool of lava, and I was back staring out of eyes in a body that felt like it was on fire and in raging pain.'

Later that day nursing staff noticed that a small patch of her long dark hair, about three centimetres in diameter, had turned white. It has regrown white in a perfect circle ever since. Ayya Tathaaloka believes it may be a mark of her consciousness having briefly left her body. 'Tibetan Buddhist monastics also believe that your consciousness leaves your body through the crown of your head when you die,' she says. 'So when they saw this mark they said my "sky door" is open.'

After this experience she felt changed and somehow 'lost between worlds', she says. She started questioning what it meant to be alive. She dropped out of school, left home, took up with a band of musicians and fell into their 'toxic lifestyle' of drugs and alcohol. At one particularly low point she was taken in by a community of Christian nuns in Spokane, Washington State, who ran a shelter for women in dire circumstances; it was known in the community as 'The Sisters' Home for Lost and Wayward Women'. Unable to stay there indefinitely, she moved back to the East Coast, where she started studying again and working part-time, first as a 'box girl', unpacking women's sportswear in a department store, and later in the bridal-wear department, where, she says, she witnessed first-hand how 'emotionally fried' many women become when preparing for marriage.

'There were just so many emotional dramas, with enormous amounts of money involved. You really had to know when to call security.' She laughs. 'I felt increasingly grossed out and disenchanted by this obsession with what the body is clothed in and the value placed on material form.'

After catching up on her studies, in 1987, in her late teens, she enrolled at Portland State University on a pre-med course. It was what happened after this that proved a turning point.

The light has almost gone by now, so I stop taking notes and rely on my tape recorder, aware that what Ayya Tathaaloka tells me is likely something she rarely speaks of. As I listen to her soft voice on the tape afterwards, I am moved by the way she chooses her words carefully, never dramatizing or blaming, simply relating events as they unfolded.

Before we met, I read in a short summary of her background that the sudden death of someone she knew prompted her to leave university and, eventually, enter monastic life. Since sudden bereavement has set a number of the women I speak to on a path towards spiritual seeking – myself included, I increasingly recognize – I imagine the person concerned was a close friend or family member. But when I ask Ayya Tathaaloka to explain, she clasps her knees further towards her chest and falls silent for some time. The night air seems suddenly heavy. The long shadows cast by the redwoods outside block nearly all light to the hut, and I feel my breathing became shallow as I sense I am on delicate ground.

'Let me think. How do I like to speak about this?' She pauses. 'Generally I brush over this lightly, like it was someone I was close to,' she begins, before hesitating again.

'A boyfriend?'

'Not a boyfriend. No, and not exactly a close friend or family member. But someone I was close to and had a strong difficulty with,' she says, going on to explain that it was someone she met at a club towards the end of her first year at college when she was back on the East Coast working.

'There was something that was going on popularly in clubs at that time. I don't know if it still does. But this someone bought me a drink and put a drug in it. Then I was kidnapped.' She pauses before continuing and in these moments I think I understand. But it is worse than I imagine.

'Some people don't remember anything afterwards. But I didn't lose consciousness. So, I still have a lot of memory. It was – how do you call it? – a date-rape drug. So I wasn't able to volitionally direct my body and speech. This person had a practice of finding people to take advantage of. This person was also a heroin addict and kept me drugged for some time before I was able to get away,' she says.

When she talks of how she had had to 'psychologize' her captor in order to be able to escape eventually, I realize her ordeal must have been lengthy. I don't press her for more details and in the silence that follows my mind flashes back to the many hours I spent, a decade before, interviewing victims of genocidal rape in both Kosovo and Bosnia in the wake of the Balkan Wars. I remember the women's faces, their tears, the details of their trauma, even some of the words they spoke in languages I needed translators to interpret. They are seared in my brain. I remember the phrase repeated again and again by one young woman who lay in a narrow cot, in the once-beleaguered Kosovan border town of Djakova, with an IV drip attached to her arm because she no longer ate or had any will to live. I remember her whimpering, '*Trupi m'leshon … Trupi m'leshon*' – my body is leaving me … my body is leaving me – as if trying to divorce her thoughts from a physical experience she could not bear. I am lost in these thoughts when Ayya Tathaaloka's words jolt me back to the darkening room where we sit.

'I didn't press charges,' her soft voice continues. 'I had seen in the past how traumatic that whole prosecution process can be and I didn't want to go through that. But when he tried to approach me again, I took out a police restraining order.'

This, however, was not the end of it. A few years later, she was contacted by the police. The man who assaulted her had contracted a heavy cold, which turned into pneumonia, from which he died within two weeks. Tests revealed he had been suffering from AIDS. Since the man's brother knew what had happened to her, he included her name on a list of women he passed to the police, after which she was advised to go for HIV testing. The reaction of those closest to her shocked her deeply.

'It was just at the beginning of the major conflagration of the AIDS scare. People didn't know if you could catch AIDS just from touching someone or breathing on someone. When I told my family and others close to me some small part of what had happened, I saw the enormous fear that arose in them,' she says.

During the time when she was waiting for the test result, she felt she became 'a kind of outcast, a pariah amongst my family and friends. I really saw how fear and ignorance can take over people's minds and cause so much suffering.' She realized that their support for her was 'not immutable. I knew that my parents loved me, absolutely, and I thought they would be there, like Mother Teresa, no matter what terrible disease I might have. But I realized then that not everyone is there for you all of the time and I couldn't rely on them 100 per cent.'

The test result revealed she was not HIV positive. But the critical illness she had contracted as a child had left her immune system severely weakened. 'I saw then the precariousness of our lives. I had a strong sense of mortality, and I knew I had to find out what was going on deeper in myself, to understand what was real and true.'

I hesitate to speak, and then find myself apologizing for continued questioning. I would not have done so as a journalist and I realize that, in the company of the extraordinary women I am meeting, my way of asking questions of the world is changing. Ayya Tathaaloka acknowledges my wavering. 'I appreciate the way you are inquiring but respectful,' she says. The room is now almost dark, so we agree to continue talking the following day.

Lending me her small torch, Ayya Tathaaloka walks me to a wide track that will lead me through the forest to the office trailer where I am to roll out a makeshift bed. 'Do you like cats?' she asks with a smile as we part, meaning the cougars sometimes spotted in these parts. That night I lie looking out at the stars, thinking over her story. I think again of the seventeen-year-old Kosovan girl whose hold on life seemed so fragile and wonder if she survived. So many of the nuns I have met have survived extraordinary circumstances and, some of them, almost unimaginable hardship. Something that Ayya Tathaaloka said earlier in the day comes back to me and resonates profoundly: 'Most people can only see their own projection of what a monastic is. Few look and see deeply.'

Throughout the time I have been writing this book, I have listened to many people's preconceptions of what sort of women become nuns, Buddhist or otherwise. But the dynamism and determination of the women I have met belie assumptions. Though some have come to the monastic path following devastating loss or as a means of escaping adversity, I slowly start to see beyond such biographical shorthand. The internal shift and deeper sense of need that most feel is both harder for them to articulate and harder for another person to understand. It requires, I realize, a different kind of listening.

Returning to Ayya Tathaaloka's *kuti* the next morning, I learn of the remarkable trajectory her life took after the assault she suffered as a teenager. It is nearing midday and a younger nun, originally from Thailand, is delivering the last meal Ayya Tathaaloka will eat until the following morning. The younger nun's name is Munissara, and her demeanour appears meek as she kneels before Ayya Tathaaloka, setting a lidded alms bowl by her side. I can't help but smile as Ayya Tathaaloka pulls out an iPad to consult a solar noon app for exact information on when the sun will reach its zenith that day, after which she cannot eat until the next break of dawn. While the seven *kutis* at Aranya Bodhi are off-grid and out of phone range, the office trailer is linked to solar panels which allow the nuns to charge laptops and run satellite internet to remain connected to the outside world. A 2,500-year-old tradition meets modern technology.

Before eating her lunch, Ayya Tathaaloka picks up the thread of her story. Following her AIDS test, she was advised by an employer to learn meditation, and it was then that her interest in Buddhism developed. After her first intensive meditation retreat, she dropped out of university to travel first to Europe, then to India and through East Asia on a spiritual quest. While on 'the dharma bum circuit' she learned that the best opportunities for spiritual training for women were in South Korea, so in the 1990s she went there in search of a teacher and ended up staying for several years, first in a meditation centre and then in a hermitage. Observing in Korean *bhikkhunis* a strength and ease in the monastic life, she says she recognized that this was a path that would allow her to address the deep questions she had about life.

While in Korea she undertook pre-novice and novice training and then ordination, before visa problems forced her return to the US in 1996. The following year she was fully ordained as a *bhikkhuni* in Los Angeles at an international gathering of nuns and monks. After completing a three-year retreat, she then returned to study and teach in South Korea, and also spent some years in Thailand, before formally dedicating herself to the Theravada path and going on to establish a permanent residential teaching base in the United States, first in the San Francisco Bay Area and finally here, in the Awakening Forest at Aranya Bodhi.

In Ayya Tathaaloka's own words, she had 'squeezed through a crack' in becoming fully ordained. As my experience in Burma has shown, as far as many conservative Theravada monks are concerned, their tradition no longer allows women to pass from the stage of a laywoman renunciant to full ordination as a *bhikkhuni*. Recent scholarship by leading Buddhist authors disputes this, however. With the ordination of several *bhikkhunis* in North America in the late 1980s and again in the 1990s, a revival of the Theravada *bhikkhuni* order is under way, spearheaded by nuns and monks from Sri Lanka and more liberal-minded monastics from elsewhere.

Ayya Tathaaloka is now an active proponent of this movement to support full ordination. In 2005 she proposed and helped found the North American Bhikkhuni Association. Since then she has played a leading role as preceptor, overseeing the ordination of nuns in the US and elsewhere. As a result she has been caught in some bitter crossfire, which led to one prominent British-born monk, Ajahn Brahm, abbot of Bodhinyana monastery in Western Australia, being 'delisted' – in effect 'excommunicated' – by traditionalists in the Thai lineage to which his monastery originally belonged. This came in the wake of a ceremony in 2009, at which Ayya Tathaaloka was the preceptor, held to ordain four nuns from Australia, Germany and Malaysia at the monastery the monk had founded outside Perth.

'In the short term it made things pretty windy.' Ayya Tathaaloka laughs as she remembers the events of 2009. 'But I can't say if this was fortunate or unfortunate. In general, disharmony, conflict and controversy are avoided because of the doubt, confusion and despair they cause. But, because of what happened, so much awareness was generated and spread through the Buddhist world that many people who were either clueless or ignoring the problems that "lay nuns" faced were galvanized and came out in support of full ordination for nuns.'

In the aftermath of this turmoil, on a clear summer day in 2010, a group of 200 supporters tossed flower petals along a path at Aranya Bodhi as four novices from California, New Zealand and Germany trod their way through the forest in the first ordination to be held here. The ceremony was conducted initially by a quorum of Theravada *bhikkhunis*, with Ayya Tathaaloka as preceptor, and afterwards by a quorum of sympathetic monks. The following year several hundred lay Buddhist teachers, supporters and friends, together with nuns and monks from the East and West, gathered at Spirit Rock Meditation Centre in Marin County, California, to celebrate the full ordination of three more western women. The intermingling of maroon, dark brown and saffron robes on a Californian hillside signalled the support of monastics from different Buddhist traditions.

Since then, *bhikkhuni* ordinations have become a more regular and accepted occurrence, not only in Sri Lanka, and to some extent Thailand, but also in the West. 'I feel as if the crack I squeezed through to become fully ordained has slowly widened,' says Ayya Tathaaloka. 'Rather than meeting with a sheer and seemingly impenetrable rock face, now aspirants are faced with very rough and rocky tilled soil.'

The significance of full ordination, Ayya Tathaaloka stresses, lies not in any sense of elevated status, but rather in affirming and supporting those women who seek it in order to undertake the full rights and responsibilities that complete membership in this ancient community entails. This includes equal participation in decision-making, leadership, teaching and giving of ordination, as originally established by the Buddha 2,500 years ago.

In recent years Ayya Tathaaloka has received a growing number of enquiries from women interested in joining her monastic community – around fifty in the first six months of 2013, a five-fold increase on previous years. 'The tradition of Christian monasticism is gradually declining,' she says, and statistics bear her out: the number of Roman Catholic nuns, for instance, has fallen worldwide from around a million in 1973 to just over 700,000 in 2013. She goes on, 'If you group together all the women now living in the East who are some form of not fully legitimized or legally ordained nun or religious recluse, including the *maechees* in Thailand [women who live the life of a renunciant], *thilashins* in Burma, *donchees* and *maekaows* of Cambodia and Laos and *dasa-sila-matas* of Sri Lanka, I think you will find these Theravada nuns might well be the largest body of religious women in the world.' The growing interest amongst many of these women in becoming fully ordained, if such an option becomes more widely available and accepted, she concludes, could then make them a powerful force for good in the world.

In Thailand, where a secular government ministry oversees many Buddhist activities, state laws now permit full female ordination in the Theravada tradition. But the country's religious authorities continue to uphold a ban. This means many women who choose to shave their heads and don the white robes of the *maechee* are sometimes referred to as 'white shadows' and are marginalized by wider society. Some greeted the first of those who dared to leave the country and become fully ordained abroad with scorn, even death threats, on their return. One account of the experience of the first Thai woman to be fully ordained in Sri Lanka in 2003, Dr Chatsumarn Kabilsingh, a highly respected former academic, tells of how some householders closed their doors when they saw her approaching on an alms round close to the temple of which she is abbess on the outskirts of Bangkok. Other lay women, meanwhile, wept at the sight of her walking the dusty streets in her saffron robes, and with shaking hands put rice in her begging bowl.

From this, it might be tempting to assume that most Thai women who aspire to the monastic life are downtrodden. Yet, from the young nun who delivered Ayya Tathaaloka her midday meal, I hear a different story. My initial impression of Munissara as shy proves to have been mistaken. Later that day, as the small community of nuns take a brief rest after lunch before returning to their rota of chores to keep the hermitage running, I sit with her under a canvas awning that serves as the dining area, and her story emerges. It is not a typical experience, since for most of her life Munissara has not lived in Thailand. But it points, perhaps, to a more enlightened future for young women who seek to follow the monastic path.

Though her passport states her nationality is Thai, Munissara was born Nissara Horayangura to Thai parents in the predominantly Catholic Philippines. After attending a series of international schools in Manila, and briefly Bangladesh, she gained a place at Harvard, where she majored in the history of international relations. She laughs as she remembers being asked at her admissions interview what her goal in life was: 'You're supposed to say that you want to be a great world leader or find a cure for cancer. But I answered that my goal was spiritual growth and to be mildly entertaining to family and friends.' As she says this, her rather serious expression changes completely and I glimpse her quirky character for the first time. 'It's amazing to me now that that's what I said,' she continues, smiling, 'as, generally speaking, I was pretty confused as a teenager.'

During her college years, she says she was struck by how 'stressed out everyone was' and remembers thinking, 'What's the point of being smart if you don't know how to be happy?' I really started asking, 'What does intelligence mean?' It seemed to me that the kind of smart that really mattered was happiness, and I didn't see a lot of that in the people walking across Harvard Yard.' Munissara speaks quickly, with a marked American accent, and I imagine her striding across campus in jeans and sneakers, one eye on her fellow students, or lost in thought. I am struck by the eloquent simplicity with which she sums up what must have been a decade of soul-searching and inner turmoil.

'I'm not saying there weren't benefits to my education. I developed a lot of critical-thinking skills,' she continues. 'But I began asking, what is the point of life? To go to school, get a good job, have small people and then get old? I was like, "Why?" There has to be more to life than this. Everyone asks these kind of questions,' she says, with an assurance I choose not to challenge for fear of interrupting her flow. 'It just depends how old you are when you ask them.'

After graduating from Harvard, she worked briefly as an intern for the Media Trust in London, before moving to New York to work first in advertising and then for a non-profit organization looking at US–China relations. 'It was a nice job. But after a couple of years of that I started suffering a "quarter-life crisis".' She laughs. 'People talk about a mid-life crisis, now we have a twenty-five-year-old crisis, where you question what you're doing much earlier.' Living in the hothouse of New York, it was the time when her contemporaries 'started thinking about grad school', she remembers. 'There they were, worrying what was on their résumé, reading the *New Yorker* so they could say well-informed, witty things, preferably smarter than other people. And I was, like, "Wow! What is this?"'

Then life stopped her in her tracks. Munissara was twenty-five when her mother fell gravely ill and she returned to be with her in Thailand. As a child Munissara had visited Buddhist temples. But when it became clear her mother's illness was terminal, nothing seemed more important to Munissara than deepening her understanding of the fundamental Buddhist teachings on the roots of suffering and how to bring suffering to an end through spiritual development. 'A path that wouldn't simply educate the brain, but would train the heart to end suffering, both for myself and others. This was the first time it occurred to me that to do this I might ordain,' she says. 'I guess I felt if I was going to go all the way with it, then going all the way was to become ordained.'

When I question why she felt it was not possible to 'go all the way' in reaching a spiritual understanding as a lay practitioner, she compares the difference to that of a student of a foreign language attending a weekly class, rather than living in the country where the language is spoken. 'To me it seemed like it would be something I needed to do full time,' she says. 'Like being a professional, rather than a dabbler.'

But it was then that the critical-thinking skills learned at Harvard appear to have kicked in. 'For a long time I kept checking myself, wondering if I was romanticizing the notion of becoming a nun or running away from my responsibilities,' she says. So rather than seek ordination straight away, she signed up for a master's programme in South-East Asian Studies at university in Thailand and wrote a thesis on how far laypeople could follow Buddhist teachings. 'There's this whole trend to laicize Buddhism, especially amongst the intellectual middle class, to think that you can be a totally dedicated lay practitioner and that monasticism is irrelevant,' she says. 'And there's no doubt there are lay people who are very dedicated and do wonderful things. But I was very struck by how some people would show up to dharma teachings in white Christian Dior clothes and then go back to a totally corporate life, taking advantage of people. There is this conflict in lifestyle, which for a monastic doesn't exist.'

After finishing her master's degree, however, Munissara felt torn. She was sure by then that she wanted to ordain one day, but still felt that maybe she was too young. 'I wanted to have fun,' she says. Then her mother died and she felt it was time. In 2009 she ordained as a novice at a temple near Chiang Mai in Thailand and in March 2012 was fully ordained in a ceremony at which Ayya Tathaaloka presided in Australia. With an obligation to be near to her preceptor for her first two years as a nun, Munissara expects to stay close to Ayya Tathaaloka for some time. When I ask what she believes the future holds for her after that, Munissara shrugs, saying that 'planning is not the way of the renunciant. Our practice is to trust that you are where you need to be.'

Four years into her monastic life when we meet, she still keeps in regular touch with friends from her former life. 'Hopefully I haven't become this pious, religious type. I'm still the same zany person,' she says.

When I ask if there is anything she misses from that former life, she pauses for a moment and then breaks into a broad smile. 'I don't really miss anything about lay life, except maybe dancing.' She laughs. 'There are times when I'm doing walking meditation and I get this urge to break out in some hip-hop moves, which, in private, I sometimes do.'

As I drive back through the forest to rejoin Highway 1, the image of Munissara, when alone, occasionally lifting her saffron robes, swinging her hips and shuffling her feet seems symbolic of the ways in which many of the women I meet are bucking some of the restrictions placed on them over the centuries: though respecting the fundamentals of traditional practice, they are forging ahead with new ways of being a Buddhist nun in the West.

EAST OF THE CASCADES

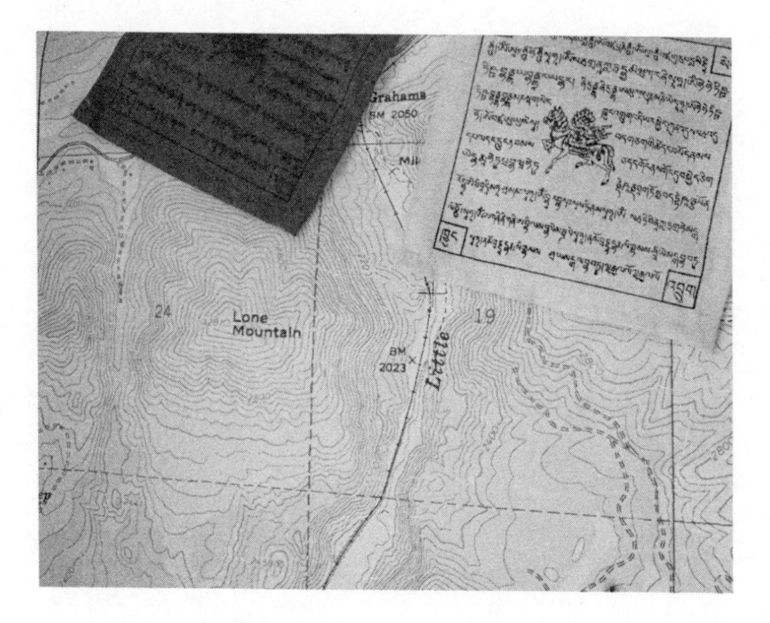

To the far north of San Francisco, close to the Canadian border in Washington State, the terrain can be harsh and unforgiving. In an area of wilderness known as the North Cascades, the very names of the mountains signal danger: Mount Terror, Mount Fury, Mount Despair. It was here, in the 1950s, that Jack Kerouac sought spiritual awakening in the solitude of nature, furiously scribbling out *The Dharma Bums* one summer while working as a fire-lookout on Desolation Peak. 'Desolation ... the place where I learned all,' he writes at the end of this autobiographical novel, before bemoaning 'the sadness of coming back to cities [with their] bars and burlesque shows and gritty love, all upside down in the void'. Little over a decade later, heavy drinking had claimed him.

The place I'm heading to is a few hours east of the Cascades. Here, in the shadow of the Selkirk Mountains, the hills and valleys close to the Idaho state line offer a more hospitable landscape, broken up by farmland and small settlements. But as in the Cascades, there are stretches of boreal forest here that run a high risk of wildfires. With temperatures soaring close to 38°C, the area is on high alert when I arrive.

The road that leads north from the former fur-trading post of Spokane grows narrower as I near my destination. Glancing left and right, I note names like Bear Tooth Road, Frost Loop and Bigfoot Lane. In the midst of this Arcadian scene lies Sravasti Abbey, a huddle of log cabins, barns and wood-shingled chalets that wouldn't look out of place in the Swiss Alps. The place appears largely deserted as I am shown to the nuns' residence. Most of the nuns, I am told, are out working in the dense woodland surrounding the abbey, having swapped their monastic robes for trousers and T-shirts. Not content, like Kerouac, to sit back, keep watch, ruminate and write, they are out getting their hands dirty. In the searing heat, they are busy cutting back deadwood to reduce the potential of forest fires spreading. It is heavy manual work and seems a fitting metaphor for the hard labour the nuns are willing to undertake in matters of metaphysics.

'Let us know when you're ready for lopping,' a tall, athletic-looking nun says to me over supper on my first evening. I smile and nod, unsure from her rather serious features whether or not she is joking; she is not. The next day we beat a path through the long grass behind the abbey and climb the slopes of a steep incline known as Lone Mountain. With only a handsaw and heavy gloves, we set about limbing the dead lower branches from towering larches, as well as pine and birch trees. Even in the forest shade, the summer heat has me flagging in less than an hour. The nuns continue working long after I have wilted; the members of the small resident community here at Sravasti Abbey are made of stern stuff.

At the entrance to the dining hall at Sravasti Abbey I notice a framed letter from the Dalai Lama, in which he acknowledges that western monastics have faced 'various difficulties' as interest in Buddhism and the monastic way of life has grown in the West. 'It is particularly refreshing to know that the Abbey will be charting a new course as a place where both traditional Buddhist teachings and innovative cultural forms will be present,' he writes. 'I am glad to know that the community seeks to provide both monks and nuns with not only equal opportunity, but equal responsibility to study, practise and teach the dharma.'

This is why I am here. Sravasti Abbey holds a unique position as the only place of its kind in the United States offering rigorous monastic training in the Tibetan Buddhist tradition for both nuns and monks, though at the time of my visit the community is comprised solely of women. Sravasti Abbey is the vision and creation of abbess Thubten Chodron. Not only is Thubten Chodron an influential teacher and the driving force behind the continuing expansion of the abbey, but for more than two decades she has also been a leading figure in a pioneer generation of western Buddhist nuns lobbying for the introduction of full ordination for women in the Tibetan Buddhist tradition.

I have come to talk to Thubten Chodron about the progress that is being made on all these fronts. But during my first few days the abbess and her nuns are busy teaching a group of youngsters here on retreat. So, together with them, I get up at 5 a.m. and make my way through the trees and wildflowers to the small log cabin that serves as a meditation hall. At this hour, the sun has yet to burn off the morning mist and Sravasti sits above the cloud line, hovering in an ethereal pink blush. The only sounds are the chorus of birdsong and the swoosh of the nuns' long robes against the grass. From behind, they look like a single file of Little Red Riding Hoods making their way in the forest.

But these women are far from ingénues. Most are in their middle years, with the exception of one young German-born nun from former East Germany. They count amongst their ranks a former Canadian military police officer, a US naval officer, a psychiatric nurse, a music teacher and a performing artist. All have lived full lives before choosing the monastic path. Some have been married, as has their abbess.

Over the course of several days I sit listening to Thubten Chodron speak to the visiting youngsters, boys as well as girls, most in their late teens, about challenges we all face, such as how to deal with anger, regret and guilt, how not to dwell on the past and how to arrive at forgiveness for grievances big and small. She has a keen eye for comedy and mime, at one point sucking her thumb and putting on a whiny voice to mimic the internal dialogue we all fall victim to when feeling wronged. The sight of this senior nun, with her broad smile, sparkling eyes, shaven head and maroon robes, acting out scenes in everyday psychological dramas in such a playful manner is a delight to watch. She has a real knack for comic timing that sees the youngsters erupting frequently with laughter; her high-pitched, almost child-like voice masks her gravitas as a senior teacher and author of many books on Buddhist subjects. But the message of what she says is not lost.

On the final day of the retreat one eighteen-year-old confides in me that he is a survivor of one of the worst mass shootings by a rogue gunman in the community in recent American history. When I ask if the time he has spent at Sravasti Abbey has helped him, he nods and smiles shyly. Although the retreat lasted only a few days, his eyes convey a strong sense that he has experienced some longed-for peace: evidence of how teachings 2,500 years old are able to begin healing the madness of the modern world.

By the time I finally have the opportunity to sit down and talk to Thubten Chodron, I have some understanding of the community she has established and the path that led to its creation. In an article she once wrote entitled 'You're Becoming a What?', she talks candidly about her early life and the dismay of her Jewish parents at the unexpected turn it took when she was in her early twenties. Born Cheryl Greene in 1950, she grew up in the Los Angeles area; her parents were middle-class second-generation immigrants, her grandparents having fled pogroms in Eastern Europe. Her father was a dentist, her mother a bookkeeper, both were non-religious. As a child, she was thoughtful and inquisitive. After failing to find answers to spiritual questions about life, many prompted by the Vietnam War and the growing civil rights protests, she became an atheist.

A bright student, she went on to read history at UCLA and at the age of twenty-one, after beginning work as a primary school teacher, she married a lawyer. Shortly after their wedding, she and her husband set off backpacking for a year and a half through Europe, North Africa and the Middle East, to India and Nepal. But her interest in Buddhism only started to grow after they returned to work in LA and attended a meditation course at a local bookshop, taught by two Tibetan monks. The monks were Lama Yeshe and Lama Zopa Rinpoche, co-founders of Kopan monastery, which I visited in Kathmandu. During their teachings, the two monks had a nun guide several meditation sessions. 'It impressed me that she was happy, friendly and natural, not stiff and "holy",' says Thubten Chodron. 'Even so, I still thought that being a nun was strange. I liked my husband far too much to even consider it!'

But as she sat listening to the monks teach, she began hearing answers to questions that had long troubled her, at the root of which lay a conviction that 'there must be more to life than having fun, working, making money, having a family, growing old and dying'. Eager to learn more, she persuaded her husband to return with her to Nepal to spend time at Kopan. Once there, she became convinced that she wanted to devote herself to following the Buddhist teachings full time, and it soon became clear to her that she wanted to seek ordination. Whilst her husband eventually supported her choice, has since remarried and remains a close friend, her parents were less understanding. They were unable to comprehend how she could abandon a promising career, marriage, friends, family and financial security.

She explains her choice by saying that she lacked the self-discipline to be able to practise the dharma as a layperson. Considering the tenacity it has taken to establish Sravasti Abbey, this is hard to envision. After becoming one of the first generation of westerners to ordain as a novice in the Tibetan tradition in Nepal in 1977, it took nine years for her to receive full ordination – known in this tradition as *bhikshuni* – by travelling to Taiwan. She acknowledges that at the time she became a novice, the priority of her Tibetan teachers was to rebuild their monasteries in exile and take care of the refugee Tibetan community. While they supported westerners ordaining, there were no monasteries where they could live and train continuously. 'While Catholic nuns enter a particular order, for example a teaching order, a contemplative order, a service order, Buddhist nuns have no prescribed living situation or work,' says Thubten Chodron. So, for more than fifteen years, she travelled from one Buddhist monastery or teaching centre to another, both in the East and in the West, some of this time spent in retreat, the rest spent studying, teaching and working in Buddhist centres.

This rootless existence sowed the seeds of a determination to establish a place where western monastics could live together, practising the dharma and training others. 'I realized that if I wanted to live in a community that would correspond more to our culture, then I would have to create it myself,' she says. In this, she was spurred on by the Dalai Lama. During the conference with western Buddhist teachers in 1993, at which he wept on hearing of the plight of Tibetan nuns and western monastics in the Tibetan tradition, the Dalai Lama encouraged the western monastics to take their welfare into their own hands. Usually both monks and nuns engage in projects begun by their teachers, but 'he told us, if we ran into problems to come to him, but that we should not rely on others to do things for us', Thubten Chodron recalls. 'This was an incredible turning point for me,' she says, her eyes widening and hands clasped. 'It made me realize, "I can act. I can try out my ideas!"' With the Dalai Lama's blessing, she felt galvanized into action.

At that time Thubten Chodron was the resident teacher at a Buddhist foundation in Seattle. It would be many years before Sravasti Abbey came into being, but she started looking for land on which to establish her own monastic community. After a number of false starts, in 2003, as if by divine providence, the former owners of the ninety-seven hectares of meadow and forest on which the abbey now stands agreed to carry the $500,000 mortgage needed to purchase the property. Over time, Thubten Chodron was able to pay them back, through donations she received from supporters and royalties from her books. The abbey continues to exist with the support of donations and offers free teaching. In order to be able to develop Sravasti Abbey in a way that is more in tune with western life, Thubten Chodron set it up to be independent of any wider Buddhist organization.

This has opened up the possibility of developing a monastic life very different from that in the East. The structure of Sravasti Abbey is more 'horizontal, more collaborative, with gender equality and with seniority based on years of experience and knowledge,' Thubten Chodron explains. Practices and ceremonies are conducted in English. The fact that the abbey is open to training nuns alongside monks is also unusual. Traditionally, in order to avoid sexual attraction, nuns and monks live in different monasteries. At the abbey they are housed in different buildings, but teaching and offering service are done together. From the beginning, Thubten Chodron says, she was clear the doors of the abbey would be open to both men and women. 'I have been excluded too much because of being a female and I don't want to exclude sincere male aspirants. I don't want to create more "exclusion karma" or say to anyone, "Sorry, you can't come here because of the shape of your body,"' she says firmly. At the time of my visit the community is still relatively small, with just nine nuns in residence, but a large hall with new kitchen facilities and accommodation is under construction.

'If people turn up here and start falling in love, then we'll have to do something else, because that's not going to work,' she says with a laugh, stressing the importance of celibacy in monastic life. This is in stark contrast to views held by some young nuns today in Japan, but Thubten Chodron is adamant on the subject and continues, 'In Buddhism, being a monastic entails being celibate. It makes a huge difference. When you are celibate, you have to be more independent, to take care of yourself. You have to deal with your sexuality, be more responsible for your emotions and deal with your attachments,' she says, referring to a core Buddhist teaching which sees craving and clinging attachment as one of the principal causes of human suffering.

'When I'm with Tibetans, my views are seen as very radical and liberal, and when I'm with westerners, because of my monastic robes, I'm seen as very traditional,' she concludes.

In addition to the teaching and retreats offered at Sravasti Abbey, its resident community of nuns is also actively involved in work in the community, not least in a programme of regularly visiting prisons and corresponding with inmates, many of whom will never be released from jail. As head of such an innovative institution, it might seem that Thubten Chodron would be fully occupied here in the Pacific northwest, but she regularly travels the world, giving teachings and attending meetings promoting full ordination for nuns in the Tibetan tradition. When I ask her about this, she downplays her role and refers me to two other leading proponents, both nuns and academics: German *bhikshuni* Jampa Tsedroen, a Tibetologist at Hamburg University, and fellow American Karma Lekshe Tsomo, associate professor of theology and religious studies at the University of San Diego. I had sought advice from Karma Lekshe Tsomo at the very start of my journey and I knew she had been instrumental in founding an organization called Sakyadhita, an international association of Buddhist women.

Since the launch of Sakyadhita in 1987, there have been numerous meetings and conferences held internationally in which the question of full ordination for Tibetan Buddhist nuns has been discussed. But, like the British-born nun Tenzin Palmo in India, Thubten Chodron stresses that this is not a matter that can be decided in the West. 'It is in Tibetan hands and always has been. It is their tradition and they have made that very clear,' she says. Given the resistance conservative Tibetan clerics still have to the notion of full female ordination, I ask Thubten Chodron how she believes they would respond to the notion of a female successor to the Dalai Lama. Like Tenzin Palmo, she does not see this as a realistic possibility. 'A woman would never be accepted as the Dalai Lama in Tibetan culture. Things may be changing, but not that much,' she says. 'After all, here in the United States, we have yet to elect a female president!'

But for Thubten Chodron, the question of full ordination has little to do with women's rights. 'It isn't that we want to do what the men do,' she says. 'It's a question of being able to take all the monastic precepts that lay out the path for ethical conduct. Living with precepts helps us to refine our behaviour and purify our actions, setting the stage for cultivating concentration and wisdom,' she explains. 'Of course you can keep ethical behaviour without monastic precepts, but it is much harder.' For her, becoming fully ordained 'completely transformed' her practice, she says. 'It made me grow up. I realized there were twenty-five centuries of practitioners behind me, whose kindness in keeping the dharma and monastic life alive allowed me to encounter these liberating teachings and become a monastic.' Her responsibility now, she stresses, is to pass these teachings on. 'Being fully ordained isn't about me,' she concludes. 'It's about benefiting others and preserving the teachings and ordination lineage so people in the future can benefit from them too.'

The sun is now at its zenith and it is time for Thubten Chodron to return to her duties. That afternoon she will retire to a secluded writing cabin surrounded by a pretty garden in the grounds of Sravasti Abbey. It is here that she now pens the books on Buddhist teachings that are published internationally. Before we part, I ask if she envisages her community inspiring similar establishments elsewhere in the West. 'Some people tell me that others are looking at us to see what we're doing, but I didn't set this up as a model,' she says. 'What happens to this place doesn't depend on just me, it depends on who shows up here. Opening a monastery is such a good example of how everything in life depends on multiple causes and conditions.'

At a time when countless monasteries of other faiths are declining and falling into disrepair, the founding of centres such as Aranya Bodhi and Sravasti Abbey reflects a wider flourishing of female Buddhist monasticism in the West. On returning to my own home shores in the British Isles, a more complex picture of the personal and social consequences of this resurgence emerges.

PART VI

BRITAIN

CHANGING GEAR

I had not intended that my first encounter back in the British Isles should be with a woman who has given up her nun's robes and returned to lay life. But her story is indicative of the challenges and difficulties involved in adopting a Buddhist monastic life in the West.

Southern England is in the grip of fierce storms as Beki and I arrange to meet on a windswept hillside on the South Downs. I fear we will hardly be able to hear each other speak amid the howling gales, but I am keen to see something of the life Beki has embraced since disrobing as a nun after seventeen years in the Tibetan Buddhist tradition. It includes duties as a part-time shepherdess, or 'lookerer' as she calls it, using the medieval term for keeping watch over the herd of Swaledale sheep grazing twenty hectares of farmland she and her boyfriend own just a few miles inland from the busy resort of Brighton.

Before we meet, I watch a short documentary made while Beki was still a nun. The film, entitled *Unusual Choices,* briefly charts how she went from being a presenter on the BBC's hit show *Top Gear* to seeking ordination in her late twenties. There is no hint that, less than a year after the making of the film, she will no longer be wearing her maroon robes. There is a warmth and joy in her voice as she speaks of her monastic life. The same warmth is there as Beki welcomes me at the gate to her farm, wearing jeans and wellington boots, her head no longer shaved.

Taking advantage of a brief break in the weather, we trudge through the mud to the highest point of their farm, which dates back to the fourteenth century and has a Bronze Age burial mound within its boundaries. Even before we sit down to talk, I sense the importance for her of being firmly rooted in such an ancient landscape. 'This was sacred land thousands of years ago,' she says, spreading her arms wide, her words whipped by the wind as we take in a breathtaking view across rolling chalk hills. 'You get a real feeling of timelessness and freedom up here.'

In the film Beki, who then went by her monastic name Ani Chudrun, talks of how the best thing about being a nun was the freedom it offered. Though she jokes that it means, for instance, never having to shave your legs, it is clear she means an inner freedom. Had she finally come to feel her celibate monastic life led her to lose too many of the liberties we women in the West take for granted, I wondered? The answer to this question does not emerge until we have been speaking for many hours.

The exposed hillside where we stand offers little shelter, and there is still no heating in the farm's outbuildings, which are slowly being reconstructed with funds from campers who stay during the summer months. To talk in peace and comfort, Beki invites me to her small home a few miles further along the coast. We take separate cars and I ask her to drive slowly so I can follow. But Beki's 'slow' has me revving my engine to try to keep up: her driving style is perhaps all that remains from her former association with a cult TV programme about cars.

It seems such an unlikely trajectory, from fronting one of the most unashamedly macho and materialistic of television shows to retreating within cloisters, that I begin by asking directly, 'How was it working on *Top Gear*?'

'I thought it was pointless!' she replies, without hesitation.

Photographs from this time show Beki with flowing blonde hair behind the wheel of various cars, a cluster of cameramen and photographers in attendance. But there is a distant look in her eyes that hints at boredom. Her stint on *Top Gear* ran from 1987 to 1989, before the show became an international phenomenon, though it was already watched by over five million viewers.

'I was treated like a star. When I walked into a car showroom, everyone knew who I was,' she says. 'But I remember looking into the camera lens one day and thinking, millions of people are listening to what I'm saying. What a waste to have your voice heard by that many and be talking about inane things, like the acceleration of a car.'

Beki had landed the job almost by accident while working on a car magazine. Invited, because of her contacts, to help organize a particular episode, she was asked by its presenter at the time, William Woollard, what she thought of the show. 'I said, "It's dull and boring," and something to the effect that its presenters were shit.' She laughs. Even after admitting she didn't think she could make a better job of it, she was invited to try. A year later Jeremy Clarkson rose to fame as the face of *Top Gear* and shortly afterwards Beki and the BBC parted ways.

From this blunt exchange Beki's next remark comes as little surprise; she mentions that, according to the sixty-year cycle of Chinese astrology, she was born in the year of the Fire Horse, 1966. 'In China they drown baby girls born in Fire Horse years because they're thought to be too unruly and difficult to tame,' she says.

Born in Sussex, the youngest of three daughters, she describes herself as a defiant child, a tomboy. But in common with other nuns I have met, it was the death of someone close that marked the most important turning point in her life. 'I had an idyllic childhood until I was thirteen. But when Mum died, my childhood ended. I had a very clear feeling that no one knew what happened when someone died and I remember thinking, "I'm sure there must be people who know. When I'm older, I'm going to find them."'

The loss of her mother meant Beki gave little thought to marrying and having children. 'It was never on my radar. I had boyfriends. I fell in love. But I remember saying to my school friends, "What's the point in getting married if you finally find someone worth getting married to and they're going to die?"' Growing up in the 1980s also had a huge impact. 'The Thatcher years, capitalism, the Berlin Wall coming down. It was all a huge deal,' she says. 'And there I was, presenting *Top Gear*, a classic example of all those things: fast cars, TV, going out with a guy who was a rock star, drugs.' She pauses with a wry smile. 'Not so great really.'

After leaving *Top Gear*, she researched possible subjects for television documentaries, one of which was the history of outlawing marijuana. To publicize the project, in March 1992 she opened a cannabis cafe in Brighton. It remained open for fifty-seven minutes before she was arrested and, very briefly, sent to jail. 'It was on the news as the shortest-run business in the history of southern England.' She laughs, her chin creasing into a dimple.

'Sitting in that cell, I had the strong feeling that this solitude was actually what I wanted. I realized I needed to go away somewhere and sit quietly.' She travelled first to India and then Kathmandu, where someone handed her a photograph of a young boy, a Tibetan lama. Without realizing who it was, she remembers looking at his eyes and feeling very strongly, 'He knows everything. He's got all the answers. What can I say? That's just what I felt,' she says, shrugging her shoulders. 'The feeling then to go and find him and ask him a few questions was overwhelming.'

It was only after returning to London that she discovered the boy was Ogyen Trinley Dorje, recognized by the Dalai Lama as the

Seventeenth Karmapa, a position widely regarded as third in line in the Tibetan spiritual hierarchy. At the time, he was just seven years old and still undergoing training in a monastery in Tibet. Seven years later, he would stage a dramatic escape across the Himalayas on horseback to live in exile in India, in a monastery close to Dharamshala. That was where I met him, several years later, whilst researching my article on the Dalai Lama's transfer of temporal power to a newly elected Tibetan Prime Minister. I too found him a compelling figure. His youthful good looks have led some to refer to him as 'His Hotness'.

In her quest to find out more about the Karmapa, Beki initially travelled to Scotland to visit Samye Ling monastery, the oldest Tibetan Buddhist monastery in Europe. Whilst there, she decided to ordain as a nun for a year: 'I had a very strong sense that when I went to see the Karmapa, I wanted him to take me seriously.' It seems a big step to take in search of gravitas, I say, to which her reply again reminds me of what other nuns have told me: 'If I do something, I do it wholeheartedly.' She then adds, 'But there was absolutely no way I thought I was going to be a nun for longer than a year. In fact I was so sure that I asked to be ordained quickly so I would be out of robes in time for a big party coming up the following year.'

Beki's family and friends also thought that it was 'just a passing phase'. But it would be several years before she was able to travel to Tibet to visit the Karmapa, and in that time she became convinced that she wanted to continue on the monastic path. 'When I started to meditate, I realized that I was just a complete mess,' she says. After renewing her vows for a further three years, she eventually took life vows. But the longed-for meeting with the Karmapa was not quite as she had expected. He was still a boy when she first travelled with a group of nuns and monks to Tibet to see him, and she was struck by his 'wild, raw energy' and 'wrathful' manner that quashed any possibility of asking questions. In subsequent meetings, after his escape to India, she describes the Karmapa, regarded by some as a possible spiritual successor to the Dalai Lama, as being kept 'like a caged lion' in a monastery near Dharamshala. Indian authorities have him held under virtual house arrest here amid spurious allegations that he has been planted as a spy for the Chinese. As Beki speaks, I recall my own meeting with the Karmapa, conscious of Indian security agents permanently posted outside his private quarters, as he talked of his deep hurt at the unfounded allegations.

During the seventeen years Beki spent as a nun, her energetic 'Fire Horse' nature was put to use by the Tibetan lamas with whom she studied. Apart from long periods in meditation retreats, both at Samye Ling and in the United States, she was put in charge of organizing a sequence of activities in the West, including helping to establish a London branch of Samye Ling. She also spent time in India, teaching English to young lamas recently arrived from Tibet. But gradually this peripatetic existence began to take its toll. No longer attached to a monastic centre and unable to stay indefinitely in either India or Nepal due to visa restrictions, she began to feel rootless.

Two years before she gave back her vows, she was sent to attend an English language teaching course in Oxford. Whilst there, she temporarily swapped her monastic robes for lay clothes, and an uneasiness about her chosen path began to creep in. 'There's a beautiful subtlety to wearing robes. They are like a protective layer on lots of levels. So in the beginning, I felt I had lost that protection. I felt dizzy, almost as if I was physically going to fall over,' she reflects. 'But in another way, when I borrowed a pair of jeans, it felt fantastic, like meeting an old friend. In the era of the Buddha, wearing robes was a way of giving up your individuality, and still, in the East, when you wear robes, you merge into the crowd. But in the West it has the opposite effect. You stick out like a sore thumb.'

As she speaks it is clear she was also beginning to feel fettered by the strict hierarchy within Tibetan Buddhism and by other East–West cultural differences. 'Because of losing their homeland, all Tibetans have a great wish to preserve their culture. But this is difficult if you also want Buddhism to take root in another culture, as it effectively becomes an obstacle for many people,' she explains, echoing a concern shared by others in the West.

But the decisive factor in Beki 'coming out of nundom', as she puts it, was the death of her father, whom she had nursed at home during a final illness. For some time she had lived in a small wooden cabin in the garden of his home and he had supported her financially. 'When he died, that was gone. I no longer belonged to any monastery and there was a sense that "This doesn't fit any more,"' she says. Even though she slipped out of monastic life, quietly returning her robes, Beki's devotion to following the dharma seems undimmed.

After we finish talking, late into the evening, she invites me to sit with her as she goes through her nightly devotional practice. Upstairs in her home she has transformed one bedroom into a quiet place of meditation and prayer. An altar, decked with water bowls, candles and photographs of revered teachers, including the Karmapa, reminds me of similar shrines in nuns' dormitories in India and Nepal. Every morning and evening Beki still recites chosen texts, moving her hands in a dance of mudras practised for more than two millennia.

Although Beki is now a passionate environmentalist and has thrown herself into restoring the Sussex farm she bought after her father died, which she hopes to offer as a venue for Buddhist teaching retreats, she does not rule out the possibility that she might one day re-ordain as a nun. Her partner is also a devout Buddhist. 'Being a nun is undoubtedly the most precious thing I could have done with my life,' she says.

From the way she speaks, it seems she is still weighing up the different ways of life she has known. Even today, she talks of wearing lay clothes as 'disguises you can play with'. When I ask what it was about her femininity that she missed as a nun, she talks not about intimacy or sex, but about other trappings most women take for granted. 'As a nun you are stripped of everything that you might associate with being a woman: no make-up, nothing that shows any curves, no hair, not even your name,' she says, before concluding that this also has its advantages. 'It means you really have to look at what it means to be a woman, and you realize it is our qualities of love and kindness and care.'

As we part Beki prepares to return to her upstairs shrine room, and I imagine her as I drive away, eyes closed, hands resting in her lap. There's a certain comfort in knowing that, as all around her settle down for the night or rush to start their day, Beki will be sitting quietly, reciting ancient blessings of harmony and peace.

After saying goodbye to Beki, I continue my trip deep into the heart of rural England to meet an older woman with many years of monastic experience. Making my way along winding country lanes, so worn with time that they have sunk between high banks of moss and overhanging trees, I see why she sometimes feels as if she is living in Tolkien's Middle Earth. She likens her surroundings, and the small wooden cabin where she spends periods in silent retreat, to the half-hidden home of a Hobbit. As the road I take twists and turns further off the beaten track, dipping into waterlogged dells and between steep earth banks held in place by gnarled roots, the countryside seems to take on an almost mystical air.

My destination is a monastery belonging not to the Tibetan tradition in which Beki ordained, but to the older Theravada school of Buddhism I encountered first in Burma and again in the secluded hermitage founded by Ayya Tathaaloka in California. Although an awareness of Buddhism reached the United States and Britain at roughly the same time, in the mid- to late-nineteenth century, the route it took was very different. While Buddhism was first introduced to the United States by immigrants arriving on the West Coast from China and Japan, in Britain it was brought back by academics and civil servants working in far-flung corners of the British Empire – places such as Ceylon (modern-day Sri Lanka) and elsewhere in South East Asia, where Buddhism principally followed the older Theravada order. Initially, there was just a handful of academic translations of Buddhist scriptures, but then in 1879 the publication of Edwin Arnold's epic *The Light of Asia,* a poetic narration of the life of Prince Gautama Siddhartha, suddenly brought the Buddha and his teachings to wider public attention. In Britain, as in the United States, the book became hugely popular, going through eighty editions and selling around a million copies.

Even so, for decades Buddhism was viewed by many in Britain as little more than a romantic oriental tradition. It was not until the mid-twentieth century that any attempt was made to found a centre of Buddhist monasticism in Britain, and the first attempts were faltering. Two small centres for a handful of British men ordained as monks in Thailand were initially established in private houses in London, the first in St John's Wood in the 1950s, and then in Hampstead in the 1960s. Neither flourished until the arrival in

Britain in 1977 of an influential Thai monk named Ajahn Chah and his American follower, Ajahn Sumedho, a former Peace Corps worker who had ordained after serving as a medical officer during the Korean War. Both adhered to the ancient Buddhist practice of leading a monastic life in the seclusion of nature. Braving both the rigours of the British weather and the dubious public, one spring morning in 1978 Ajahn Sumedho accompanied several British monks on an alms round through the streets of north London and across Hampstead Heath. That day they passed an early-morning jogger who was so struck by their devotion he offered to donate them woodland he owned, but could no longer maintain, in West Sussex so they could lead the lives of secluded forest monks.

This plot of land, Hammer Wood, could hardly be more English. Parts of it have lain untouched for more than 500 years and are designated as ancient woodland. With almost fifty hectares of oak, birch, ash and willow trees, it sits to the west of the historic picture-postcard English market towns of Petworth and Midhurst. It is in this unlikely setting that the first Theravada Buddhist monastery in the Thai Forest tradition was established in Britain. Since they were unable to build accommodation within the boundaries of Hammer Wood, a half-derelict mansion nearby, Chithurst House, its grounds littered with scores of abandoned cars and accumulated rubbish, was purchased for the monks from the proceeds of selling their Hampstead home. In 1979 the house was renamed Cittaviveka, or 'Heart Without Attachment'. Here, over the next thirty years, a flourishing community grew to accommodate growing numbers of both monks and nuns. When their number became too large for the mansion, an abandoned school was purchased thirty miles north of London and converted into an additional monastery complex called Amaravati.

As I pull into the drive of Cittaviveka I am greeted by the sight of a line of saffron-robed monks making their way in single file from the now immaculately restored house to a large oak-beamed worship hall newly built in the grounds. There are no nuns to be seen. A few years ago a major rift tore this monastic community apart, after which all the nuns here either disrobed or moved elsewhere. In recent years, just one has returned, and she now lives in a secluded cottage some distance from the main monastery buildings. Walking through the grounds, I spot her 'Hobbit' home by the edge of a deep pond. Thin whispers of smoke curling up from the cottage chimney signal that Sister Metta is there and waiting for me. She ushers me into the warmth and draws two chairs up to a wood-burning stove for us to sit and talk.

I quickly sense Sister Metta's reluctance to discuss the events that shattered harmony at the monastery. She prefers to talk instead of the period when the community of nuns at Chithurst and Amaravati flourished in the years after she ordained in the mid-1990s. Born in northern Germany, Sister Metta was drawn to leave her homeland to become a nun at Chithurst because at the time it was the only place in Europe that offered women the opportunity to follow the strict monastic life of the Theravada tradition she had encountered while travelling in Thailand. Unlike in Thailand, however, where women who don religious robes are often still marginalized, the Chithurst nuns lived in a similar way to its monks.

From the earliest days of the monastery, the small but growing number of women wishing to ordain here had been given a special dispensation that has never existed in the Thai tradition. After a period following the same basic vows as those observed by Thai *maechees*, the nuns of Chithurst and Amaravati took an additional two vows that, crucially, prohibited them from handling money and confirmed their status as true renunciants, withdrawn from the world and reliant on alms. Officially, however, their standing within the community was considered junior. So when, for instance, monks occupied an elevated platform during ceremonies, nuns often sat in a slightly lower position; and, irrespective of how many years a nun had been following the monastic path, she would be expected to defer to any monk, no matter how new to the order. While nuns were just as actively engaged with ceremonies and activities involving lay followers in the wider community, their voice and opinion carried less official weight. All Sister Metta will say on the matter is that she and the other nuns 'were under the impression we were moving more and more towards equality'.

That this impression was mistaken became painfully apparent in the autumn of 2009. Although Sister Metta prefers not to expand, I already know the broad facts from two former resident nuns I met briefly while in San Francisco. In the wake of the fracture, both had chosen to leave in order to establish their own community in the more liberal climate of California. From them, I know that the trouble started in 2007, when some lay followers expressed their concern that the organization of both monasteries was lagging far behind wider society in banishing unequal treatment of the sexes. Following open debate of the thorny question of full ordination for nuns in both the Theravada and the Tibetan traditions at an international gathering of Buddhists in Hamburg, Germany, in 2007, the position of the monks at Chithurst and Amaravati was made quite clear. The American-born co-founder of the monastery, Ajahn Sumedho, who has since returned to Thailand, issued a 'Five Point' declaration that amounted to an ultimatum for all nuns under his jurisdiction to either accept the status quo or face the prospect that ordination of any kind for women at both monasteries would cease.

In the years that followed, a succession of nine nuns chose to disrobe or leave, to the point that there were fewer than a dozen at Amaravati and none at all remaining at Chithurst. In 2012 Sister Metta was transferred back here from Amaravati, in the hope that a female monastic presence would once again flourish in Sussex. But as the shadows lengthen in the room where we sit talking and her sorrow at what has happened remains unspoken, hers seems a lonely vigil.

'When you move into monastic life, you become part of a larger body and your individuality is secondary,' Sister Metta says, by way of explaining her decision to remain. 'The practice is to let go of the desires of the ego and a sense of self-importance. What you gain in relinquishing your individuality is peace of mind.' To a western ear, which fêtes individuality and the fight for equality, such self-effacement might sound defeatist, especially when so much is at stake. But Sister Metta argues that it is a question of taking a wider perspective very different from the one commonly held in the West. From a Buddhist viewpoint, it is the grasping and delusions of the ego that lie at the root of much human suffering.

Notwithstanding this metaphysical stance, as I say farewell to Sister Metta I can't help but reflect on the efforts to rectify outdated discrimination being made by many of the Buddhist nuns I have met elsewhere: the nuns in Nepal practising kung fu, those at Dolma Ling in Dharamshala engaging in fierce debate, Tenzin Palmo ensuring the novices in her care receive the highest standard of education, Daw Zanaka and Daw Molini struggling against the odds of a still restrictive regime in Burma to do the same for their charges, Ayya Tathaaloka and Thubten Chodron in the United States lobbying for full ordination for women in different Buddhist traditions.

To gain another perspective on the hurt caused by the authoritarian handling of the question of full ordination at Chithurst and Amaravati, however, as well as on the relevance of this strict monastic practice in a modern western society, I must journey much further north in the British Isles. There I will meet one of the first women to ordain at Chithurst just after it was founded. Although she still remains affiliated with the community, it is no coincidence that she now spends most of her time far removed from both Chithurst and Amaravati, though I had not expected to find her in quite such an isolated location.

As far as human suffering goes, there are few more poignant reminders of its depth than the memorial I visit at the end of my train journey north of the English border. In the cathedral nave of the small Scottish town of Dunblane stands a tall stone erected in the year 2000 in memory of sixteen young children and their teacher killed by a deranged gunman who had gone on a shooting spree in their primary school four years before. The massacre happened towards the end of winter, when snowdrops were in bloom, and two species of this fragile flower have since been named after one of the five-year-olds and her teacher whose lives were cut short.

Great clusters of snowdrops lie nestled in hedgerows as I travel on beyond Dunblane into the foothills of the Highlands in search of a newly established hermitage called Milntuim, meaning Mill on the Hillock. After many wrong turns, I eventually find it tucked in a fold of moorland, barely visible from the road. I am greeted at the door by the hermitage's founder, the rosy-cheeked, freckle-faced Sister Candasiri. She quickly suggests that we take advantage of a rare sunny afternoon to go for a walk across the moors before we sit down to talk. Just as Beki had felt rooted by the ancient markers of her surroundings on the South Downs, I am struck by how the nun twenty years her senior, who leads the way at a brisk pace, has also chosen to anchor herself in a place believed to date back 4,000 years. Battling against the wind, we climb to a high point where one of Perthshire's many mysterious standing stones towers over the landscape. As she rests her hand against its mossy granite face, I sense that Sister Candasiri takes comfort from physical phenomena predating even the primal origins of Buddhism.

After a light supper, from which Sister Candasiri abstains – observing the monastic custom of fasting from noon to dawn – we settle in an upstairs room of the hermitage looking out across still-snow-capped peaks. When I ask Sister Candasiri about her early days at Chithurst, she rummages in a drawer to find a well-thumbed copy of *Woman's Own* magazine, dated 17 May 1980. There, on its cover, beside a large picture of a bronzed model posing seductively in one of that summer's 'sexiest swimsuits', is a small photograph of three young women with short cropped hair, all swathed in the white monastic robes still worn today by Thailand's novice *maechees*. 'British Buddhist Nuns in Sussex – Their Amazing Story' runs the headline. Inside, spread across two pages, an article charts the founding of Chithurst monastery, and gives brief details of the first four women ordained there as novices in 1979 – a time, it says, when there were 'plenty of hopefuls queuing up to join them'. The article heralds Sister Candasiri and her companions as 'the only Buddhist nuns in the Western world', describing them as 'women devoted to a philosophy and way of life totally at odds with the materialistic Eighties'. While the former claim is exaggerated – given the community of ordained women dating from the early 1970s I had encountered at Gold Mountain monastery in the heart of San Francisco – the latter is undoubtedly true.

Flicking through the faded magazine, full of models sporting Farrah Fawcett flowing locks of the type I once tried to emulate, I think of the turn my own life took at the end of the 1980s, when Margaret Thatcher's free-market revolution was in full swing. In my late twenties by then, I left a safe desk job as a junior reporter on the *Sunday Times* to work as one of its foreign correspondents, covering the civil wars raging at the time throughout Central America, in Guatemala, El Salvador and Nicaragua. Aside from a burning desire to dive headlong into the journalistic thick of things abroad, I remember feeling relieved at escaping Britain's prevailing 'loadsamoney' mindset, which was driving an ever thicker wedge between the country's haves and have-nots. These were the years that had also cemented Beki's determination to seek a more spiritual life.

Tracing the very different decisions other women were taking around the same time makes me reflect on all our choices. Nothing could have been further from my mind then than the life of a nun. By the early 1990s, I was living in Mexico with a young daughter, my professional focus being reporting on bloody combat. Had I known anything about the lives of women whose focus was to understand the struggles of our interior landscape, would I have paid them much attention? Probably not. It took more than two decades of covering the aftermath of war in hotspots around the world, looking outward rather than inward, for me to appreciate that any true understanding of conflict can only come from facing up to our own inner battles.

For Sister Candasiri, the catalyst for her spiritual journey was the serious illness and subsequent nervous breakdown of a close friend at university. 'For me this was very shocking and upsetting,' says the nun, who talks of having had a 'wild time' at the University of St Andrews in the late 1960s. Raised in Scotland, by a Scottish solicitor father and Canadian mother, to say her prayers every night, she says she had 'given all that up by the age of sixteen because I didn't want to have to believe in anything. I wanted to find out for myself'.

I remember having similar feelings after my own brief flirtation with devout Christianity as I was reaching puberty. Looking back, it seems clear that I was far more interested in the handsome Californians who turned up on the doorstep of my all-girls grammar school in Wales than in the Bible study classes they encouraged me to attend, though perhaps it signalled an early inclination towards spiritual searching. As it turned out, I had a lucky escape. The bronzed, blond-haired hippies belonged to the Children of God movement, later denounced as a cult after it emerged members engaged in what was known as 'Flirty Fishing' – using sex 'to show God's love' and win converts. But I also remember quite clearly waking up soon after becoming embroiled and deciding there was little point in leading an adventurous life, which I was determined to do from a young age, if I was simply going to swallow much of the way the world worked on faith.

In Sister Candasiri's case, her friend's mental illness prompted her to train as an occupational therapist specializing in psychiatric care. 'But quite quickly I saw that drugs and other treatments like electroshock therapy were a really coarse way of dealing with mental problems,' she says. After travelling to India with a boyfriend and then settling with him in Belsize Park in London, she heard about monks offering meditation lessons nearby in St John's Wood and started attending regularly. The monks were Ajahn Chah's followers, who were just about to establish Chithurst monastery in Sussex.

'I had a job, a flat, a boyfriend and no thoughts of becoming a nun. But I decided to move to Sussex to help them clear the grounds at Chithurst, because I wanted to practise meditation,' she says.

Within two years, her head was shaven and she had become a novice nun, known as an *anagarika* in the Theravada tradition. Her parents were distraught, 'wondering where they'd gone wrong', she says. But she was happier than she had ever been, meditating under the guidance of the monks, cooking for them and helping establish the community. When she and three other women who had ordained as novices took further vows four years later, progressing to what in the Chithurst–Amaravati community are known as *sila-dhara,* they no longer handled money, drove cars or cooked for themselves; these tasks were performed by lay supporters, confirming their status as true renunciants, dependent, like the monks, on alms. As in the East, the intended dynamic this creates is for lay people to provide food for the body, while monastics provide food for the mind.

As the number of women seeking ordination at Chithurst grew, most were transferred in the mid-1980s to Amaravati. Sister Candasiri clutches her hands tight under her armpits as she begins to talk of how things progressed from there. By 2000 the community of nuns had swollen to around two dozen, with women coming from elsewhere in Europe as well as from South Africa and the United States. 'Even though we were clearly still junior to the monks, attempts were made to downplay the disparities. But this was a time when real efforts towards gender equality were being made in wider western cultures, so when we began to talk about this within our monastic community it was not appreciated,' she says, appearing to choose her words carefully. 'For the monks, we nuns are an awkward phenomenon. Sometimes I think it would be easier for them if we didn't exist. In some ways we are a challenge to the situation in Thailand.'

When the nuns were then issued with the 'Five Point' ultimatum to accept their junior status or see the community of *siladhara* die out, most initially agreed to sign. But as time went by, some who had grown increasingly disenchanted at what they saw as their harsh treatment found the conflict impossible to reconcile with living as a practising nun; they took the decision to disrobe, preferring to practise Buddhism outside any institution. Others became wandering nuns with no fixed means of support. 'We were left with a very slender community and it was touch and go whether we would survive,' says Sister Candasiri, one hand slipping up to her head, the other remaining in a clenched fist.

Sister Candasiri says she stayed at Amaravati out of a sense of loyalty and also because she believes 'living in community with others who are following the same practice is like living with a mirror, forcing you to look at things you otherwise wouldn't, both within yourself and in those around you . . . it's both unbelievably painful and unbelievably powerful.'

Although the community of nuns is now slowly growing again, it is still at a 'very delicate stage', she says, explaining that she organized the purchase of the hermitage to provide the recovering order of nuns with an alternative place to practise, away from any restrictions imposed by monks. Though Sister Candasiri currently lives most of the time here alone, but for the assistance of a changing succession of lay helpers and visiting nuns, her intention is that this will eventually grow into a flourishing centre of female monasticism. She remains convinced that full ordination for women is 'inevitable, though it may not happen in my lifetime'.

'The aspiration of our Buddhist practice is towards harmlessness and moral integrity, to live with a sense of honour and provide an opportunity for people to hear the Buddhist teachings if they choose,' she continues. It is hard to view the way she and other women aspiring to full ordination have been treated by their monastic brothers as either honourable or harmless. But given the struggles of women in the Anglican Church to be consecrated as bishops, such treatment has a familiar ring.

When I ask what she feels the relevance of her hermit-like existence is in western society today, she describes her strict practice of Buddhist monasticism as 'a very powerful symbol'. 'Generally in this society there is a sense of people wanting to get as much of everything as possible, and yet this leaves so many miserable and confused,' she says. 'So it can be inspiring to know there are others living much more simply and according to clearly defined ethical guidelines.

'For me, the most useful thing I can do is to just be here as an encouragement towards certain values,' she goes on, stressing how everyone can benefit from a short daily meditation practice. 'You may not want to shave your head or live away from your telly and mobile phone. But everyone can spare a little time in the day to sit still and tend to their own mind and body,' she concludes. 'You don't have to be fully enlightened or have a mind that goes perfectly still every time you sit. Anyone can do it. You just start from where you are. Even from small beginnings you can feel benefit.'

Tucked away in this quiet corner of the Highlands, it might seem that Sister Candasiri and her hermitage could have only a limited impact on the wider community. But she believes otherwise. 'We act like yeast,' she says as she waves me farewell at the gates of Milntuim. 'It works very quietly in society, but it has an effect.'

14

'WE ARE PIONEERS!'

By sad coincidence, the nearest train station to my next destination is in the town of Lockerbie, a community, like Dunblane, marked by human tragedy. To the west of this small locality in the Scottish Lowlands lies a garden of remembrance to the 270 people killed in the terrorist attack on Pan Am Flight 103 on 21 December 1988.

But my route takes me in the opposite direction, north-east towards the small village of Eskdalemuir, where I quickly pick up road signs to Samye Ling Tibetan Buddhist Monastery. There is no mistaking it as my taxi approaches and a white stupa, eighteen metres high, suddenly emerges through the trees. A further eight smaller stupas line a driveway leading off the main road to a huddle of low buildings, behind which stands a grand temple built along traditional Tibetan lines: brightly coloured tiles circle its lower storeys and above this rises a gold-painted, winged pagoda roof. Despite the grandeur of its design, Samye Ling turns out to be a more compact complex than I had expected, given its sizeable reputation and long history.

Evening is drawing in as I arrive and the monks and nuns of Samye Ling are still seated in the temple, attending a special week-long service to celebrate the coming of the Tibetan New Year. Slipping in a side door of the temple, I settle myself at the back and watch the row of nuns seated to my left chanting in the rhythmical way I am now familiar with from my travels in India and Nepal. Closing my eyes, I am transported back to nunneries on the outskirts of Kathmandu and in the Tibetan refugee settlements around Dharamshala.

Samye Ling too was founded by Tibetan refugees fleeing the Chinese invasion of their homeland. Although the first influences of Buddhism in Britain followed the older Theravada tradition observed at Chithurst and Milntuim, Samye Ling was not only the UK's first full Buddhist monastery but also the first Tibetan Buddhist monastery in the West. Its founders, Chögyam Trungpa Rinpoche and Akong Rinpoche, both monks revered as reincarnated high lamas in Tibet, were first invited to England in the early 1960s, just a few years after escaping across the Himalayas. Of the 300 fleeing refugees in their group, only thirteen survived this perilous trek. Akong Rinpoche would later write of the hardships they suffered traversing the highest mountain range in the world, boiling leather shoes and shoulder bags to make soup, unsure who would be alive each morning.

It was Chögyam Trungpa's reputation as an outstanding scholar that led to the offer of a scholarship to study at Oxford University and, in the years that followed, the two monks were in great demand, giving talks around the country. In 1968, though still in their twenties, they were given the opportunity to found a monastic community on the site of what had once been a Theravada Buddhist meeting place in Scotland. From these small beginnings, Samye Ling grew to become a thriving centre of monasticism and Tibetan culture, which, by the 1990s, had a six-month waiting list of westerners wanting to ordain as monks and nuns.

Much of the early draw was the charismatic personality of Chögyam Trungpa, who turned out to be a brilliant, if unconventional, teacher. In the late 1960s, musicians David Bowie and Leonard Cohen were amongst those drawn to Samye Ling; Cohen later went on to ordain as a monk and Bowie reportedly came close. But as a descendent of the Karmapa's Kagyu lineage, Chögyam

Trungpa embodied what some call 'crazy wisdom'. With the hippie movement in full swing, he began taking a relaxed approach to spiritual enlightenment, eventually returning his monastic vows, marrying a young English aristocrat and turning to drink, drugs and free sex. On one drunken binge, he drove a car through the window of a practical-joke shop, an accident that would leave him partially paralyzed for the rest of his life. When his behaviour led to a rift at Samye Ling, he left and moved to the United States, where he dedicated himself to presenting Buddhist teachings, largely stripped of any eastern cultural trappings to make them more accessible to westerners. After Chögyam Trungpa's departure, Samye Ling was run for more than four decades by Akong Rinpoche and latterly by his younger brother, Lama Yeshe Losal Rinpoche, who took over as abbot in 1995 to allow his brother to devote more time to international humanitarian work under the umbrella of the Rokpa Trust he founded. It was this work that eventually led to Akong Rinpoche being murdered in Tibet, together with two other monks, apparently in a dispute over money, just a few months before my visit to Samye Ling.

As the evening service draws to a close I watch Lama Yeshe Losal file from the hall and sense a pervading sadness in all present. Treading lightly by his side is the slight figure of one of Samye Ling's most senior nuns. Ani Lhamo, a former computer programmer from Glasgow, became part of this order in her thirties, when Lama Yeshe broke with tradition by offering temporary ordination, not previously available in Tibetan Buddhism. The move drew growing numbers of westerners to take the first step to enter monastic orders but, unlike Ani Lhamo, many did not continue on the path. In order to maintain a more stable community, it was subsequently decided that this option should only be offered to those with a sincere intention of ordaining for life. This has meant the number of monks and nuns at Samye Ling has dwindled from several dozen at the turn of the millennium to a nucleus of around fifteen nuns, ranging in age from their early twenties to one in her eighties.

A particular feature of Samye Ling and other centres opened under the umbrella of the Rokpa Trust in London, Edinburgh and elsewhere in Europe and Africa is that many of its leading figures are women. Of the four westerners named as lamas, or master teachers, three are female. One, a Danish nun named Lama Zangmo, heads the centre in London; another, Lama Tsondru, oversees five centres in Spain. Since Lama Yeshe supports the full ordination of nuns, and was one of those who participated in the high-profile international ceremony held in Bodh Gaya, India, in 1998 to fully ordain novices in both the Theravada and Tibetan Buddhist traditions, several of Samye Ling's nuns are also fully ordained, including Ani Lhamo.

'We are pioneers!' Ani Lhamo says with a broad smile as we sit down to talk on my first evening at Samye Ling.

While much of the focus of those at this Scottish monastery is to make Buddhist teachings more widely available and to continue Rokpa's international humanitarian work, they also put great emphasis on long periods of contemplative retreat. Traditionally, these last for three years and three months, but at Samye Ling they have been extended to four years and are open to small numbers of devout lay practitioners. 'If Buddhism is to become a permanent fixture in this culture and society, there has to be a real spiritual depth amongst western people, not just Tibetan lamas, and the only way to achieve this is through this practice of retreat,' says Ani Lhamo.

Since the 1990s these lengthy retreats have been held in a series of converted lighthouse cottages on Holy Island, an islet off the west coast of Scotland purchased by the Rokpa Trust in 1992. Ani Lhamo, who completed one of the earliest long retreats, speaks at one point of the virtues of sleeping there in a meditation box, like the one Tenzin Palmo used during her twelve years in a cave in the Himalayas. She talks of the 'almost womb-like sense of security it instils' and the way it promotes lighter sleep, which, contrary to perceived wisdom, she describes as 'better for the mind'. 'In Buddhism there is a saying that sleep is the sleep of ignorance,' she tells me. 'In our modern, western culture we have an obsession with getting eight hours, but a lot of the time this is totally unnecessary.'

It is relatively rare that a lay person who has participated in a retreat will then want to commit to monastic life, but Ani Lhamo is convinced the path she followed has much to offer. 'For the right person, it is an ideal life.'

'Who do you feel is the right person?' I ask, even though I know it is a question to which there can be no simple answer.

'As I'm sure you've discovered, women who become nuns come from all walks of life!' she says in her Scottish lilt, and I recall my meetings with the princess, the pilot, the actress, the journalist, the celebrated composer, the policewoman and the writer of erotic fiction. 'Sometimes the most unlikely people become ordained and it's very successful,' she continues, pointing out that the Kagyu lineage to which Samye Ling belongs is often called 'the chaos lineage'. 'This is because it offers such opportunity for a wide range of people,' she says. 'One of its core practices is that every single second is seen as an opportunity, which means you're carrying no baggage from the past or expectations of the future. You're just in the moment. How free is that?'

My next encounter is with a woman who embodies this ethos of living purely in the present. Ani Rinchen Khandro, whom I meet the following evening, prefers not to dwell on her past, except to say, with refreshing bluntness, 'I surprise myself a bit by being a nun.' Some of the more high-profile aspects of her former life are, however, a matter of record. In the Swinging Sixties Jackie Glass, as she was then, worked as a model and became known for her striking resemblance to one of the world's first supermodels, Jean Shrimpton. For two years she was the girlfriend of soccer star George Best, at the time when he was named European Footballer of the Year. When I Google their names, a striking black-and-white photograph of them in profile pops up. The Manchester United winger has an unusually tender look about him as he looks into her eyes. Her long blonde hair frames stunning features.

At this time she was living in London and counted amongst her friends the French screenwriter Gerard Brach and the Polish film director Roman Polanski, who once asked her to help him choose clothes for his then-wife Sharon Tate, just weeks before the actress and four of her friends were murdered. As a budding writer, she once collaborated on a Hollywood movie and also wrote a hit single, before moving to Bali, where she designed clothes for export. On returning to England eight years later, she became a committed conservationist, working on film projects about endangered wildlife.

'But once I know I can do something, I lose interest,' Ani Rinchen Khandro says matter-of-factly about the whirlwind of youthful activity that came before her decision to ordain in her mid-forties. 'I've done a little of a lot of things in my life. But this is the only thing I've ever committed myself to for any length of time.'

Born in Manchester to an Irish Catholic mother and a Russian Jewish father, her upbringing was largely Jewish. But following the death of her mother and shortly afterwards that of her sister, just a few months before her own daughter was born, she started reading books about Buddhism. This interest deepened after she almost died from malaria while travelling. But it was not until she met Akong Rinpoche in the 1990s, and then attended a teaching given by the Dalai Lama at Samye Ling in 1993, that she began to feel drawn to life at the monastery. 'I didn't see myself becoming a nun at all,' she says. 'I don't like uniforms of any description and I didn't want to advertise what I believed. I thought it was my private business.'

The turning point came suddenly, when she realized she had the opportunity to take ordination vows with an eminent Tibetan meditation master paying a rare visit to Samye Ling. 'Much to my surprise, and everyone else's, I became ordained,' she says, pulling her maroon robes tighter across her shoulders. Only afterwards did she tell her grown-up daughter, with whom she says she has something of an Edina and Saffy '*Ab Fab* relationship'.

'I called her and told her, "I've had a rather radical haircut,"' she says, mimicking a sheepish voice.

'And what did she feel about it?' I ask.

'She was cross that I hadn't told her beforehand. She wasn't cross that I'd become a nun. We'd lived in Bali, so she was used to eastern spirituality. She just said, "At least I know where you are now and you're not gallivanting around the world,"' Ani Rinchen Khandro says with a raucous laugh.

As she talks I have the feeling of someone who became a nun almost in spite of herself, and tell her so. 'In spite of my ego, certainly, and I've never ever regretted it. Not only that, I've enjoyed it,' she says, her clear blue eyes and aquiline features growing increasingly animated.

'Do you know what I really feel about ordination?' she asks. 'My feeling is that if you are a very good person, you probably don't need to get ordained. But if you're someone like me, a bit adventurous, shall we say, it can be very helpful. The robes become your armour, the vows too. Once you've made a decision to take the vows, you don't have to think about it any more. Of course you have to keep them,' she says, with disarming candour. This is certainly an argument I've not heard before. 'Well, yes, that's because people have very preconceived ideas of what a nun is,' she says. 'What ordination gives you is the opposite of what most people would think. It gives you freedom. The only things that you give up are things that are not really beneficial for you.'

'What about relationships?' I ask, thinking back to my meeting with Beki.

'I'd been there and done that. I'd had long and precious relationships. But I was ready for something else. On the spiritual path, relationships are a distraction. I've always had a rebellious streak,' she goes on, talking again of the reputation the Kagyu lineage has for 'taming the untameable'. 'I'm still a rebel. I'm still funny. I still like a laugh. You don't go through a total personality change when you become a nun. You have to be authentic.'

Despite her jocular manner, the work she now does marks her out as a seasoned and serious practitioner. For many years, after completing a long meditation retreat, she oversaw the fundraising and course programme on Holy Island. Then, in 2008, she established, and now runs, the Kagyu Samye Dzong centre in Edinburgh, a thriving city-centre resource for anyone interested in Buddhism. She is also the honorary Buddhist chaplain to Edinburgh University, as well as a regular visitor to schools and hospitals, and is on various media panels, regularly debating faith on the BBC and in publications such as the *New Statesman*.

As the evening draws in and Ani Rinchen Khandro prepares to leave, I take a closer look at the pictures lining the walls of the formally designated 'Interview Room' where we have been talking. Amongst the photographs are several of celebrity supporters of the monastery, including singer Annie Lennox and comedian Billy Connolly, together with pictures of Prince Charles, Princess Anne, Mother Teresa, the Pope and the Archbishop of Canterbury in meetings with Akong Rinpoche and Lama Yeshe. The contrast between Samye Ling's mix of rock and royal backing and the low-key feel to places like Chithurst highlights the way Tibetan Buddhism has acquired a sheen of glamour in the West, making it one of the most widely recognized forms of Buddhist practice.

Away from the spotlight, however, there are aspects of what has happened as Buddhism has transferred to the West that many would prefer remained hidden. While in Scotland I had hoped to meet another former Tibetan Buddhist nun named June Campbell, author of a book called *Traveller in Space*, which was published in 1996 to a storm of publicity over some of its revelations. While the feeling I have, after speaking to Beki and one or two other former nuns I have met along the way, is that they stepped away from their ordained life with a certain sense of reluctance, I can only imagine that June Campbell did so with relief.

She ordained as a nun in the Kagyu tradition, to which Samye Ling belongs, while travelling in India in the 1970s. After living in a nunnery there, she became the personal translator to one of the most revered Tibetan Buddhist lamas in exile, Kalu Rinpoche, as he travelled through Europe and America. Though the book, subtitled 'In Search of Female Identity in Tibetan Buddhism', is a deeply academic treatise, in it she revealed that she had for years been Kalu

Rinpoche's secret sexual consort, or 'sky dancer'; she was told that if she ever disclosed the relationship, it would lead her to 'madness, trouble or even death'.

Trouble there certainly was. On one of the rare occasions when she has spoken publicly of her experience, during a lecture at a non-sectarian Buddhist college in Devon in the late 1990s, she described how she had been 'reviled as a liar or a demon'. To his devotees, Kalu Rinpoche was a reincarnated master. Before fleeing into exile, he had held an influential position as a high-ranking abbot of a monastery in western Tibet. By the time of his death in 1989, he had helped found dozens of teaching centres in the West, most notably in France, one of which has also been rocked recently by allegations of sexual misconduct by one of its resident lamas, who has since been dismissed.

In her book June Campbell writes an unsparing critique of some of the Tantric rituals in Tibetan Buddhism, the roots of which lie in India's ancient past and are based on powerful beliefs about the union of male and female energy required in order to be able to withstand any inner and outer turmoil. While monastics of lower status take vows of celibacy and confine themselves to visualizing imaginary sexual relationships during meditation, Campbell speaks of the belief of some Tibetan Buddhist masters that they are able to reach a point where they can engage in sex without being 'tainted' by it. While a lama would then be 'viewed publicly as a celibate monk', she writes, 'in reality he was frequently sexually active'. The reason such liaisons were invariably kept secret, she argues, was in order to keep control over the women involved, like herself, as well as to maintain the prestige and power of the Tibetan Buddhist lineage.

Both Tibet's image as a kind of lost paradise or Shangri-La and the Dalai Lama's reputation as a Nobel prize-winning champion of peace and human rights have done much to boost interest in Buddhism around the world. But the Dalai Lama himself has warned against being wooed into Tibetan Buddhism because of some exotic Tantric aura, with hints of arcane sexual practices. In recent years intimate revelations by Hollywood A-listers on the subject of Tantric sex have exposed a gap in understanding between westerners who crave physical gratification and those in the East who are steeped in ancient traditions that see sexual energy as something to be channelled into spiritual practice.

So, when June Campbell exposed the way in which such practices were abused, 'It was like claiming Mother Teresa was involved in making porn movies,' she told her Devon audience. The reason she took eighteen years to expose what had happened to her, she explained, was because it had taken her that long to overcome the trauma of the experience. Given the venom with which her revelations were received by some Buddhists, I do not hold out much hope that she will be willing to delve back into such a painful past, and when I do finally manage to speak to her on the phone, she declines a meeting. Since disrobing more than thirty years ago, she has carved out a new life for herself, working in Scotland as a psychotherapist. Even though I explain my interest is wider than what one newspaper described as her time as a 'tantric sex slave', she assumes this would be my focus and keeps our conversation brief. 'Everything I have to say on the subject is in my book,' she says in a soft but weary voice. 'That is as far as I wish to go. I wouldn't have anything further to add.'

During my own journey, I have not met any nuns who intimated that they had experience of abuse, but both before and since the publication of June Campbell's book, other sex scandals have emerged involving Buddhist teachers and their followers, particularly in the Tibetan and Zen traditions. In 1994 the high-profile lama Sogyal Rinpoche, author of the international bestseller *The Tibetan Book of Living and Dying*, was the subject of a $10 million civil lawsuit in the United States following allegations of sexual assault. The case was settled out of court with undisclosed damages paid, but rumours of alleged misconduct have continued since then. More recently, a number of Zen centres in the United States have been hit by allegations of repeated sexual misconduct by senior teachers, including one of the most revered Japanese masters, Joshu Sasaki, who migrated from Japan to California in the 1960s and became well known as the teacher of Leonard Cohen. After ordaining as a Buddhist monk, Cohen was inspired in his writing by Sasaki, whom he refers to simply as 'Roshi' in his 2006 poetry collection *Book of Longing*.

One reason such alleged abuse has often gone unchecked is because of the strong Buddhist caution against gossip and the emphasis on loyalty to teachers. It is no coincidence that there is a greater prevalence of alleged misconduct amongst those affiliated to the Tibetan and Zen Buddhist schools, both of which place particular importance on a student's commitment to, and personal relationship with, a teacher. Less emphasis on such a relationship exists in the Theravada tradition. In the case of Tibetan Buddhism, there are also the problems involved in the custom of taking boys, sometimes at a very young age, away from their mothers to begin monastic training. The psychological repercussions of being deprived of female influence at such a tender age are now well understood.

In the past the Dalai Lama has spoken movingly about how much he missed his mother and elder sister after leaving his family home in a remote corner of Tibet to receive monastic training at the Potala Palace in Lhasa following his recognition as a reborn *tulku* at the age of two. This was at a time when no woman was permitted within the walls of the cavernous Potala Palace after dark. The pain of such separation also hung in the air as I sat in the spacious private quarters of the Gyalwang Drukpa at his nunnery in Nepal. Listening to him extol the feminine virtues of love and compassion, I couldn't help but think of him as a small boy taken from his parents for training at a monastery where he was beaten for writing with his left hand.

The efforts the Gyalwang Drukpa is now making to empower the nuns in his care by encouraging their training in kung fu, along with the Dalai Lama's support for full female ordination and many of the other initiatives I have witnessed in individual nunneries, are all evidence of a growing appreciation of the feminine within the Buddhist leadership.

As Buddhism has evolved in the East and transferred to the West, gradual changes have taken place in the way both ordained and lay people engage with their practice, bringing it more in line with modern life and current social mores. To witness more evidence of this evolution, I travel on down through the Scottish Borders and on to a Zen Buddhist abbey on the windswept moors of Northumberland.

15

'ZEN IS NOT A SPECTATOR SPORT'

As the train travels south, hugging the wild coastline of Northumberland, I am captivated by its landscape of hidden coves, ruined castles and wild headlands crowned with circling gulls. In the distance lies another Holy Island: this one the ancient tidal isle of Lindisfarne, where the ruins of a Christian priory are silhouetted by the setting sun. Such threads of contemplative history seem to loop back and forth across my path as if weaving an invisible meditative net.

Though firmly based in Japanese Soto Zen, the tradition to which those at my next destination belong is quite uniquely western in style. The monastic community at its core is known as the Order of Buddhist Contemplatives. Theirs is a path of practice developed relatively recently by an indomitable English church organist turned Buddhist nun, which is now followed by an expanding group of Zen Buddhists in both Europe and North America. Their principal UK base is Throssel Hole Abbey, a monastery and retreat centre in the northern Pennines, to which I travel onwards by taxi. Turning off the main road, the taxi takes me through wooded valleys and exposed slopes before a winding drive, lined with towering pines, leads up to what looks at first like a traditional farmhouse with outlying cottages. But in amongst this collection of old buildings, a modern elevated meditation hall has been built. When I arrive, I find a small group of laywomen and men already gathered ready for an evening service and meditation session here. Joining them, I climb the stairs to the hall and we sit in traditional Zen fashion facing the wall.

After a period of silence, the thudding of a great drum signals the arrival of the resident monastic community. My eyes are closed and I am still turned away from the centre of the room. But then singing that would not sound out of place in a Christian monastery fills the hall. The sacred harmony is sung in the style of Gregorian plainchant. Only the words, ancient Buddhist texts translated into English, make it clear this is something quite different. Opening my eyes and turning, I see two rows of women and men wearing traditional black and brown Zen monastic robes with purple, black or saffron-coloured *kesa* cloaks fastened across their shoulders.

In this tradition, as in some others linked with Japanese Zen, both men and women are known as monks, though here they are also referred to as 'Reverend', again echoing Christian tradition. Even the terms used in the daily programme of worship conform more to Christian custom, the earliest being Morning Office and the last Vespers. I also notice that the golden Buddha statue the monks bow to as they file from the hall at the end of the service has western facial features, instead of the usual oriental ones. When I am shown later to my room in a converted annex, I pass along corridors where I see this is true of all the Buddha images tucked in alcoves and on shelves throughout the abbey.

All these western variations bear testimony to the particular, and often difficult, spiritual path of its founder, Reverend Master Jiyu-Kennett, both during the time she studied in Japan and on her return to the West. Born Peggy Kennett in the south of England in the 1920s, her childhood was overshadowed by the Second World War and the loss of her best friend, who drowned after becoming entangled in barbed wire strung up for defence across a beach in Sussex. The sight of the Sussex night sky stained red from the glow of far-off London ablaze during the Blitz is said to have stayed with her throughout her life. She first became interested in Buddhism through reading Edwin Arnold's *The Light of Asia*, and afterwards met and studied with many of the Buddhist teachers who visited London in the 1950s. Her professional training was as a musician and she worked for some time as a church organist. But then, in 1960, she was invited by a visiting Japanese Zen master to study in Japan and whilst there decided to ordain and begin monastic training.

As the only woman, and a western one at that, training with several hundred monks in a deeply patriarchal society that had suffered at the hands of Allied western forces, she received harsh treatment. But her spiritual accomplishment was quickly recognized. At the age of forty, she was appointed abbess of a small Japanese temple. Shortly after this, in anticipation of her returning to London, she was the first woman appointed by the Soto school to teach in the West and was named Soto Zen Bishop of London. But Britain also proved less than welcoming. The founder and president of the London Buddhist Society at the time, Christmas Humphreys, resisted her appointment, saying he wanted a 'real' Zen master, the assumption being that this master would be both male and Japanese.

Jiyu-Kennett decided to relocate to California, where Zen Buddhism was already flourishing, and in 1970 founded a training monastery called Shasta Abbey. It was only then, in 1973, that Throssel Hole was established by a group of British Buddhists inspired by her way of teaching. Much of the draw was her emphasis on making Buddhist practice more accessible to westerners, largely through translating texts into English and setting some to music, while at the same time retaining much of the discipline and tradition of Japanese Zen. Jiyu-Kennett died in 1996, but a number of smaller priories, temples and meditation groups following her Serene Reflection Meditation tradition have been established in different parts of the UK. This tradition is just one of many that is now flourishing in Britain in response to a growing interest in Buddhism, and while few might connect their interest with early pioneers of its teachings reaching the West, the influence of women like Jiyu-Kennett is both subtle and undeniable. As I wait on a crisp bright morning to speak to one of her female monastic heirs, I stand for some time before a large portrait of her hanging in Throssel Hole's dining hall. It shows a large woman, with an ample chin and girth and an expression of quiet determination. Looking back on my time at Nisodo in Japan, I reflect on how different her experience was from that of those receiving Zen monastic training there today.

I am then joined by Reverend Olwen, a senior monk and former music teacher, in her mid-fifties, who explains Jiyu-Kennett's legacy: 'Through having her as our founder, we have a strong sense of what's known in the tradition as "old woman Zen". This is a form of Zen which is very compassionate, has a certain softness and a sympathetic heart,' she explains. Earlier that day, during the morning service, I have seen Reverend Olwen standing at the front of the temple with a rather stern expression and a striking crimson tassel hanging from one shoulder, denoting her official standing as a Zen master. But in person, she is friendly and informal, settling into an easy chair in one of the adjacent cottages to talk about the practice here.

'One of the phrases in our texts talks about how Buddhism only lasts as long as bowing lasts,' she says, explaining that this isn't meant to signify a blind kowtowing to authority, but rather a respect and recognition that there are those who have travelled further along the path of understanding and practising Buddhist teachings. Monks like Reverend Olwen, who have followed in Jiyu-Kennett's wake, focus their efforts on meditation and giving guidance and teachings in small groups; theirs is not a practice that emphasizes wider work in the community – rather, it involves giving instruction on an individual basis.

'Our practice does not have bells and whistles in the same way that some others do,' says Reverend Olwen, whose own upbringing by Quaker parents accustomed her to a more simple tradition. 'It's never going to appeal to a lot of people. Zen is not a spectator sport. It's very undramatic,' she concludes. 'But sitting practice is an extraordinary practice and it takes years to come near the depth of what it is.'

The intimate nature of this approach reminds me of Sister Candasiri's metaphor of Buddhism acting 'quietly … like yeast' within society, and I see its appeal as a counterpoint to our turbulent, driven, instant-fix modern culture. There are, however, other traditions taking root in the West whose monastic life is focused on what has come to be known as 'Engaged Buddhism'. To visit the centre whose founder first coined this term, a place where such a practice lies at the heart of a thriving community of monks and nuns, I must cross the Channel, to the halcyon depths of rural south-west France.

PART VII

FRANCE

16

QUIET REVOLUTIONS

Travelling eastwards from Bordeaux, away from the Atlantic coast, the route I take inland follows the course of the Dordogne River. A low afternoon sun casts long shadows across the rolling landscape as I drive on through this region world famous for its wines. Though this land was, for centuries, a battleground between the French and English, in recent years the Dordogne has seen a more peaceful invasion of '*les Rosbifs*', with thousands crossing the Channel every year from Britain to settle here permanently or pass the summer months. At the height of the tourist season, it is a case of '*cherchez les Français*', says one local shopkeeper when I stop to ask directions. With a shrug of her shoulders, she then points the way to my next destination, a loose cluster of monastery buildings spread over hills and quiet valleys, known collectively as Le Village des Pruniers, or Plum Village.

The community was founded by Vietnamese Zen Master Thích Nhất Hạnh, who was nominated as a Nobel peace laureate in 1967 for his global efforts to end the escalating carnage in his homeland. That year no peace award was made. The Nobel committee deemed protocol had been contravened because Martin Luther King Jr openly lobbied for Thích Nhất Hạnh, saying he knew of no one more worthy of the prize 'than this gentle monk from Vietnam', whose ideas for peace, he said, if applied, 'would build a monument to ecumenism, to world brotherhood, to humanity'. Vietnam's warlords did not agree. Afraid of the devotion Thích Nhất Hạnh inspired, they banished him from his homeland, refusing to allow him to return even after peace accords were signed. Since then, he has lived in exile in France.

After first founding a meditation centre close to Paris in the mid-1970s, Thích Nhất Hạnh sought more space in which to establish a monastery and place of retreat for the growing number of lay practitioners drawn to his clear and gentle way of transmitting profound Buddhist teachings. In search of cheaper land, he travelled south, in the company of a fellow peace activist who later ordained as a nun, Sister Chân Không. When the slight Vietnamese and his follower found themselves lifted off their feet by the strong mistral winds of Provence, they journeyed further west to the borders of Dordogne and Lot et Garonne. Here, over the past three decades, nestled in a string of hamlets close to the medieval town of Duras, they have established a monastic community that is the hub of global efforts to apply Buddhist teachings to the challenges of modern life.

By day, the silent figures of nuns and monks from Plum Village can be seen treading along the verges of these narrow country lanes as they make their way from one hamlet to another. Their silhouettes are unmistakable, with earth-brown robes sweeping close to the ground and conical Vietnamese *nón lá* hats to shield them from the sun and rain.

More than 150 nuns and monks live here and more than half are from Vietnam. Many are still in their teens or early twenties, having fled to France in recent years following a crackdown on religious freedom by Vietnam's communist government. But several dozen of the nuns at Plum Village are western women who have given up full and varied lives to follow Thích Nhất Hạnh's monastic path. Amongst them are a former aide to the mayor of Washington, DC, a former concert violinist with the Mahler Chamber Orchestra, and a former BBC news journalist who came to Plum Village with her boyfriend while still in her twenties, after which both she and her boyfriend ordained. The linchpin of the community is Sister Chân Không, now a revered teacher in her own right.

Before agreeing to speak to me, the sisters of Plum Village had asked that I gain some familiarity with their practice by attending one of their annual summer retreats, a core event in the Engaged Buddhism of the community. Every year thousands of lay people from all over the world flock to this quiet corner of the Dordogne to practise meditation and listen to talks given by Thích Nhất Hạnh, or Thây, meaning teacher, as he is often called. During these summer retreats, however, the monks and nuns are so busy cooking and caring for guests they have little time to sit in conversation. The lightness with which they juggle these demands, all performed with what they describe as 'mindful presence', is reflected in the terms they use to describe their daily duties: cleaning chores, for instance, are called 'household delights'.

Apart from the periods set aside for meditation, I found the busy pace of this summer retreat affords little time for reflection. In the morning I used to get up early to enjoy the company of a solitary nun signalling the start of the day by striking a giant bell in an open-sided Vietnamese-style pagoda. As she pulled at a heavy shaft of wood to strike it against the metal her chants of a chosen sutra would echo through the grounds and surrounding plum orchards with perfect clarity.

Now I have returned and the crowds are gone. It is nearly dark by the time I step through the iron gates of the old manor and out-buildings that house the forty sisters at New Hamlet on the outskirts of the small village of Dieulivol. To my left I can just make out the inky water of a small pond, where the stalks of withered lotus flowers are swaying gently in the wind. The last time I was here, this pond was lush with lotus flowers in full bloom.

After setting a time for my meeting the following morning with Sister Chân Không, I settle down to finish reading a book she wrote many years ago about her life so that I won't have to ask her to repeat too many biographical details. During the summer retreat, I had only been able to observe Sister Chân Không at a distance, but in the guided meditations she led I was struck by her crystal-clear singing voice, which seemed to belong to a much younger woman, and her gentle delivery of instructions reminding all present to relax and return to their true feelings. But I sensed a harder edge, a steely determination and a certain impatience in her too. I read long into the night to understand more of what she had been through.

The next morning I am ushered into Sister Chân Không's small spartan room close to the kitchen in New Hamlet and am met by a sweet smile and soft eyes in an almost cherubic moon face. But she quickly announces that she has little time to talk and my hunch that she is a woman who prefers action to words is confirmed. Almost immediately after we begin speaking, Sister Chân Không closes her eyes and falls silent at the sound of a bell chiming in the dining room. It does so every fifteen minutes throughout the day and night at Plum Village as a reminder to all who hear it to stop for a few moments and become present.

In these moments I glance around the small room in which we sit and notice above her bed a sign with calligraphy, written in French, in Thích Nhất Hạnh's distinctive thick brush strokes that reads: '*Les larmes que je versais hier sont devenues pluie*' – the tears that I shed yesterday have become rain. I cannot help but think back over what I had learned the previous evening of her history.

Born into a large family in the Mekong Delta in 1938, Sister Chân

Không spent much of her youth helping the needy in the slums of Saigon. As a bright schoolgirl, she tutored wealthy pupils in order to be able to buy food for the poor. Later, as a student leader, she spent much of her time working to improve the lives of the sick and dispossessed. Even before she committed herself to the Buddhist path, she felt an early yearning to become a nun, but was disillusioned by the narrow views of Buddhist priests who viewed her good work as a way of simply earning merit to benefit her in future lives. 'With all the generous work that you do, you will be reborn into a wealthy family. Perhaps you will be a princess,' one told her. Another suggested her good fortune would be to be reborn as a man.

Alienated by such attitudes, Sister Chân Không continued to concentrate her efforts on social work. But when, in 1959, she met Thích Nhất Hạnh, she felt she had found her true teacher. Thích Nhất Hạnh was then in his early thirties and had been a monk since his teens. At the time, the Vietnam War was gathering pace and he was already drawing many supporters through his visions for peace and the development of pioneer villages dedicated to social harmony. Together with Sister Chân Không, who quickly became his devoted follower and co-worker, he went on to found a Buddhist university and a grass-roots organization rallying thousands of students to help rebuild bombed villages, resettle homeless families, organize agricultural cooperatives and set up schools and medical centres.

As Vietnam descended deeper into the war that pitted the communist North against the US-backed South, the persecution of Buddhists by South Vietnam's Catholic government led to the first acts of self-immolation. On one June morning in 1963, Sister Chân Không happened to be riding her motorbike past the street junction in Saigon where the Buddhist monk Thích Quảng Đức chose to set himself alight to focus international attention on the conflict. 'I witnessed him sitting bravely and peacefully, enveloped in flames. He was completely still, while those of us around him were crying and prostrating ourselves on the sidewalk,' Sister Chân Không wrote of that agonizing day. When film footage of the monk's final moments was shown around the world, pressure on the regime of Ngô Đinh Diệm to introduce reforms increased. But there was little respite. The conflict continued to escalate.

Four years after the monk killed himself, one of Sister Chân Không's closest friends, a teacher, chose to do the same. After writing a letter calling for Catholics and Buddhists to work together, the young woman sat on the steps of a pagoda, with both a Buddhist statue and one of the Virgin Mary in front of her, and set herself alight. Writing movingly of this many years later, Sister Chân Không describes the death of her friend as one of the greatest sorrows of her life, an act that left her immersed in sadness. But it is one she also defends, saying, 'When you want something ordinary, you can just go out and buy it, but when you want something extraordinary, like love, understanding and peace for a whole nation, you have to pay for it with something more precious than money.'

After witnessing the emotional repercussions of the immolations carried out more recently by Tibetan Buddhist nuns, I fear stirring memories by raising the subject, but when I ask her what she feels about such protests, she closes her eyes and breathes deeply before speaking with firm conviction. 'Immolation can reach the attention of many people. One life is lost, but many people around the world take notice,' she says, in a slow, clear voice. 'If what is in the heart of the person who immolates is widely known, then this can move many others.'

The same year that Sister Chân Không's friend committed suicide, seven fellow social workers were abducted and killed. Helping the poor was considered a communist activity, and those who worked to bring about non-violent social change had many enemies. In the late 1960s Sister Chân Không left Vietnam to join Thích Nhất Hạnh campaigning in the West for peace. It would be another forty years before either would set foot in their homeland again. Although Sister Chân Không had been living a monastic life committed to celibacy for more than two decades, it was not until 1988 that she asked formally to be ordained by Thích Nhất Hạnh, receiving her monastic name, which translates as Sister True Emptiness. While the word 'emptiness' carries a negative emotional undertone in English, its meaning comes from the essence of Buddhist teaching that all life and living beings are profoundly interconnected and so 'empty of a separate self'. This teaching lies at the heart of Thích Nhất Hạnh's Order of Interbeing, established at the height of the Vietnam War.

Out of this war-torn background, this deep philosophy of interconnectedness evolved into the practice of Engaged Buddhism. Given its potent origins, it is little wonder that the Order of Interbeing attracts so many dynamic characters from diverse backgrounds. But Sister Chân Không is keen to stress that the focus of this practice is not only on its work in the wider community but also on helping people find peace within themselves. 'People think that Engaged Buddhism is only about social work and stopping war. But at the same time that you stop the war outside, you have to stop the war inside yourself,' she explains, her own life proof that suffering can be transformed into enlightenment through mindfulness.

At Plum Village they teach this discipline through practical techniques and exercises; central amongst them is the simple act of conscious breathing, practised by the Buddha until he died. 'Thây is the only one who really teaches us how to deal with strong emotions like anger. In other monasteries they may say, "Don't be angry. Let go." But let go how when a situation is so bad?' asks Sister Chân Không, before continuing: 'Thây brings us back to the teaching of the Buddha; that you have to touch the Buddha in you, your own peace, by constantly coming back to the in-breath and out-breath. This helps you disassociate from anger and fear. It brings you back to the present moment.'

A bell is chiming again in the dining room and I know my brief time with Sister Chân Không is at an end. Before leaving, she closes her eyes once more. I close mine too and feel a moment of shared peace.

A little later I sit to the side of the meditation hall at New Hamlet and watch Sister Chân Không walking serenely beside Thích Nhất Hạnh as he leads the entire monastic community into a formal lunch. She treads one step behind him as a sign of respect, and, lined up in single file behind her, in order of the number of years they have been ordained, are all the sisters of Plum Village. They walk side by side with the community's monks, who are lined up similarly, in order of seniority, behind Thích Nhất Hạnh. Walking shoulder to shoulder as they enter the hall, the nuns file off to the left, the monks to the right, and both groups sit facing each other as they eat a simple meal in silence. Given the belief still prevalent in some communities that a Buddhist nun, no matter how many years she has been practising, should defer to a monk, no matter how young or inexperienced, this seemingly unexceptional scene represents a quiet revolution.

*

The following morning I sit talking about the gender inequality that runs through the history of Buddhism with one of the nuns at Plum Village and she throws back her head in amusement at how outmoded such beliefs now seem. Sister Peace works in the administration office of New Hamlet, helping to ensure the smooth running of the community, a task for which she is well qualified after many years spent in the crucible of American politics. 'I'm glad I didn't know about those old customs when I first became interested in Buddhism, otherwise I could have been turned off completely,' she says, regaining her composure. 'Can you imagine this western girl growing up as an "urban urgent" in Washington, DC being considered in any way "less than"?'

Looking at the warm and confident African-American woman sitting opposite me, her dark eyes shining as she speaks, it is inconceivable. Some years ago Sister Peace wrote a moving article about her ancestors' experience of slavery. In it she talks of the internal struggle she felt when she first came to wear the simple brown headscarf that nuns at Plum Village sometimes tie around their shaven heads. For Sister Peace it carried echoes of the now-abandoned trademark of the Aunt Jemima baking products, showing a stereotyped image from the American South of a smiling African-American domestic servant, head wrapped in a cloth bandana. Her own grandmother had worked all her life as 'the help' in an antebellum mansion in Virginia, and the generations before that had been 'house slaves'.

Her own path through life was a far cry from such servitude. Born in Washington, DC, one of six children in a Baptist family that converted to Catholicism, she had, she says, 'a high resistance' to religion when she was growing up. 'Every Sunday we had to get up to go to Mass and I'd tell my mom, "They say God's everywhere, so

I don't need to go to church." She'd shout up, "You get your lazy butt out of bed!" And off we'd go,' she recalls with more hearty laughter.

But after graduating from Georgetown University with a business studies degree and setting up her own small beauty business, she started asking herself, 'Is this it?' She was convinced there must be more to life, and a spiritual seeking began. The stance of the Catholic Church on such issues as divorce and abortion meant that she began enquiring gradually into other spiritual traditions. Then her life took a different turn. After being invited to help with the grass-roots campaign of a candidate for the position of mayor of the District of Columbia, she became immersed in Washington's all-pervading creed of politics. Once he was elected, she continued to work for his administration, and became deputy campaign manager when he ran for a second term. 'But after about ten years I was getting tired of the power play,' she says. 'I started peeling off. I was disillusioned, exhausted. I'd given everything I had. I was left spiritually bereft.'

Through her spiritual enquiry she had come into contact with the teachings of Thích Nhất Hạnh and when she heard he was to hold his first retreat for people of colour at Deer Park in California, one of three American monastic communities affiliated to Plum Village, she signed up. The experience was, she says, 'life-changing'. In a documentary made of the gathering, which I watch after we meet, it is just possible at the end to make out her immaculately groomed figure as she embraces others there with a look of calm wonder on her face.

In the years that followed she dedicated more and more time to attending Buddhist teachings and gatherings. When in 2005 Thích Nhất Hạnh made his historic first return visit to Vietnam since having been banned from his homeland, she joined the group of lay followers, monks and nuns who accompanied him. The deep joy on the faces of thousands of Vietnamese who came to greet the Zen master as he stepped from the plane left an indelible impression on her. The visit took place at the time of the Vietnamese New Year, when it is customary for oracle readings to be given at Buddhist temples. That day she was given a red envelope containing a message that read: 'Why do you need to bother yourself with red dust [earthly affairs] when everything you need is here behind the temple walls?'

With this message, a seed was sown. In the months following her return to Washington she began to progress towards what is known as 'release': the process by which those interested in ordaining settle their worldly affairs, or 'red dust', by closing bank accounts and giving away their belongs. To prevent any conflict of interest and avoid aspirants believing they are somehow 'owed something' by the monastic communities they wish to join, the Buddhist tradition is that these worldly goods be given away elsewhere.

In June 2006 Sister Peace flew to France to attend a summer retreat at Plum Village; when it ended, she stayed on and wrote a letter of aspiration to become a nun. 'I had found something that resonated with me deeply,' she says. 'I thought, "Why wait?"' She was forty-nine. Today Sister Peace says she wears her brown headscarf with a deep appreciation that it was the determination of her forebears to survive and overcome servitude that has enabled her to lead the life she does. Any hint of discrimination against her as a woman following the monastic path would clearly have been anathema. The ordination precepts taken by both the nuns and the monks in Thích Nhất Hạnh's Order of Interbeing are the same, without any of the additional vows required of nuns in some lineages.

'Here monks and nuns get the same training,' she says. 'It's just one of the ways Thây has been revolutionizing Buddhism. He is constantly opening doors, keeping the dharma current, making teachings that are more than 2,000 years old relevant to what is happening today.'

Late that evening I stand in the moonlight in the grounds of New Hamlet, listening once more to a young nun striking the giant bell that signals silence will be observed until the following morning. As I pass the administration office I see Sister Peace, shoulders bent over a computer, making preparations for Thích Nhất Hạnh's next teaching tour. Though in his late eighties at the time of my visit, he still spends several months a year leading retreats in mindfulness around the world, accompanied by an entourage of monks and nuns. He is now regarded as one of the most popular Zen Buddhist masters of all time, and his teachings reach many more than those who read his books or attend his meetings. Instant access afforded by live streaming of such events on the internet, together with other uses of new media, has now opened his public talks up to millions.

One of those in this monastic community well qualified to understand the power of the media is the former BBC journalist Sister Natasha, who, like Sister Peace, grappled with a fast-paced professional career before choosing to ordain. Sister Natasha asks that we meet outside the dining hall of Lower Hamlet the following day so that I might join the nuns there in a silent walking meditation before we speak. The sun is shining as we set off along a country lane that winds through gentle hills. Treading slowly and in silence, I am struck by how much more I notice than I would were I walking at my normal fast pace: the glint of light on a stream running beside the path, the way a breeze ruffles the manes of horses grazing in a field beyond, the sound of birdsong, bells ringing in the distance.

'What better way to begin our meeting?' Sister Natasha says with a broad smile as we settle later on cushions she has arranged in one corner of a spacious meditation hall filled with golden light from a large stained-glass window. Sister Natasha has brought two nuns with her, the quietly spoken abbess of Lower Hamlet, Sister Jina, who stays mostly silent, and Sister Tri, from Australia. After laying out delicate cups and a pot of green tea, the three women sit in silence for a short while and I sense the familiar reticence. Speaking about themselves is something most have become unaccustomed to. One of the Buddhist practices particularly cherished at Plum Village is that of deep listening: listening not so much with the ears, as with the heart and complete presence.

But, slowly, Sister Natasha begins to explain what led her to ordain and it is clear she had a deeply questioning nature from a young age. She remembers, for instance, as a teenager, 'trying to understand life, asking questions like "What's all this about?"' She says this with a wide smile lighting up her striking features. 'I felt I was getting swept along on this conveyor belt that we all get caught on, until I realized you couldn't find the answers in books.' Her keen intellect led her to study history and political philosophy at Cambridge University, followed by a further degree in women's history at London's Royal Holloway College. 'I had a great time at Cambridge,' she says. 'I was involved in theatre, sport, a lot of activities. But by the end I felt I hadn't really learnt anything important about life. I felt very short-changed.'

Sister Natasha first came to Plum Village on a summer retreat in her early twenties after hearing about the monastic community from friends. Despite reservations about what spiritual seeking might involve, she was struck by how 'authentic and normal people here were, very international', she says. 'It was a very peaceful place, full of joy, with very helpful practices of breathing, walking meditation, looking deeply. It was the first time I came into contact with the nuns here and I remember thinking, "Ah ha, so there are wise women in the world and I've found them!"'

After returning to London, she started working for the BBC, both in the newsroom and as a researcher. It was 2003 and the Iraq War was in its early stages. The environment, both at work and politically in the UK, where there was mass public opposition to the war, was 'toxic', she says. 'It was certainly not conducive to wisdom, clarity or compassion.' Within three years, she had asked for sabbatical leave to return for an extended stay at Plum Village, though, at the time, she had no intention of becoming ordained.

But within a few months of returning to France, she began to feel an extended stay as a lay practitioner was not enough. 'I was blessed with a happy relationship and I think that is what kept me following the lay path as long as I did,' she continues. 'But I began to realize that the monastic life would offer me the chance to devote myself 100 per cent to the path I wanted to follow.' When she discussed it with her boyfriend, who had also spent time at Plum Village, both decided they would seek ordination. 'It was one conversation. Very easy,' she says, as if the couple had been having a casual conversation about choosing a holiday destination.

It seems incredible that such a momentous decision could have been reached so easily, and I press her to explain. 'Even in healthy relationships there is some kind of limitation,' she says. 'It had become clear that neither I nor he could fit into this box of two people any more, that our wish to practise, to learn and connect with others, was greater than that. So together we made this decision to liberate ourselves from the attachment of the relationship and continue our path as spiritual companions.'

'How has that been?' I ask.

'I am very happy. I feel very lucky. By becoming a nun, I didn't feel I was checking out of life in any way,' she says. 'The decision to ordain was not an outward decision that I wanted to live away from England or live a celibate life. It was a choice made to understand life and understand myself, to heal, transform, learn, and do it in such a way that I can share this with others.'

After resigning from the BBC, she took the vows of a novice in 2008 and three years later became fully ordained. Sister Natasha is thirty-two when we meet. I wonder if it was hard for her to let go of the prospect of becoming a mother, but it seems she had made up her mind about this much earlier. 'I remember thinking when I was a teenager, "How can people have children when they don't know about life?"' she says. Now, much of the work she concentrates on at Plum Village involves an international programme fostering mindfulness in young people, both through retreats and through the introduction of mindfulness and applied ethics in schools. This programme is coordinated through another centre founded by Thích Nhất Hạnh called the European Institute of Applied Buddhism, or EIAB, close to Cologne in Germany.

From the passion with which she speaks about her chosen path, it seems the number of people Sister Natasha will touch through such teachings will outweigh any number she might have influenced by continuing to work in the media. But in the years since she became a nun, she has maintained contact with some former colleagues at the BBC, who have recently asked her to return to teach mindfulness workshops there.

Throughout most of the time I talk with Sister Natasha, the other two nuns in her company remain quiet, listening. Sister Jina describes herself as a private person and deftly diverts most questions I ask of her towards the younger two women. Before becoming a nun, Sister Tri had been married in Australia before moving to Europe and living for many years in Switzerland. During this time she practised *zazen* in the Japanese Zen tradition and attended meditation retreats that emphasized long hours of sitting meditation practice. But she found this led to only temporary feelings of euphoria that were not sustainable in her daily working life. Following the death of her sister in a plane crash in Australia in 2003, she says she found the emphasis placed on community living in Plum Village and the practice of mindfulness in all aspects of daily life far more supportive for ongoing personal transformation and peace.

Over the next four years she visited Plum Village many times and says the aspiration to ordain emerged gradually. 'It was the lightness and joy I saw in the faces of the sisters that convinced me,' she says. 'It showed me that happiness was possible. I wanted to be like them. I wanted the joy I saw in their lives in my life too.' Although Sister Tri was in her late forties at the time, she had no doubts that this was the path she wanted to follow. At Plum Village the age limit for ordination is currently set at fifty, partly, I am told, so that it is not viewed as a 'retirement option'. Most of the sisters here become fully ordained while still young, in their twenties or thirties. But in recent years the possibility of temporary ordination for a period of five years has also been introduced to give young people who are unsure, or unable to commit to a lifetime calling, the opportunity to live the life of a Zen nun, or monk, for a limited period of time.

Sister Tri is fifty-three when we meet and she describes the four years since she ordained as the happiest of her life. Like Sister Natasha, she too now devotes much of her time to the programme promoting mindfulness and applied ethics in education. 'People think the life of a nun is a joyless one of frustration and renunciation, with no friends and no fun. But it is the exact opposite,' she says with a laugh, as we prepare to part. 'If more people knew what life was really like at Plum Village, they would flock here.'

The light is beginning to fade in the large hall where we sit and it is time for the three sisters to return to their duties. As I drive away from the cluster of low stone buildings that make up Lower Hamlet, I reflect on Sister Tri's words. For those able to withstand the rigours of community living and an unrelenting timetable with no recourse to most usual forms of entertainment, I can see the appeal. From a monastic point of view, the sense of inner freedom such a life affords more than compensates for the difficulties. But the path is far from easy.

Only one of the nuns I meet at Plum Village seems to have envisaged a quieter, more contemplative life than the frequently busy schedule of this outward-looking community. Sister Trai is the slight, swaying figure who can often be seen standing close to Thích Nhất Hạnh, violin tucked under her chin, accompanying the nuns and monks on stage, during the teachings and retreats he leads around the world. But this is not the music that Sister Trai trained most of her life to play.

It is a cold afternoon when we meet and we seek the warmth of cushions close to a radiator in the old manor house at New Hamlet. At first, Sister Trai talks hesitantly about her past. Born Akemi Uchida, in Texas, to Japanese parents, she was taken back to Japan as an infant and spent the early part of her childhood there. When she was thirteen years old, her father urged her mother to take their daughter back to the United States to be educated. It was an excuse to leave him free to pursue an affair. For nearly twenty years father and daughter would have no contact.

Akemi sought solace in music. She had begun to play the violin at the age of five and in her mid-twenties moved to Europe to pursue post-graduate studies before joining an orchestra, first in Athens, then the Mahler Chamber Orchestra in Berlin. For several years she played in concerts all over the world. A photograph from those days shows Akemi cradling the neck of her violin against a dark purple silk blouse, her head tilted to one side with a wistful smile, her face framed by lustrous dark hair.

'I was enjoying my career. I felt I was doing exactly what I wanted to do. I wanted to create something beautiful and see how far I could reach as a violinist,' she says, her hair now shaven, but the warm smile and dimpled cheeks the same. 'It was a glamorous and colourful lifestyle. I had relationships, though none very deep. But there was a lot of pressure and stress to always stay on top.'

Her smile fades as she goes on to talk of the turning point in her life when she was in her late twenties and her mother was diagnosed with breast cancer. She returned then to the United States to care for her until she died. 'My mother's death was life-changing,' she says, and I feel a pang of recognition. 'I had contemplated death and impermanence before, but it is completely different when someone close to you is dying. Many of the things that I used to think mattered – career, status – I realized then didn't matter much at all.'

Some years earlier, she had been struck by a quote from Plato, which she wrote on a slip of paper and still keeps: 'It is not he who produces a beautiful harmony in playing the lyre or other instruments whom one should consider as the true musician, but he who knows how to make of his own life a perfect harmony in establishing an accord between his feelings, his words and his acts.' After her mother died, the meaning of this became unbearably poignant. 'Every musician knows about creating harmony on stage. But if you don't have inner harmony, then what sense is there?' she continues. 'For me, performing had been a spiritual experience in some ways, a way of going deep within, contacting the beauty of life, having a conversation with myself.'

But in the years following her mother's death, these internal conversations took her in a different direction. Frustrated at not having been able to do more to alleviate her mother's suffering, and determined to do more to help others, she first trained as a yoga teacher and for a couple of years combined teaching yoga with concert work. She also started a period of spiritual enquiry. Growing up in Japan, she had been influenced by what she describes as 'the pervading allergy to religion'. But, increasingly, her interest turned to Buddhist teachings, and a chance conversation with another member of the orchestra brought her on her first visit to Plum Village. 'I immediately felt at home with the whole energy of the place,' she says.

Following her mother's death, she also went in search of her father in Japan. 'I felt I needed reconciliation to find peace,' she says. She found her father bankrupt and abandoned by his girlfriend, who had left him to look after their child. 'But my father was not a person who was able to talk. After all that time, he behaved as if nothing had happened,' she recalls. While in Japan, Akemi visited Nisodo nunnery but did not feel drawn to its strict regime and emphasis on ritual. Returning to Berlin, she continued with her music. But a few months later her father was also diagnosed with terminal cancer and she flew back to Japan to be by his side.

'When I came into the hospital room, he broke into tears and kept apologizing for all the suffering he had caused. I realized then how much pain he was in, both physically and from the way he had lived. It was a very powerful moment,' she says, her voice softening.

'Until then I thought I had wanted to hear him say he was sorry. I thought I needed to find the compassion to forgive him. But in that moment I realized that everything I had understood of Buddhist teachings until then had been intellectual. In that moment I realized that there was no forgiver and no forgiven, that we were the same. I really felt there was no distinction between my father and me, that we were one from the beginning. That we are all one.' The room falls silent for a few moments as Sister Trai recalls her awakening to the truth that lies at the heart of all Buddhist teaching.

After her father died, she felt drawn to return to Plum Village. 'It was then that I started thinking about remaining here permanently. I knew that by transforming myself I could help many people. At first I thought, "That's crazy. How can I give up my career?" But slowly I realized it was exactly what I wanted and needed to do. It was because I'd had the career I wanted that I was able to give it up – otherwise I might still have been chasing after that,' she says. Sister Trai was by then in her early thirties. The option of returning to lay life and teaching the dharma in some way, while continuing to work as a musician, seemed too daunting; despite the demands of monastic life, she says, 'Life is short so why make it harder?'

When we meet, Sister Trai is about to become fully ordained and she has a vision that by the time she reaches her fifties she wants to be a senior dharma teacher. At first she imagined her monastic training would take place as she led a quiet life at Plum Village, perhaps tending the vegetable gardens on which the community depends. Instead, she now spends much of the year travelling with Thích Nhất Hạnh, who, as the author of best-selling books that now sell in the millions, is in great demand to teach and lead retreats around the world. 'Thây has a way of challenging preconceptions,' she says with a laugh.

After we finish speaking, Sister Trai agrees to take me briefly to the bedroom she shares with two other nuns, and I finally glimpse the simple monastic living quarters that are generally off-limits to visitors. While those who stay at Plum Village are housed in rooms or shared dormitories with only basic facilities, the simplicity of the rooms the nuns share is still striking. There is little adornment. Their belongings are stored in large wooden boxes that serve as bed frames. There are no mattresses, sleeping bags being rolled directly onto hard board. In a narrow gallery beneath the bedroom are three small writing desks with a lamp, and just a few books, mugs and pens. Witnessing such simplicity leads me to reflect on how much paraphernalia I am accustomed to travelling with, even in conflict zones, when, to my mind, I am travelling light.

After leaving Sister Trai, I take a walk in the grounds of Upper Hamlet and witness there an extraordinarily beautiful scene. Half hidden amongst the trees, I come across eight life-size seated stone Buddhas, carved of dark lava, all facing towards a distant hill, as if in silent contemplation. As the seasons change their upturned palms catch leaves, seed heads and flowers carried by the wind.

Settling close to these Buddhas, I sit for a while and think about Sister Trai's words on forgiveness. My mind wanders back to events in my own life when I have struggled to forgive wrongs. I think also of some of the areas of conflict around the world from which I have reported, where forgiveness between warring factions seems impossible, yet without it there will never be peace. One question I ask of some of the nuns I meet is what lesson from monastic life they would most cherish and carry with them were they ever to return to lay life. More than one says it would be simply 'to constantly let go'.

The most basic tool taught at Plum Village for doing this is through repeatedly coming back to awareness of the breath. Reminders of this can be seen everywhere in Thích Nhất Hạnh's distinctive calligraphy, carrying the simple exhortation in English, French and Vietnamese, 'Breathe, My Dear.' Sitting beside the stone Buddhas, I become aware of my own breath and a letting go begins.

17

CHANGING TIMES

At the dawn of the new millennium, the Netherlands inaugurated the West's first independent Buddhist Broadcasting Foundation. In France too, every Sunday, a state television channel broadcasts a programme boasting an audience of more than a quarter of a million called *Sagesses Bouddhistes*, 'Buddhist Wisdom', in recognition of Buddhism having now become the country's fourth largest religion after Christianity, Islam and Judaism. The number of French who, while not formally registered as Buddhist, profess a closer affinity to Buddhism than to any of these other religions reaches into many more millions. In some areas of France, particularly the Loire, Dordogne, Auvergne and Touraine, dozens of Buddhist retreat centres and temples lie tucked away in the countryside.

In every country to which Buddhism has travelled, there are different historical and cultural reasons why the teachings have taken hold. Throughout Europe there are Buddhist monasteries or nunneries and other centres where ordained women are responding to a growing interest in Buddhism as belief in other faiths declines. While it is still lagging behind the Buddhist boom in America, some estimate that the number of those drawn to Buddhist teachings on this continent now runs into several million. Further afield too, there are flourishing dharma centres in Africa and South America.

In France the growing interest in Buddhism is partly a result of the country's colonial past in South East Asia, with many Asian immigrants who arrived in the 1970s and 1980s retaining the religion of their ancestors. But there are also centres here which follow newer traditions and, after leaving Plum Village, as I travel north through France I stop at one such Zen temple in the heart of the Loire Valley.

Unlike many grand chateaux lining the banks of the river Loire, in this area of France that was once the playground of kings, La Gendronnière does not announce itself to the world. In fact, it takes some time to find. The directions I am given point to it sitting on the outskirts of a small village called Les Montils, just a few miles south-west of the historic city of Blois. But I exhaust all roads leading out of the village before finally stumbling across a muddy track at the end of which I can just make out a darkened building. A small sign low to the ground confirms this is the 'Temple Zen de La Gendronnière.'

From a distance, through the trees, La Gendronnière appears imposing and deserted, its tall gabled windows and chimney stacks jutting skywards from a steep slate roof. It is growing dark and I hesitate before turning off the road and driving on through the trees and mud. But as I approach the small chateau I make out lights in a low modern structure off to the left. Drawing closer, I see figures moving around inside, setting a table. It is early evening and I am expected.

The headlights from my car bring out a young man, dressed in jeans and plaid shirt, to direct me where to park and usher me inside. In the dining hall I am greeted by the monk responsible for running the temple, and his girlfriend, Christèle, the nun who has coordinated my visit. Both she and her partner have just been to see the latest James Bond film, *Skyfall,* Christèle explains, taking a seat beside me and pouring herself a glass of wine. Christèle is in her early forties, has bow-shaped lips, large blue-grey eyes and, on this first evening, is wearing jeans, knee-length boots and a thick pullover. The only thing that marks her out as a Zen Buddhist nun is her shaven head. In the days before my arrival La Gendronnière has hosted an intensive meditation retreat attended by more than 100 lay practitioners from all over France. The small group of temple staff who reside permanently at La Gendronnière are exhausted. This is their night to relax.

La Gendronnière was founded in 1980 by the Japanese Soto Zen teacher Taisen Deshimaru, one of the first and most influential Buddhist teachers to travel to France, after being considered too radical by Japan's Buddhist establishment. His arrival in the 1960s coincided with the tumult of social unrest sweeping the country. In 1968 the streets of Paris and other cities, both in France and elsewhere, were ablaze with protest against war and injustice. The spirit of the age was to buck conformity, and Deshimaru's way of teaching was anything but conventional. His burning mission was to establish in the West the essence of Zen without the formalism of the practice in Japan. Within three years he had founded the Association Zen d'Europe, and quickly developed a devoted following.

One of his early devotees has arranged to meet me at La Gendronnière the following morning. After breakfast is cleared away, I am shown into an airy conservatory where I find Françoise Laurent, a former fashion model and a mother, who was ordained as a nun by Deshimaru in 1976. Now in her early sixties, Françoise is tall and striking, and the graceful poise with which she perches on the edge of a sofa as we speak makes it easy to imagine her treading the Paris catwalks in her twenties.

The daughter of doctors, Françoise grew up in comfort, and when she started modelling for the house of Louis Féraud she was moving in glamorous circles. But the allure of that life quickly wore thin. 'I was happy working in high fashion in Paris. But I also knew that something important was missing,' she says. 'I saw first-hand the misery of very rich people. This was when I started searching and practising meditation.'

Françoise first met Deshimaru at a small dojo in Paris and describes him as a 'very cheerful and warm person, who never forgot the importance of laughter'. That first meeting was an eagerly awaited *mondo* session, where pupils are given a chance to ask their *roshi*, or teacher, questions. When Françoise asked what the difference was between meditating as a layperson and doing so as a monk, Deshimaru shot back an abrupt and enigmatic reply. Pointing at her, he said, 'OK, directly nun!'

'I didn't understand what he meant and thought maybe the translator had left something out, so I asked the question again,' Françoise recalls. 'But he repeated the same words and the second time made a chopping gesture as if I should cut off my hair. Then I understood he meant that I should become a nun.' A few months later Françoise shaved her head and became ordained. She admits that the move provoked some hostile reactions. In the fashion world many thought she was simply seeking attention, while on the streets of Paris there were those who still remembered that French women who had collaborated with the Nazis had had their heads shaved; their response was, she says, 'not positive'.

Shortly after ordaining as a nun, Françoise married a monk who also followed Deshimaru's teachings, and the couple set up home together in an apartment close to a temple founded by Deshimaru in Paris. As is the custom in Japan, where monks have long been allowed to marry, those who ordain in Deshimaru's tradition are permitted relationships providing they observe an ordination vow 'not to engage in sexual relations without love'. The couple had a daughter and Françoise took over the care of two young children from her husband's previous marriage. But when this marriage foundered too, Françoise found herself responsible for raising three children. At first she returned to work as an assistant to Louis Féraud, but eventually took a post as a librarian. Throughout this time, Françoise says she continued to consider herself a nun. For all but a year, when her children were young and her marriage was crumbling, she has continued a regular practice of *zazen* sitting meditation. When we meet, she is wearing, over the top of a cream cardigan, a black *rakusu*, a small apron-like piece of cloth worn at chest height to symbolize in daily life the traditional *kesa* mantle worn by monks and nuns on ceremonial occasions.

As Françoise describes this, I find myself asking the same question she had posed before becoming ordained. What difference has it really made to her life being a nun? Though she comes often to La Gendronnière, which has only a small resident community and functions principally as a place of meditation, she does not live here. Françoise answers my question by saying that, for her, her *kesa* – the most potent symbol of becoming a nun – has been her greatest gift in life. 'I feel my *kesa* has always protected me and made me feel, very deeply, that I am a child of the Buddha,' she says. 'Although tradition is important, I found my own way of practice. For me it was important to have a child and my children became my daily Zen practice,' she continues. 'Through being a nun, I see everything in life with the eye of the dharma.' The challenge of living in the community rather than cloistered in a monastery is what has tested her conviction and sense of inner strength, she believes. 'This everyday social life was the best place for me to practise the Buddha's teachings.'

Recently, Françoise was diagnosed with breast cancer, and the depth of her commitment to Zen practice has, she says, helped her cope with the disease. She struggles to describe how, except to say, 'When you become ordained, it's like jumping into the centre of a stream, and this feeling inside of being a nun never disappears. It's very strong. It goes beyond thought and somehow beyond explanation.' I try to press her further on this, before recognizing, once again, that there are limits to what can be understood through asking questions.

After leaving La Gendronnière, the road I take skirts along the banks of the Loire; here the river, the longest waterway in France, is wide and its current strong. As my eyes follow the rapid drift, I am reminded of how often life itself is seen as a river, a continual flow of unstoppable change. In Buddhism, change and impermanence are recognized as the very essence of existence, something not to be feared, but to be appreciated as giving rise to a ceaseless stream of grace.

At different points along my own journey in writing this book I have encountered Buddhist nuns whose life work has been to guide others through some of the most turbulent waters of human experience, at times when life seems unbearable and, ultimately, when life itself is ebbing away. Rather than basing themselves within a nunnery, monastery or other form of Buddhist monastic residence, some choose to live in the wider community, often travelling tirelessly, engaging with people in extreme situations. From here, my onward journey no longer follows a clear geographical arc, but twists and turns through different places and lives, just as Buddhism itself now flows through many streams of our modern world.

PART VIII

BEYOND BOUNDS

18

INSIDE

METROPOLITAN POLICE
Division
PAUL LOVES
I will get REVENGE

A former maximum-security courthouse with the remnants of bullet holes still pockmarking its walls might not seem the most auspicious place to find enlightenment. There was a time when police marksmen regularly took up positions on the roof of this building in Lambeth, south London, and helicopters would hover overhead as prisoners deemed a serious danger to the public were brought before judges here. Amongst them were accused IRA terrorists, some of whose names remain scrawled on the walls of what were once holding cells. But some years after this courthouse was closed in the 1990s, it was bought at auction and converted into a Buddhist meditation and study centre called Jamyang.

Today a golden Buddha statue sits in the place once occupied by the judge's bench. Gone are the courtroom's bulletproof glass screens, replaced by delicate white stucco frescos depicting scenes from the Buddha's life. When builders were converting Jamyang's barred cells into rooms for overnight guests, old radiators were torn from walls and scraps of paper were found stuffed into crannies behind. Amongst them were secret notes written by prisoners in moments of quiet desperation, one bearing a declaration of love, another vowing revenge.

As I pass through the corridors of this old Victorian building both the pain of those once incarcerated here and the pain of the people whose lives they scarred are still somehow palpable. Yet in spite of its troubled past, or perhaps because of it, and the extraordinary transformation it has undergone, there is an exceptional sense of peace in this place, and it seems a fitting venue for the nun I am about to meet.

It is a Saturday morning and Jamyang's shrine room slowly begins to fill. An audience of assorted ages and nationalities sits in quiet anticipation. Then a bell is rung and everyone rises as the sounds of rapidly approaching footsteps are heard pounding along an outer hallway. Some make a small bow of respect as a short nun in her sixties powers into the room, her stocky frame and determined walk the only hint of her background as a former martial arts enthusiast who once served as bodyguard to the Dalai Lama.

Robina Courtin is a bundle of ferocious energy. Over the course of two days she talks and answers questions from the audience with a quick-fire delivery that is at times hard to keep up with. Her subjects are wide-ranging and include an explanation of Buddhism as a form of psychology well suited to dealing with difficult emotions such as anger, guilt, regret and remorse. On occasion she makes reference to her own background. But it is only through delving deeper into her biography that it becomes clear to me how much of what she says has been informed by her own early experiences.

Born into a Catholic family in Melbourne, Australia, to an abusive and sometimes violent father, she was a gangly girl determined to stand out from the crowd by breaking into a bigger smile than anyone else every time she was photographed. As a young woman, she lived life on fast-forward. After moving to London and training as a classical singer, she passed rapidly through phases of passion for men, drink and drugs, left-wing politics, radical lesbian feminism and Afro-American causes, until, finally exhausted, she turned her back on them all.

When she was introduced to Buddhism in her early thirties, she embraced it with the same intensity she had shown everything else in her life. But this was something she did not abandon. Within two years, she had taken the decision to ordain as a nun in the Tibetan

Buddhist tradition in a ceremony in Dharamshala. After this she was sent to the United States, where she went on to become editorial director at a leading Buddhist book publisher and editor of an international Buddhist magazine. In the years since then, her spirited manner and down-to-earth style have led to a growing demand for her to give teachings around the world, as a result of which she now travels constantly.

She is perhaps best known, however, for her work over the past two decades with those whom most of the rest of society shuns: prison inmates, many of them men serving life sentences, some of them on death row. This work began when she answered a letter from an eighteen-year-old Mexican gangster who had been incarcerated in a Los Angeles jail since the age of twelve. In the years that followed, she received many such letters and began visiting prisons across the United States. Then, in 1996, she founded the Liberation Prison Project, a spiritual foundation which now offers Buddhist teachings and spiritual counselling to thousands of prisoners worldwide, principally in the US and Australia, but also in Europe and as far afield as Mexico and Mongolia. Several years ago it was reported that Buddhism was the fastest-growing religion amongst British prison inmates.

On her visit to south London, she makes passing references to her prison work as she talks of Buddhism as a psychological 'toolkit' for deconstructing the mind and getting in touch with reality. 'There are no bars worse than the prison of one's own mind,' she tells her audience, describing some of the inmates she has worked with as being 'among the most dedicated practitioners she has ever met'.

Many believe that those who have committed some of the worst crimes deserve retribution rather than redemption, but for others, working with prisoners has always been a calling. The powerful effect Buddhist practice can have on prisoners was something I had been able to see for myself during my time in the United States, when I was offered a rare opportunity to accompany a group of Buddhist nuns from Sravasti Abbey on one of their regular visits to a men's prison in Washington State. Of the many rich experiences writing this book has afforded, for me this prison visit was one of the most poignant.

Before we set off, I was aware that the nuns are mindful of the men's right to privacy and I follow their lead in not asking for the names of those we are to meet. When I ask what crimes the men have committed, the nuns reply that they do not make a policy of asking. All I know is that there will be a group of around twenty inmates awaiting our arrival and that the prison is classed as a minimum and medium security institution. I assume this means those incarcerated have not been convicted of the most serious offences. I am wrong.

After rising at dawn and squeezing into a battered old car the nuns share as communal property, we drive some distance beneath an overcast sky before the horizon fills with rows of watchtowers and rolled razor wire. Only then do I get a clearer idea of the size of the facility. There are more than 2,000 inmates held here. This is just a fraction of the two million men and women incarcerated across the United States – a quarter of the world's prison population. As a journalist, I have visited prisons in the past: once to interview former Panamanian dictator Manuel Noriega, jailed in Miami after his capture and extradition as a prisoner of war; another time, to expose the practice of imprisoning girls alongside hardened adult criminals in a British prison, in direct contravention of international law. I remember the noise, the claustrophobia, the sense of despair, and I feel my chest tighten as we sign in at the front desk.

Following behind the nuns, I pass through three sets of bullet-proof glass doors and we line up in front of a raised bank of surveillance cameras for guards to check that we match the photographs in our identity papers. In the face of all this high-tech security and wardens with semi-automatic weapons on their hips, the four nuns, who visit this prison throughout the year, stand patiently and smile. This is, after all, a day of rejoicing. It is the one day in the year when the inmates who follow Buddhism hold a 'Buddha Fest', an opportunity to mark their commitment to Buddhist teachings by talking with the nuns and, if they wish, making a symbolic offering to the Buddha.

After the security vetting we are ushered into a large room and seated in a row of chairs facing the exit door. The men then slowly file in. Dressed in white T-shirts and beige trousers, some are clearly freshly shaved for the occasion. They range in age from late thirties to sixties. The younger ones settle on meditation cushions on the floor, those with creaking bones sit on metal chairs facing us. First, there is a short motivational ceremony conducted by the nuns. Then comes the time for the men to make any offering they choose. What follows is both sad and beautiful.

One man with a long thin plaited ponytail steps to the front. His offering is to be a performance. As a fellow inmate presses a button on a portable CD player and the sound of a melodic Buddhist chant fills the room, the man closes his eyes and raises himself on tiptoes. Very slowly, he begins to weave a dance of such grace and elegance that I find myself holding my breath. With his arms circling slowly around his waist, his body pirouettes, bends and twists in intricate manoeuvres that blend the refinement of classical ballet with modern dance. His movements have a delicacy that defies his harsh surroundings and strike me as extraordinarily brave in the company of convicted and frustrated criminals. When the music stops, he brings his hands together in prayer, bows at the waist to everyone in the room and then resumes his place on a cushion on the floor. Later, he confides that he used to be a professional dancer.

Over the course of the next hour, other inmates make different offerings. One reads a poem. Another plays the guitar. Another talks about how he gets up at 3 a.m. every day, as this is the only time he can find any peace and quiet in which to meditate.

'This is a population that most people want to ignore and throw away. But not only do they learn from us, we learn from them,' says the nun who has organized the visit. 'When we get a letter from a prison inmate describing how he's sitting on his top bunk, a few feet away from a bare bulb, meditating, with noise and commotion all around, it cuts down on our complaining radically.'

When the inmates get up to stretch their legs and take refreshments, I stay seated, lost in thought, until a prisoner comes and sits beside me. It is the only brief opportunity I have to talk with one of the men and I ask how long a sentence he is serving. 'Life,' he says, 'without parole.' Often those most receptive to Buddhist teachings, I am told, are 'lifers', who will never be released. Those whose only chance of freedom is an inner sense of liberation that comes from truly accepting who they are and acknowledging what they have done and consciously transforming their minds.

'I've been inside nineteen years,' the man by my side continues. 'For the last thirteen I've been following the dharma.'

'Has it helped?' I ask.

'The first year inside was the worst,' he says. 'That year was longer than all the rest put together, because you're going through grief for the loss of yourself and everything that has been taken from you.' I can only imagine that the severity of his sentence means he must have taken the life of another person, maybe more than one. But I let him speak, conscious of the nuns' policy of not asking for details.

'I know I'm the only one responsible for why I'm here,' he says. 'I know I'm never going to be released. But through the dharma I've found an inner freedom. For the first time in my life, I've come to terms with who I am. That's the same for most of us here. These are men I trust,' he says, glancing around the room. 'That's unusual. A lot of the guys inside go to meetings clutching Bibles, but they're not the sort of guys you'd want to meet in the bathroom.'

When it comes time for us to leave, a bell is rung. As I get to my feet the prisoner with whom I've been speaking confides that he has not had any relative visit him for many years. 'It means everything to us that the nuns come to see us. It's like having family come. When the nuns are here, we walk taller,' he says. 'That feeling lasts a long time, until the weight of this place grinds us down again.'

As we are escorted back through an exercise yard, then a windowless corridor and the same series of bulletproof security doors, I sense something of that weight and I feel enormous relief at being able to leave. But then, directly opposite the prison, I see the neon lights of a giant casino. Attached to it is a luxury hotel and spa, so that gamblers can check in for days and be pampered while they play the tables. It's a stark reminder that it doesn't take barbed wire or watchtowers to keep us mentally behind bars. We are quite capable of imprisoning ourselves.

All this is going through my mind as I sit listening to Robina Courtin speak to her south London audience. Keen to learn more about Robina's work in prisons, I wait for her audience to leave before joining her in an upstairs room at Jamyang. It is late by this time and she is relieved to have time to rest, kicking off her shoes as she beckons me to take a seat.

In person, Robina is more mellow and reflective than her rapid-fire public delivery suggests. But when I ask her why she was drawn to prison work, she talks of being attracted to working with people who are trying to control the sort of chaotic energy she feels she has had to deal with all of her life. 'I admire people who have a crazy mind and are really working on it,' she says, easing herself back in her chair. 'Crazy people, angry people, violent people don't faze me. I had a pretty violent upbringing myself.' Was it this violence that led to her spiritual seeking, I wonder? 'No, I don't think so. I became a Buddhist because I wanted to understand the world,' she says. 'I wanted clarity and truth. I wanted answers.'

Although her introduction to working with prisoners happened by chance, it answered her need to understand the rawness of life, she explains, and work with it in a significant way to bring about change. 'The men I work with are in the garbage dump of the world. Their back is against the wall,' she says. 'So when you see it is possible for them to really change the way their mind works, in such a dire situation, it is very moving.'

It might seem that the reason those in prison are turning to Buddhism in growing numbers is of little relevance to the rest of us, but this is not a view she shares. 'It's not just prisoners,' she says. 'All of us benefit from Buddhist teachings in the same way. You could say the Buddha was an expert psychologist, because he deals with the mind.'

In Buddhism, the words 'soul' or 'spirit' are rarely used; instead, teachings refer to 'mind' and 'consciousness'. Because there is no creator God in Buddhism, no sense of a Supreme Judge or Deity-in-Charge, but rather an acceptance that life is determined by constantly evolving causes and conditions – karma – there is no concept of sin either, in the sense in which it is understood in most religions, as a transgression of God's will. The emphasis instead is on personal accountability for moral conduct. Robina explains that guilt is dismissed as a function of the ego, anger turned inward, a destructive emotion; this is quite distinct from remorse, which requires true acceptance of responsibility for one's actions and a sincere effort to discover what changes for the better are needed.

'Buddha didn't believe in trying to squeeze information into your head, or in getting you to believe anything without you testing it out for yourself,' she continues, barely pausing for breath. 'You could say he was more of a scientist with a working hypothesis on how to end suffering.'

More than once, she refers to Buddhist teachings as a way of becoming your own therapist, looking deeply at negative states of mind and transforming them. 'There's nothing holy or wishy-washy about it. It's got nothing to do with a person with a silly grin on their face. It's practical and intelligent. A calm mind can be a busy mind. I have a busy mind, believe me,' she says with a laugh, and there's no disputing that. Keeping up with her stream of consciousness, as lucid as it is, can be a challenge.

She finds such inspiration in working with prisoners because they live in 'violent, insane asylums' and yet they are working hard at changing their own mind. 'If you think that you can't work on your own mind, that you're stuck with what you have, how depressing is that? No wonder so many people kill themselves.'

The rising rate of suicide globally is a powerful sign of just how many people find themselves backed up against the wall of their own mental prison; it is an issue that Robina cares about deeply. Just before we part she searches out an old copy of a *Newsweek* article that touched her deeply. On the train ride home, I take a closer look at it and am staggered. According to its findings, in the year 2010 more people died by their own hand around the world than were murdered or killed in wars and natural disasters combined. In that year alone, 36 million years of life, the sum of the ages of all those who died by suicide, were lost globally to self-harm. In high-income countries, suicide is now the leading killer of women in their thirties, and the leading cause of death for men in their forties, and none of these figures includes the terrible toll of twenty-five attempts for every death. With suicide rates increasing in almost every country, the article comes to the following grim conclusion: 'More and more of us are living through a time of seamless black; a period of mounting clinical depression, blossoming thoughts of oblivion and an abiding wish to get there by the non-scenic route.'

As I read these bleak statistics I think back to the fate of the young Tibetan nuns I heard about while in India, whose desperation at being evicted from their nunneries by Chinese troops drove them to kill themselves. I think too about Jakucho Setouchi's confession that she was on the brink of suicide when she sought comfort in Buddhism and took the decision to ordain. It is, of course, more difficult to gather statistics for those who have been able to find a way out of their anguish than to count the toll of those who succumb to it by taking their own lives, but it seems that an increasing number of people are turning towards Buddhist teachings as a way of calming their troubled minds.

Many of the nuns I have met have become the public face of this wisdom, and their lectures fill auditoriums worldwide. Many more seek out their teachings and those of other high-profile nuns, such as the engaging American teacher and best-selling author Pema Chödrön, in books or online. But even for those who might never feel drawn to listen to such women, the influence of Buddhism has now become so widespread that certain aspects of it have entered into many people's everyday lives without them ever realizing their monastic origins. To explore more about how Buddhist practice has found its way into mainstream psychology, including offering solace to those who find themselves in despair, my journey takes me back to a once-familiar place.

19

FULL CIRCLE

There is a cobbled square at the heart of Oxford that I know better than any other. It is a misty morning when I retrace my steps here to get my bearings. In the many years since I donned the black subfusc gown students here wear on formal occasions, I have spent so much time in foreign countries that I have revisited this place rarely. But as the Palladian roof of one of the university's most iconic buildings, the Radcliffe Camera, comes into view, I feel the years slip away. For a fleeting moment I sense a knot in my stomach as I remember the endless hours spent hunched over books in this library in an effort to meet some looming essay deadline. As an undergraduate at neighbouring Brasenose College, I used to climb up to work in the Camera's topmost reading room, where windows offer undisturbed views across the rooftops of this 'city of dreaming spires'.

Much of my time high up in this circular gallery was spent looking out of those windows and cherishing dreams of travelling the world. Even then, I knew that whatever I could learn from books was a pale imitation of what I really longed for. It had little to do with acquiring academic knowledge, cramming in facts that would be quickly forgotten. It seems strange in retrospect, but I remember quite clearly thinking then that what I wanted from life was maybe not what others craved. I didn't yearn for fame, or fortune, or even, at that stage, family life. What I wanted more than anything was what I thought of as wisdom, though I had little idea what that really meant. It seems to me now that I was seeking answers to questions about the way the world worked, and it was this that drove me on during much of the following twenty-five years in my work as a foreign correspondent.

Perhaps the books I burrowed into at Oxford were of the wrong kind. My eagerness for exploration led to studies in physical and political geography, and while I have always cherished the feeling this has given me for natural landscapes, when it came to examining the deeds of some of those I have encountered as a journalist, I have sometimes found myself floundering. When trying, for instance, to explain the actions of suicide bombers, war criminals, serial killers, dictators, drug lords, terrorists, torturers and megalomaniacs, I have struggled to understand their inner terrain.

Perhaps if I had travelled East rather than West earlier on in my journalistic career, I might have gained some of the insight that meeting the women in this book has afforded. Or perhaps this only comes at a certain time, when you are open to it and ready. When I first came to base myself abroad, I felt torn in two directions. In my naivety I wrote to the foreign editors of several national newspapers, asking if they might consider employing me as a correspondent either in the Far East or in Latin America; my hope was that a positive answer either way would resolve my indecision. It was hardly surprising that none responded with enthusiasm. If I had received such an equivocal pitch when I later worked as an editor on the *Sunday Times* foreign desk, I might well have dismissed it too.

In an attempt to make up my mind, I eventually set off on the Trans-Siberian Express, crossing what was still the Soviet Union from Moscow to Vladivostok, before travelling by boat to Japan, then on to Hong Kong and into China. But while I've always had a reasonable ear for picking up languages, shortly after arriving in China I became convinced that learning Mandarin was beyond me. So I took myself west, to Mexico, to cover Latin America for the *Sunday Times,* with brief periods covering the American political scene in Washington, DC. After this I was based as a correspondent first in Paris and then in Berlin; on returning to London, I then spent fifteen years undertaking assignments all over the world as a staff writer for the *Sunday Times Magazine*.

Looking back on all this, a phrase of poetry comes to mind that has played in my thoughts in the course of this present journey. I don't know how it came to be stuck in my head. I didn't even remember who the writer was or which poem it came from until I looked it up and discovered it comes from T. S. Eliot's *Four Quartets*. But the words come back to me now, as I stand in the lodge of my old Oxford college, looking up at the Camera windows.

We shall not cease from exploration
And the end of all our exploring
Will be to arrive where we started
And know the place for the first time.

I have a strong sense in these moments that my life has, in some ways, come full circle. That it is only through my recent journey in the wise company of Buddhist nuns that I have begun to glimpse some of the deeper truths I have sought for a long time.

As I leave the cropped lawns and cobbled walkways of Brasenose College and Radcliffe Square behind me, I realize that this return to Oxford completes a circle within the circle of my journey with the nuns, too, for there is a connection between this city that was once so familiar to me and my first introduction to the unknown world of the nunnery all those months ago in Kathmandu. In 2012 the Twelfth Gyalwang Drukpa travelled to Oxford from Gawa Khilwa in the Himalayas, accompanied by a handful of the 'kung fu' nuns

I met there, including my patient translator Rigzin and my curious walking companion, the beautiful Migyur. One morning Migyur and four other Gawa Khilwa nuns stood in damp grass on the banks of Oxford's river Cherwell and gave a short kung fu demonstration to enthralled onlookers in the grounds of Wolfson College. Inspired by their visit, the college invited the Gyalwang Drukpa to send one of his nuns, or more if the funding could be found, to study English and comparative religion at Oxford University for a year. The intention was 'to encourage meaningful dialogue between two cultures' and help the nun's Oxford hosts 'access greater depths of understanding of the philosophical and spiritual roots of the Buddhist tradition'.

The nun is due to arrive from Kathmandu later in the year, as the chill of autumn sets in, and I imagine her here then, pulling woolly layers over her maroon robes to keep out the cold, and wonder what she will make of her new surroundings. However alien the environment, she will at least find herself in an institution where the influence of Buddhism has recently started to flourish, as I discover after heading east from the centre of Oxford and crossing over the river Cherwell, taking the Headington Road towards a district of hospitals and medical-research labs. At the heart of this sprawling complex of modern steel and glass is an old Victorian building that was once known as the Oxford Lunatic Asylum. This is now the Warneford Hospital, a major teaching facility that forms part of Oxford University's Department of Psychiatry. Much of the focus of the Warneford today is on scientific research into the way the brain works. In the grounds of the hospital there is an airy modern building with a small sign by its front door announcing it as the Oxford Mindfulness Centre.

The building is surrounded by lawns and some newly planted

trees. A number of these trees have been planted in memory of those who have succumbed to suicide, by relatives wanting to show gratitude for the work of the centre, founded in 2008. Its stated mission is 'Preventing Depression and Enhancing Human Potential by Combining Modern Science with Ancient Wisdom'. As I step through the centre's front door I am greeted by a beautifully crafted reminder of one of modern science's major achievements. On one wall of an open atrium hangs a striking glass artwork showing a cross section of the brain as it appears in the deep blue, red and yellow contours of computer-generated neuroimaging. There are no visual reminders of the 'ancient wisdom' referred to in the OMC's mission statement. But, as the centre's founding director Professor Mark Williams acknowledges, this stems from Buddhist monastic practice.

Professor Williams is now retired from his OMC post and so, before I visit the centre, we speak on the phone. He tells me how, more than twenty years ago, long before plans for the OMC were conceived, he attended a Buddhist retreat in the north of England at which the principal teachers were a small group of Buddhist nuns. He no longer remembers any details about the tradition they belonged to, but he remembers well the profound effect their teachings had on him. At the core of the retreat were instructions on how participants could develop a practice of meditation through using the breath as a focus to remain anchored in the present moment.

'What the nuns pointed me to was the part of their tradition kept alive through monastic practice for 2,500 years,' he says. 'This was the importance of staying in the present moment, the importance of calm abiding, the practice of concentration in Buddhism known as *samatha*.' This time spent in the company of nuns, listening to their guidance, was 'a seminal moment'.

For decades, the professional focus of this softly spoken clinical psychologist has been to find ways of helping people suffering from depression, particularly those whose depressed state leads them to consider suicide. Just as shocking as the statistics on those who succeed in taking their own lives are the facts outlining the current global epidemic of depression. Professor Williams tells me that between ten and twenty per cent of the world's population will get seriously depressed at some time in their lives, and of these half will harbour suicidal thoughts. 'This means that up to one in five people will get depressed and one in ten will be suicidal at some point.'

While most therapies, both pharmaceutical and psychological, concentrate on treating those suffering from depression at the time they are ill, Professor Williams' focus has been to seek a prophylactic treatment: a way of teaching people skills to stay well and prevent relapse into depression once they have suffered one or more episodes. In this search he has been joined by two academic colleagues: John Teasdale, first of Oxford, then Cambridge University, and Zindel Segal, a professor of psychiatry at the University of Toronto.

In the 1990s the three men began to look to the work of an American pioneer in the field of mindfulness, Jon Kabat-Zinn, a medical professor at the University of Massachusetts Medical Facility. Kabat-Zinn's initial focus was to find a way of helping patients handle long-term chronic pain and illness. As a student of Zen, he realized how effective the Buddhist practice of mindfulness could be in helping treat chronic medical conditions and, in the 1970s, set about adapting teachings on mindfulness to develop a structured secular eight-week programme for his patients, which combined both meditation and hatha yoga. The programme, which came to be known as Mindfulness Based Stress Reduction, or

MBSR, has since become so popular it has spread around the world as a highly effective way of helping people, whether ill or not, lead healthier, more stress-free lives.

The essence of this programme, as Kabat-Zinn defines it, is 'the ability to pay total attention to the present moment with non-judgemental awareness of both inner and outer experiences'. Since it is the brain's habit of reliving past stresses and worrying about the future that so impairs mental well-being, a major principle of the programme is to teach practitioners a way of becoming more anchored in the present. This is achieved through techniques such as meditation, focus on the breath and awareness of bodily sensation, so that thoughts about the past and future lose their power. Although the programme is secular, its non-judgemental element stems from crucial Buddhist teachings rooted in compassion, both for others and for the self.

While recognizing the possible application of this technique for those suffering from depression, Professor Williams admits that at first he resisted looking into it in any depth because of its Buddhist origins. In addition to being an eminent academic, he is also an ordained Anglican priest, though one released from pastoral duties, and an honorary canon of Oxford's Christ Church Cathedral. But during the retreat he attended led by Buddhist nuns, he says he recognized that their practice of meditation and mindfulness shared many elements with the Christian contemplative tradition. This was, he says, 'like a sudden surge of electricity going from one thing to the other, enlivening both'.

After acknowledging this universal wisdom, he joined his colleagues in looking at ways in which Kabat-Zinn's secular MBSR programme could be adapted to better suit those suffering from depression. Over time, they developed a similar practice that also incorporated aspects of Cognitive Behavioural Therapy, and Mindfulness Based Cognitive Therapy, or MBCT, was born. This too is taught via an eight-week programme, at times when those suffering from depression are well enough to cope with its rigours. As any practitioner of mindfulness will acknowledge, while simple in essence, it requires hard work and perseverance to put into practice.

For several hours every week, practitioners of MBCT are led through a series of exercises and guided meditations which they are encouraged to continue at home. The courses at the Oxford centre are held in the relaxed surroundings of a large, light-filled meeting room adjacent to the central atrium; for those attending, the only reminder of the despair they are trying to shake is a statue near the entrance of a black dog, the metaphorical beast to which depression is sometimes likened.

After early trials of MBCT showed it cut the risk of relapse into depression by half, the programme became increasingly accepted as a highly effective treatment. Less than a decade later the UK's National Institute of Clinical Excellence, NICE, endorsed MBCT as a recommended treatment for the prevention of relapse into depression, particularly for people who have been clinically depressed three or more times, sometimes over a period of twenty years or more. Following this endorsement, a growing number of GPs in the UK now refer patients to attend MBCT courses, and several regional health trusts are training qualified clinical practitioners to be able to teach the programme.

'When we started this work twenty or so years ago, we thought it would be a minority aspect of health service work and that no one would be interested in it,' says Professor Williams, who has authored a best-selling book on mindfulness and now teaches the practice around the world. 'Not least because we wondered who would teach it – in order to teach it, you have to learn to meditate, and we knew how resistant we had been to that ourselves. But we've been extraordinarily surprised by the enthusiasm both from the health service and in schools. It's almost unheard of for something to spread so rapidly.'

What the professor says is reflected in much of the media today. Open many a magazine or newspaper and the word 'mindfulness' leaps from the pages. It has become a buzzword and, increasingly, a big business, to the extent that some have dubbed it 'McMindfulness' and concerns have been raised about underqualified teachers presenting themselves as mindfulness experts. Many variations of mindfulness programmes are being run by a growing number of individuals and companies worldwide who are hitching their fortunes to what some see as a mindfulness bandwagon, with promises of increased productivity and creativity, and a reduction in workplace torpor and days lost to stress-related illness. There are now programmes promoting the practice for employees at global corporations such as Google, Apple, Yahoo! Barclays Bank, Deutsche Bank, Heinz and McKinsey & Co, to name just a few. When the French Buddhist monk Matthieu Ricard attended the World Economic Forum in Davos in 2014, he found a long queue of delegates waiting to hear him speak. 'Meditation,' he told them, 'is about mastering your thoughts. It's about being in charge of your mind. It's real freedom.' Aside from the business sphere, there are also programmes around the world applying the practice of mindfulness in schools, universities, the military, amongst politicians, performers, those coping with chronic pain and parents wanting to cope better with the challenges of raising children. Inevitably, there are even mindfulness smartphone apps.

In the interests of research, and because I too felt in need of some stress reduction after a difficult few years, I signed up for an eight-week MBSR mindfulness course to understand more about its benefits. Though taught in a secular way, the course was run at the Drukpa Buddhist centre in leafy Primrose Hill, north London, where photographs of the nuns at Gawa Khilwa in Nepal adorned the walls. Gradually, week by week, the small group I join is led through a series of meditation exercises by a warm-natured female lay teacher, who encourages us to pay careful attention to everyday activities and 'weather patterns' in the mind, observing how ephemeral thoughts are.

One of the longer exercises, known as 'the body scan', calls for attention to be paid to sensations in successive parts of the body, during which any thoughts arising are simply to be acknowledged, without judgement, before refocusing the mind on the breath. A shorter, three-minute 'breathing space' meditation encourages briefer moments of awareness throughout the day in which thoughts and feelings, together with bodily sensations, are recognized before attention is once again brought back to the rhythm of breathing. The focus of much of this work is an encouragement to recognize thoughts as 'mental events' from which you can, figuratively, step back in order not to be carried away by them. It also acts as a practical means of anchoring attention in the present moment.

In a very visceral way, this practice leads to a sense of living life from the inside out, depending less on external circumstances for a fundamental feeling of well-being. In the same way that the mindfulness programme designed to help those with depression provides tools to prevent relapse, the aim of the MBSR course is to create a greater awareness of every aspect of life in order, ultimately, to make it more enjoyable and certainly more manageable when difficulties arise. As Jon Kabat-Zinn puts it, the practice is to 'weave your parachute every day', rather leaving it until the point where you have to jump from a plane. Within just a few weeks, I notice the practice begins to instil a renewed sense of calm. But, as with any discipline, the benefits evaporate unless honed daily.

Amidst the hype heralding mindfulness as little short of a miracle cure for all manner of ills, Professor Williams sounds a note of caution, warning that exaggerated claims serve neither science nor the kind of patients he has dedicated his life to trying to help. He stresses that the OMC and similar academic institutions in the UK, at Bangor and Exeter universities, and elsewhere in the world, notably at the University of Massachusetts Medical School in the United States, are firmly founded in up-to-the-minute medical research and quantifiable scientific analysis. Much of this rests on neuroplasticity, the relatively new field of neuroscience research involving the ability of the brain to adjust to change and reshape itself.

Until quite recently, neuroscientists believed the structure of the brain was practically fixed during early childhood. Now modern science has proved, with the help of technology such as MRI scans, that neural pathways and synapses can be altered long into adulthood as a result of changes in behaviour, environment, experience and physical activity. As far as the science of brain circuitry and emotional balance is concerned, such scans have shown that brain patterns change significantly as a result of long-term meditation practice, and that such changes are perceptible after just weeks of a regular twenty- or thirty-minute daily routine. One key area of the brain that has been shown to become more active during meditation is the insula, part of the cerebral cortex that controls self-awareness, cognitive functioning and key aspects of our humanity such as empathy. Research has also shown that a regular meditation practice boosts the immune system, lowers blood pressure and reduces levels of cortisol, a hormone released in response to stress.

In addition to such tangible medical benefits, Professor Williams believes that Buddhism 'offers a path through suffering' because, as he puts it, 'it is mostly about what it is to be truly human'. While not disavowing his deep Christian faith, he describes Buddhism as 'the most compassionate form of humanity you can have, because Buddhism is much more a psychology and anthropology than other religions. It's not theistic, and that's a very useful thing for a secular society. It offers a way of guiding people to come home to their best selves.'

While mindfulness is now taught in the West in a mainly secular context, its techniques are also taught by many of the nuns I have met. A number of Zen Buddhist nuns I speak to are also qualified psychotherapists. Since some do not shave their head or wear monastic robes when working, they are unrecognizable as ordained women in their counselling rooms. For reasons of practitioner confidentiality, some prefer not to be recognized as such. Several women I encounter who spent varying lengths of time on the ordained Buddhist path, but who have since disrobed, have also found that secular life has taken them in the direction of therapeutic work deeply informed by Buddhist teachings.

Mindfulness is not only being incorporated into the treatment of those who are seeking to find ways to live more fully, it is also being integrated into the therapeutic care offered to those facing the greatest challenge of all: the time when life is coming to an end. Of all the ordained women I talk to, the one who conveys perhaps the greatest sense of urgency in her work is one whose focus throughout much of her life has been on helping others face just that.

20

THE DESERT

As I set out to meet Joan Halifax, it seems somehow fitting that our encounter will take place in an oasis in the desert, in the barren upper reaches of New Mexico in the southern United States. For Roshi Joan has made it her mission for more than forty years to provide sanctuary to those in the final wilderness of human experience – terminal illness.

The Upaya Institute and Zen Centre is a haven of lush greenery and ochre adobe dwellings, tucked in a canyon to the east of Santa Fe. This teaching centre and monastery sit in the lee of a striking mountain range, its gardens watered into life from the surrounding dry earth. On the day I visit, Upaya is awaiting the arrival of a group of lay practitioners embarking on a meditation retreat. There are few of those who live or work at the centre in evidence, except in the kitchen, where a small handful of volunteers are preparing lunch, and in the grounds, where others tend the plants.

Arriving early for my appointment, I rest briefly in the cool interior of a dimly lit Zen temple, before following a pathway up to a low sprawl of buildings where Joan Halifax has her private quarters. There I am ushered to take a seat in a deep leather sofa. While I wait for Roshi Joan to arrive, I take in the richness of my surroundings: a room adorned with the eclectic collections of a seasoned traveller and anthropologist.

After an email exchange lasting several months to arrange my visit, and having travelled more than 1,000 miles to be here, I am taken aback by Roshi Joan's hurried manner when she arrives to greet me. Even before sitting down by my side, she looks at her watch and opens our conversation with the words every interviewer dreads: 'I've only got about fifteen minutes,' she says, her piercing blue eyes searching mine with an intentness I find unsettling.

Joan Halifax trained as a medical anthropologist and psychologist and, as a young woman in the early 1970s, spent several years working with her then husband, the Czech psychiatrist Stanislav Grof, researching the use of LSD as a complement to psychotherapy in support of those dying of cancer. She went on to work with the renowned mythologist Joseph Campbell and carried out extensive field research into the healing systems of indigenous people in the Americas, Africa and Tibet.

After two decades spent studying Buddhism, both in the Tibetan and the Zen traditions, she helped found the Buddhist-based Ojai Foundation in southern California, its mission to explore the interface between science and spirituality. She then moved to Santa Fe, New Mexico, where she set up Upaya. In 1990 she was ordained as a lay Buddhist teacher in the tradition of Vietnamese Zen master Thích Nhất Hạnh. But several years later she chose to shave her head and become fully ordained as a celibate Zen priest in the Zen Peacemaker Order founded by New Yorker Roshi Bernie Glassman, whose life focus has been social activism and peace work in the community.

With the clock on our allotted fifteen minutes already ticking, I scramble to mentally prioritize my questions. But in the end our conversation extends to more than an hour and we roll back the years to her formative experiences. In many of my meetings with the remarkable women in this book I have been struck by how often a determination to ordain has been forged in the shadow of suffering, and sometimes conflict or war. In the case of Roshi Joan, born in 1942, the global events that moulded her early life were those that came in the wake of the Second World War: the cold war, the

American civil rights movement and anti-Vietnam War protests. 'I grew up in the period of the cold war with profound fear-based concerns about nuclear weapons,' she says, explaining her conviction that history forms the character of a generation. 'The qualities of altruism, compassion and concern for human rights can be found in the lives of many of us war babies,' she continues.

Aside from the influence of world affairs, her own personal history seems to have primed her for a life of putting compassion into action. As a small child she was rendered blind for two years when a viral infection attacked her ocular muscles, and again in her early forties temporarily lost her sight after having tumours removed from both eyes. This second experience of darkness, along with the death of her mother, led to a period of deep introspection that fuelled her desire to make working with the dying central to her life's path. It is a conviction graphically reflected in the ceremonial *kesa* robe she stitched together for her ordination as a Zen priest.

According to ancient tradition, this robe was often made from scraps of material salvaged from death shrouds, a reminder of the Buddhist tenet of impermanence. Roshi Joan's way of honouring this custom was to ask those in the throes of terminal illness and relatives of the recently deceased for an item of personal clothing from which she could garner material for her monastic garment. The patchwork robe she then sewed included remnants of an old silk nightgown, a wedding dress, a Chinese wool coat, a handkerchief from her father, a silk scarf from a man who had suffered from prostate cancer, and a dress from a woman who had died of AIDS.

Ever since the Middle Ages, the dying have been helped by those affiliated to different religious orders, often at way stations on pilgrimage routes. In recent times the modern hospice movement sprang from roots in the Christian tradition, with Catholic nuns founding such pioneering centres as St Joseph's in London, where in 1958 Dame Cicely Saunders began her trailblazing work in the field of palliative care. What Roshi Joan has brought to her work in this field is the Buddhist perspective and an emphasis on cultivating compassion in all encounters between those who care for the dying and the dying themselves, having recognized early on that the dying are often the most marginalized in modern hospital systems and, in a western context, a person's death is sometimes regarded as a form of medical failure.

Twenty years ago she pioneered a training programme in contemplative end-of-life care which has become one of the core projects at Upaya. The programme, Being with Dying, now draws health-care workers from all over the world, the majority of whom are not Buddhist. The programme, which includes some Mindfulness Based Stress Reduction techniques and other practices that enhance an awareness of the inner life, aims to provide clinicians with essential tools for taking care of dying people with skill and compassion. It is a relationship-centred approach that emphasizes community-building around a dying person, fostering honest and open communication, care of the care-giver, and strategies to support those who are grieving.

In addition to time spent at Upaya, Roshi Joan travels extensively, both in the West and in the East, to teach aspects of this programme and others she has developed focused on 'compassion in action'. For many years she also worked with prisoners and those on death row. Working with people in 'catastrophic situations' has much to teach us all, she argues. 'It's all about what it is to wake up and what it is to serve,' she says.

'I think there is a greater emphasis on engaged Buddhism in the West,' she continues. 'Those of us who were in our twenties in the

1960s and were social activists and became Buddhists, we see the importance of applying these practices to the suffering in the world and that's been my emphasis for the past almost fifty years.'

Unlike most of the ordained women I have met, Roshi Joan no longer shaves her head. She keeps her graying hair short, framing fine features. Instead of monastic robes, she mostly prefers to wear what she calls 'subdued clothing', simple black tunics and soft beige wraps, in order to be able to work in secular settings without any feeling of being constrained by religious garb. She sees her path as 'bridging many worlds, medicine, technology, neuroscience'. In the early 1980s she helped found the Mind and Life Institute, presided over by the Dalai Lama, which every year brings those involved in cutting-edge scientific research together with Buddhist practitioners and monastics in Dharamshala. In 2011 she also addressed world leaders at the World Economic Forum in Davos on the subject of socially engaged Buddhism, and speaks passionately of the dangers of secularizing and 'commodifying' Buddhism, stripping it of the ethical framework that lies at the heart of monastic practice.

In addition to her role as a Zen priest and abbot of Upaya, she regularly leads groups of volunteer health workers on a medical pilgrimage, known as the Nomads Clinic, offering free treatment to those in some of the poorest and most remote regions of the Himalayas and Tibetan Plateau. After a lifetime spent journeying across the globe, she was recently named a *National Geographic* Traveller of the Year. Though in her early seventies when we meet, she still spends many months of the year travelling and teaching. But as our time together draws to a close I sense a weariness creeping in. 'Even though my schedule would be considered by most as still vigorous, I want now to have some more internal, sequestered time,' she says.

For part of every year she retreats to the mountains north of Santa Fe to live as a hermit. High up in the heart of the Sangre de Cristo Mountains, in the lee of the Truchas Peaks, made famous by the expansive paintings of Georgia O'Keeffe, she and others at Upaya have fashioned a simple forest refuge centre. There, in the subalpine meadows, in a small cluster of cabins where black floor cushions are laid out for Zen meditation, she takes time to sit in peaceful solitude.

As we part Roshi Joan first takes my hand and then draws me close in a surprisingly gentle embrace. For all her energy and extraordinary drive, I am taken aback by how delicate she feels. Later I watch a short film she has made about the place in the nearby mountains where she goes into retreat. There is a verdant panorama of pine forests, a still lake and sun-drenched peaks, and I resolve to drive there before leaving Santa Fe.

Rising early the next day, I take Highway 84 north in the direction of Española. But instead of branching off to the east, towards Truchas and the retreat centre, I choose a trail that climbs to the west, scaling the outer ridges of a vast plateau. This route twists and turns, following the contours of a sloping tableland formed from lava and ash spewed by ancient volcanic eruptions. It is a spectacular drive that soars to a height where the atmosphere thins.

This road ends at a place that was once known as 'The Town That Never Was'. These days, signs at its entrance welcome visitors with a sense of pride rather than any suggestion of secrecy. One giant, rough-hewn stone slab carries the words 'Los Alamos'; another below it boasts that this is the location 'Where Discoveries Are Made!' Los Alamos is the former site of the covert Manhattan Project, the genesis of the first atomic bombs dropped on Hiroshima and Nagasaki during the Second World War.

I don't know what it is that draws me here. But it is more than mere curiosity or journalistic instinct. After meeting a woman whose life work has been concern for the dying, there is something compelling about finishing my journey in this desert region by standing in the place where human intelligence devised the means to destroy life on an unimaginable and unprecedented scale. There is little reference now to this dark chapter of the past at the public science museum of Los Alamos, apart from explanations of the technology behind the greatest lethal force ever unleashed by man. This came in the form of two bombs, nicknamed Fat Man and Little Boy, which in a matter of minutes obliterated the lives of more than 100,000 Japanese. Instead the emphasis is on the lives the bombs are said to have saved by hastening the end of the war, and on groundbreaking discoveries in the field of medicine and technology that are being made by the small army of scientists working here today.

But as I stand on the outskirts of Los Alamos, looking out across the vast horizon of desert, deep canyons and mountains beyond, I recall words spoken by Roshi Joan in a series of recordings of her thoughts and experiences. Death, she says, is 'the mirror in which the entire meaning of life is reflected'. In these moments, I know why I have driven to this high plateau.

I think back to the long-forgotten custom of the Japanese nuns of Tokeiji, meditating for hours before a giant mirror to see into their own true nature and, through this, into the nature of life itself. After a worldwide odyssey in the footsteps of Buddhist nuns, it seems East and West, ancient and modern, come into touch. As if all that I have witnessed and felt are finally joined.

In the same way I have seen nuns bringing their palms together before bowing at the waist in respect, I bow to them all now. With a feeling of deep gratitude, I know it is time to take my leave.

ACKNOWLEDGEMENTS

A heartfelt thank you to all of the following.

First to my former editor at the *Sunday Times Magazine*, Robin Morgan, without whom the seed of the idea for this book might never have taken root. To my agent Carrie Kania, who had faith in it from the start. To Philip Gwyn Jones, former executive publisher of Granta Books and Portobello Books, whose enthusiasm set me on my way, and editorial director Laura Barber, whose brilliant editing and sensitive guidance brought *The Saffron Road* to fruition. Laura and the whole Granta–Portobello team have been a joy to work with.

There are many women throughout this book with whom I could not have spoken without the patient help of interpreters, including Jigme Rigzin at Druk Gawa Khilwa in Nepal, Tenzin Tsering and Tenzin Tselha in Dharamshala, Hiroko Kawanami and her husband U San in Sagaing, Burma, and Hisako Koizumi and her husband Tetsunori Koizumi in Japan.

The kind hospitality of Hisako and Tetsunori during my time in Japan is remembered with gratitude, as is that of Hiroko and U San in Burma, Mary O'Callaghan in the south of France, Ellen Hampton and Claude Urraca in Paris, Merle Lefkoff in Santa Fe, and Sandra Cate and Robert Gumpert in San Francisco, to whom I am also indebted for their long drive to the desert of southern California to undertake the one interview for this book I was unable to conduct myself. Bob's edit of the many photographs I took while travelling, already patiently sifted through by Nichola Webb, helped whittle them down to the few used as illustrations in this book.

As my journey neared its end and the writing of *The Saffron Road* gradually drew to a close I am extremely grateful to those who took the time to read all or part of the manuscript and made thoughtful suggestions. They include Martine Batchelor, who read the first completed draft on the look out for factual errors (any errors that remain, or that crept into later drafts, are entirely my own); Carrie Kania, whose skilled eye and sympathetic reading provided constant encouragement; Sir Peter Stothard, but for whom *The Saffron Road* would have begun one sentence earlier; Emma Vickers and Greg Neale, whose keen insights and kindness sustained me when the road was rough; John Cornwell, who cheered me on as I neared the finishing line; and my sister Elaine, who listened patiently on the phone to updates as I sought breaks from writing on strolls through my local park.

For their moral support and much more I owe sincere thanks to many others, including Mick Brown, Kate Saunders, Jane Moore, Sharon Salzberg, Gavin Kilty, Frances Howland, Philippa Russell and Helen Russell, Angela Gruber, Faustomaria Dorelli, Angie Herzberg, Louise Stanion, Jacqueline Russell, Caroline Starkey, Terry Morgan, Ilana Pearlman, Diana Blanchard, Di Cook, Fernando Lanzas, Professor Junko Nishiguchi, David Williams, Joah McGee, Sik Fa Ren, Thubten Samdup and Keiko Sugiura.

A debt of gratitude and love goes to my daughter Ines for the beaming smile and embrace that always welcomed me back from my travels.

Finally I would like to say a special thank you to all the women in this book, and others with whom I spoke but whose stories I was not able to include, for their profoundly wise company as I followed their journey along *The Saffron Road* and whose warmth and welcome I shall never forget.

FURTHER READING

Aoyama Shundo, *Zen Seeds*, Kosei Publishing Company, 2011

Batchelor, Stephen, *The Awakening of the West*, Echo Point Books, 2011

Batchelor, Stephen, *Confession of a Buddhist Atheist*, Spiegel and Grau, 2011

Batchelor, Martine, *Women on the Buddhist Path*, Thorsons, 2002

Caplow, Florence and Moon, Susan (eds), *The Hidden Lamp*, Wisdom Publications, 2013

Chödrön, Pema, *When Things Fall Apart*, Element, 2003

Chodron, Thubten, *Don't Believe Everything You Think*, Snow Lion, 2012

Chögyam Trungpa, *Cutting Through Spiritual Materialism*, Shambala, 2002

HH Dalai Lama and Chodron, Thubten, *Buddhism: One Teacher, Many Traditions*, Wisdom Publications, 2014

Fields, Rick, *How the Swans Came to the Lake*, Shambala, 1992

Gyalwang Drukpa, *Everyday Enlightenment*, Penguin Books, 2012

Haas, Michaela, *Dakini Power*, Snow Lion, 2013

Hạnh, Thích Nhất, *Heart of the Buddha's Teaching*, Rider, 1999

Hạnh, Thích Nhất, *The Miracle of Mindfulness*, Rider, 1991

Halifax, Joan, *Being with Dying*, Shambala, 2008

Kabat-Zinn, Jon, *Full Catastrophe Living*, Piatkus, 2013

Lama Yeshe, *Introduction to Tantra*, Wisdom Publications, 2001
Palmo, Jetsunma Tenzin, *Into the Heart of Life*, Snow Lion, 2011
Palmo, Jetsunma Tenzin, *Reflections on a Mountain Lake*, Snow Lion, 2012
Suzuki, Daisetz Teitaro, *An Introduction to Buddhism*, Rider, 1991
Suzuki, Shunryu, *Zen Mind, Beginner's Mind*, Shambala, 2011
Tsomo, Karma Lekshme, *Daughters of the Buddha*, Snow Lion, 1988
Williams, Mark and Penman, Danny, *Mindfulness*, Piatkus, 2011